Vault Reports Guide to the Top Investment Banking Firms

VAULT REPORTS™

The Team

DIRECTORS

Samer Hamadeh

H.S. Hamadeh

Mark Oldman

VAULT REPORTS, INC.

80 Fifth Avenue

11th Floor

New York, NY 10011

(212) 366-4212

Fax: (212) 366-6117

www.VaultReports.com

EXECUTIVE EDITOR
Marcy Lerner

MANAGING EDITOR
Edward Shen

ASSOCIATE EDITOR
Doug Cantor

NEWS EDITOR
Nikki Scott

SENIOR WRITERS
Andrew Gillies
Chandra Prasad

ART DIRECTION
Robert Schipano
Jake Wallace
Amy Wegenaar

INFORMATION SYSTEMS
Todd Kuhlman
Karson Clancy

MARKETING & SALES
Benjamin Burkman   Roberta Griff
Eric Grollman   Neil Goldstein
Thomas Nutt   Katrina Williams
Noah Zucker

BUSINESS DEVELOPMENT
Lianne Gilbert
Abigail Margulies

CUSTOMER RELATIONS
Slavica Naumovska
Agatha Ponickly

ACCOUNTING
Chris Casso

RESEARCH ASSISTANTS
Kofo Anifalaje   Alex Apelbaum
Al Gatling   Kevin Salgado
Candice Mortimer   Thomas Lee
Joan Lucas   Kelly Guerrier
Sylvia Kovac   Austin Shau
Angela Tong

VAULT REPORTS GUIDE TO THE TOP INVESTMENT BANKING FIRMS

ED SHEN AND H.S. HAMADEH

For information about permission to reproduce selections from this book, contact Vault Reports Inc., P.O. Box 1772, New York, New York 10011-1772, (212) 366-4212.

Library of Congress CIP Data is available.

ISBN 1-58131-038-2

Printed in the United States of America

ACKNOWLEDGEMENTS

Warm thanks to:

Hernie, Glenn Fischer, Carol and Bart Fischer, Lee Black, Jay Oyakawa, Ed Somekh, Todd Kelleher, Bruce Bland, Celeste and Noelle, Rob Copeland, Muriel and Stephanie, Michael Kalt, Ravi Mhatre, Tom Phillips, Bryan Finkel, Geoff Baum, Gary Mueller, Ted Liang, Brian Fischer, Glen and Dorothy Wilkins, Sarah Griffith, Russ Dubner, Kirsten Fragodt, Aldith and Robert Scott-Asselbergs, C., J. Nilsson, Geoff Vitale, Dana Evans, Olympia, Marky Mark, Katie T., Rachel, Jen, and Rudy's Bar (9th Avenue between 44th & 45th).

And to:

Amy Wegenaar, Angela Tong, Kofo Anifalaje, Alex Apelbaum, Al Gatling, Kevin Salgado, Candice Mortimer, Samir Shah, Thomas Lee, Joan Lucas, Kelly Guerrier, Sylvia Kovac, and Austin Shau

And Artists:

Robert Schipano and Jake Wallace

I-BANKING JOB SEEKERS:

Have job openings that match your criteria e-mailed to you !

VAULTMATCH™

FROM VAULT REPORTS

A free service for I-Banking job seekers!

Vault Reports will e-mail you job and internship postings that match your interests and qualifications. This is a free service from Vault Reports. Here's how it works:

1 You visit www.VaultReports.com and fill out an online questionnaire, indicating your qualifications and the types of positions you want.

2 Companies contact Vault Reports with job openings.

3 Vault Reports sends you an e-mail about each position which matches your qualifications and interests.

4 For each position that interests you, simply reply to the e-mail and attach your resume.

5 Vault Reports laser prints your resume on top-quality resume paper and sends it to the company's hiring manager within 5 days.

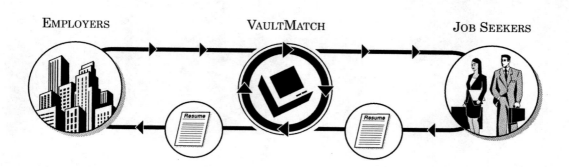

EMPLOYERS: PUT VAULTMATCH TO WORK FOR YOU. CONTACT VAULT REPORTS AT 888-562-8285.

www.VaultReports.com

Contents

Contents

A Guide to this Guide

If you're wondering what all those snazzy icons in our company entries are for, or how we developed our information, read on. Here's a guide to the information you'll find in each entry of our book.

THE METERS

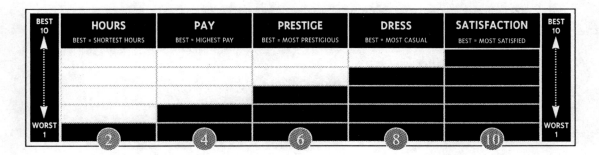

The Vault Reports Meters are scored on a 1-10 scale, with 10 being the highest. The scores are based upon how a particular firm compares to the average employer (including industries other than investment banking). A firm with a score of "5" in pay signifies that the firm has an average salary. In determining our ratings, we looked at both company data and our own surveys and benchmarking of companies (derived from years of research).

The meters attempt to give an at-glance look at a company. However, keep in mind that the issues they measure are complex, and a closer look at the entry is necessary for a fuller view.

Work Hours: The shorter the workweek, the higher the score. We did not adjust these scores based on the company location or to account for the long hours in the investment banking industry in general. Working 70 hours a week may be a vacation at some a New York I-bank, but it's still a mighty long workweek.

Pay: A company's pay score is based on home office pay, with bonuses (and likelihood of achieving them) factored in. We did not factor in cost of living or stock options.

Prestige: The higher the score, the more prestigious the firm. This score is based on our written and online surveys of bankers (see our description of our rankings on p. 2), as well as our interviews with investment bankers.

Dress: The higher the score, the more casual the dress code. A score of 10 means shorts and ripped T-shirts; a score of 1 means strict business formal.

Satisfaction: Employee satisfaction is based on our extensive interviews and surveys of employees at each firm.

THE BUZZ

In surveys that we used to compile our prestige rankings, we asked our respondents not only to rank firms, but also to give us their impressions of each company listed. We've collected a sampling of their comments in "The Buzz." We did this in order to gauge the nuances of the reputations of the top investment banks. In choosing three or four quotes for each firm to include, we tried to include quotes representative of the common perception of the firms, even if the quotes, in our opinion (based on interviews with insiders at that company), did not accurately describe the firm. Some of the comments are fair, some rather nasty, a few hilarious.

THE GRAPHS

The information given in the graphs for our top 10 banks are drawn from a variety of sources. Much of the basic financial and employment data for public banks (net revenues, number of employees, etc.) comes from business information provider Hoover's Online. In some cases, the companies and firms themselves supplied data.

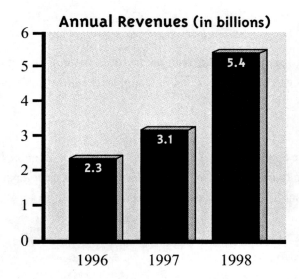

Annual Revenues (in billions)

- 1996: 2.3
- 1997: 3.1
- 1998: 5.4

I-Banking Job Seekers: Receive free e-mailed job postings matching your interests & qualifications! Register at www.VaultReports.com

VAULT REPORTS™

iii

www.vaultreports.com

THE ENTRIES

Each of our entries is broken into three sections: The Scoop, Getting Hired, and Our Survey Says.

The Scoop: This section includes information about the firm's history, strategy and organization, recent business performance, and other points of interest.

Getting Hired: This section includes information about the firm's hiring process, concentrating on on-campus recruiting and summer programs.

Our Survey Says: This section is based around quotes and comments from employees at the firm, and covers topics such as company culture, pay, perks, social life, as well as many others.

Introduction

Tom Wolfe called them "Masters of the Universe" in *The Bonfire of the Vanities*; Michael Lewis called them a few unprintable things in *Liar's Poker*. Who are they? Investment bankers, salespeople and traders. Investment banks aren't like your local branch office with ubiquitous ATM (those are commercial banks, like Citibank or Bank of America); instead, investment banks work with corporations, governments, institutional investors and extraordinarily wealthy individuals to raise capital and provide investment advice.

However, the legal barrier between commercial and investment banks has been rapidly decaying since the 1980s, and this decade has witnessed the arrival of huge commercial banks entering the investment banking market. Firms like Germany's Deutsche Bank have been spending enormous amounts of money to establish and assemble their own investment banking arms, while other commercial banks have been acquiring small- to-medium-sized investment banks at a rapid rate. Baltimore-based Alex. Brown, the oldest investment bank in the nation, was acquired by Bankers Trust in 1997 – which itself was snapped up by European leviathan Deutsche Bank in 1998. Commercial titan Bank of America bought fast-growing boutique Robertson Stephens – only to sell it to BankBoston after merging with NationsBank. Mergers between investment banks are another trend – witness the recent conjoinings of Morgan Stanley and Dean Witter, Discover (now known as Morgan Stanley Dean Witter), and Salomon Brothers and Smith Barney (now called Salomon Smith Barney). These combinations and mergers mean big changes and big opportunities in the investment banking industry – and indeed, positions in these temples of lucre are still highly sought after, though the collapse of markets in Asia and Russia may temper the ardor of applicants – and douse the eagerness of banks to hire.

1

OUR 1999 TOP TEN INVESTMENT BANKS

As part of the Vault Reports Guide to the Top Investment Banks, we've selected what we believe to be the ten most prestigious investment banks in the country. Our picks are based on the results of a battery of prestige surveys we've administered at investment banks, and our interviews and conversations with hundreds of bankers. Our choices range from the largest investment banks in the world, to some of the best-known, to a few select high-powered boutiques.

We believe our 1999 Top Ten offers an accurate view of the most desirable and prestigious investment banks in America in 1999.

RANK	FIRM	HEADQUARTERS
1	Goldman Sachs & Co.	New York
2	Morgan Stanley Dean Witter	New York
3	Merrill Lynch	New York
4	Donaldson, Lufkin & Jenrette	New York
5	J.P. Morgan	New York
6	Lazard Freres	New York
7	Salomon Smith Barney	New York
8	Credit Suisse First Boston	New York
9	Lehman Brothers	New York
10	Hambrecht & Quist	San Francisco

VAULT REPORTS™
www.vaultreports.com

The Scoop

What do investment bankers do for 100 hours a week? Investment banks serve clients who wish to raise capital, and clients who want to invest capital. (Yes, it's all about money.) Investment bankers help huge clients, such as corporations, conglomerates and major world governments raise capital, go public, divest or acquire businesses and business assets, and assist clients with their financial strategies. Investment banks also help those who want to invest money, both high net worth individuals (i.e., rich people) and corporations or other institutional investors. Backing up operations are a cadre of skilled researchers and analysts who follow companies and industries, some so savvy and influential that their recommendations can greatly affect the value of the stocks and companies they follow.

MAJOR DEPARTMENTS OF INVESTMENT BANKS

INVESTMENT BANKING – CORPORATE FINANCE

Corporate finance's most prominent function is the raising of capital for clients. To raise money, investment bankers determine the client's financial requirements, whether the company should raise the money by issuing equity (stock) or debt (bonds), or a combination of both, and how to price these securities. After researching the financial background of the company (called due diligence) to uncover risks and to assuage any potential concerns the Securities and Exchange Commission may have (the agency must approve any large securities offering), the investment bank usually prepares documents (called a prospectus) that detail the company's business, historical performance, and the terms of the securities offered. As soon as the SEC okays the prospectus, the investment bank sells the securities to the public. Among the splashier offerings a bank can handle are IPOs (initial public offerings), the process of taking a company public.

Investment banks underwrite stock and bond offerings. That is, they purchase either an entire issue or a portion thereof, in order to ensure that the cash the client needs will be raised. The bank then immediately sells the securities to clients at a slightly higher price (the difference is called the spread). It is the bank's goal to accurately price an offering, or perhaps to price it at a bit below its true market value. For example, assume an investment bank has convinced a company that it should go public by issuing 1 million shares at $30 a share. After the shares hit the market, they balloon to $40 a share. The rationale for this underpricing? The bank's clients are pleased because they bought a stock at well under market value. The rationale for this underpricing? If the bank values the company at just under its market value, its clients will receive a nice immediate boost, and the company has generated good buzz for its shares because the offering is viewed as successful.

INVESTMENT BANKING – MERGERS AND ACQUISITIONS

In the heady field of mergers & acquisitions, the investment bank advises a client that is either selling or purchasing an entire company, a division, or other business assets (like a factory or a hotel). The bank counsels either the seller or the buyer, decides on an appropriate valuation range, and negotiates terms that favor the bank's client. Mergers & acquisitions can take myriad forms, from a friendly stock swap (increasingly common) to a hostile takeover (increasingly rare). (Note: "Mergers" and "acquisitions" are essentially the same thing – the words are merely legal terms that depend on the amount of stock swapped and other arcane details of corporation law.) Investment banks may also be hired to advise on only one aspect of an M&A transaction, for example to help find the right partner, purchaser or seller, to arrange financing, or only to value businesses or assets to be sold.

Often, investment bankers will approach companies to propose M&A deals they may not have otherwise considered. Proposing such deals – or providing advice to a client – requires heavy research and knowledge of an industry, it also means gaining the trust of top company officials. It means lots of schmoozing. Although bankers generally drive the overall strategy of a company's decision to merge, acquire, or be acquired, lawyers are the ones who typically negotiate over the fine points of a deal.

M&A has been a robust business in the past recent years. In fact, eight of the top 10 mergers ever were announced in the first half of 1998, including the Travelers Group/Citicorp merger, the SBC/Ameritech marriage, and the Daimler Benz/Chrysler combo. The increased merger activity has greatly improved Wall Street's bottom line – M&A is a high-margin business.

SALES

Salespeople cultivate relationships with institutional (and sometimes retail, or individual, investors) to convince them to buy or sell securities. Working with traders, who execute the actual trades, salespeople call their clients to pitch securities, both those underwritten by the bank and others. Salespeople, who earn a commission on their clients' trades, may vend either fixed-income products (typically bonds and fixed-income derivatives) or equity (stocks and equity derivatives).

TRADING

Wall Street traders follow the ever-changing securities, commodities and currency markets, earning or losing thousands or millions of dollars with the click of a mouse and the passage of a millisecond. Traders at Wall Street firms typically have two roles: (1) traders may either buy and securities on behalf of a customer's account at the customer's order (this role is called making a market), or (2) traders may buy and sell securities for the investment bank's own account in order to earn profit directly for the investment bank, based on changes in the market the trader anticipates (this role is called proprietary trading). Most traders specialize in a certain type of security, for instance, foreign currencies, technology stocks, or U.S. Treasury bonds. The tension of trading leads one trader to describe it to Vault Reports as "warfare, waiting for the next shell to be lobbed over your head."

I-Banking Job Seekers: Receive free e-mailed job postings matching your interests & qualifications! Register at www.VaultReports.com

VAULT
REPORTS™

5

www.vaultreports.com

PRIVATE CLIENT SERVICES

Salespeople in the Private Client division of an investment bank cater to the (usually wealthy) individual investor, making investment recommendations and executing trades on their behalf. Private Client agents spend much of their time on the phone, conferring with their clients and attempting to obtain new ones, often by cold-calling names in directories of small business owners or other professionals. These salesmen and women also study the markets (often through research provided by the investment bank's Research department) to better make buy and sell recommendations to their clients. (Note: You might recall that the ill-fated Bud Fox from the movie *Wall Street* worked in Private Client Services, and always dreamed of moving to the investment banking side.)

RESEARCH

Research analysts follow industries, geographic regions or particular stocks, and make predictions about the near future of particular companies or industries. Most research analysts specialize in a particular industry, such as health care, software, or defense stocks. Research analysts keep tabs on stock prices, company developments, industry and regulatory changes, and expected future earnings, and write research reports outlining their predictions. (The research reports are circulated to the firm's clients, as well as to the bank's traders, salesmen, and investment bankers.) Based on this reservoir of knowledge and their own research, analysts make short-term predictions on the movement of stocks or bonds, which can cause dramatic changes in stock prices. An analyst's prestige – and salary – is often influenced by his or her ranking in the annual analyst survey in *Institutional Investor* magazine. Having powerful analysts is becoming increasingly important to investment banks as a way to attract investment banking clients. The media concurs: in 1997, *Fortune* magazine called the 1990s the Age of the Analyst.

VAULT
REPORTS™
www.vaultreports.com

ASSET MANAGEMENT

While generally more province of mutual fund giants, such as Fidelity Investments, asset management is a major part of the operations of many top investment banks. The department does exactly what it sounds like it does – a client (a pension fund, a wealthy individual, a country) gives the investment bank money, and the bank invests it to meet the client's objectives. These days, many banks are looking to grow their asset management business because it is largely protected against the volatility of the market. In contrast, businesses such as underwriting and M&A are stronger during bull markets (when the market is strong, companies want to issue stocks and bonds on favorable terms, and are encouraged to expand), and sales and trading is strong in active markets (the more stocks and bonds move through a bank, the bigger the commissions). In asset management, however, banks are generally paid a percentage of the assets managed, whether they make or lose money for the client.

Career Path

ANALYST

The investment banking analyst position is aimed at recent college graduates. To nab an analyst position, you don't need to have an undergraduate degree in economics or accounting, but you must have solid quantitative, organizational and analytic skills. Some banks offer analysts rotations through different departments before the new recruits settle on one. Departments that hire the most analysts are typically: corporate finance and mergers & acquisitions, followed by fixed income, derivatives, tax-exempt securities, and foreign exchange. Analysts usually perform data gathering and modeling functions, and may also field client calls or prepare material (called "pitchbooks") to be used in client presentations (also called "beauty contests"). Most analysts remain at their jobs for two to three years, after which time they are expected to go to graduate school, although a small number of analysts are promoted directly to the associate level without an MBA. (Note: Differentiate "analysts," who are recent college grads, from "research analysts," who are senior members of the firm's Research Department.)

I-Banking Job Seekers: Receive free e-mailed job postings matching your interests & qualifications! Register at www.VaultReports.com

VAULT REPORTS™
www.vaultreports.com

7

College graduates are also hired for sales and trading positions. Traders have the authority to commit bank funds on securities, stock and bond speculations, while salespeople generally spend time on the phone taking buy and sell orders, and advising clients on investment gambits. Generally, college grads will have responsibility for only small accounts and work their way up to greater responsibility. Moving up as a college graduate without an MBA is much easier in sales and trading than it is in investment banking.

ASSOCIATE

Associates in investment banking are almost invariably MBA holders, although some hold law degrees or other graduate degrees. (Occasionally, extraordinary third-year analysts are promoted to the associate level without a graduate degree.) While a few investment banks have initial rotations through different departments for associates, most assign them to a specific group, often based on industry (for example, Communications & Media, Energy & Power, or Financial Institutions). Often associates will have already interviewed with the particular department they join.

Associates will also assemble pitchbooks (though it's easier for them to delegate such tasks to analysts), prepare analysis for pitchbooks (such as "common stock comparisons," to show clients where the stocks of comparable companies are currently trading as a multiple of revenues, earnings, and other measures), liaison with clients, supervise analysts, create financial models in the ubiquitous Excel, sometimes lead client meetings, and, after some experience, call on clients alone and manage deals unsupervised. Associates can expect to be promoted to vice president after three to five years.

MBAs also join as associates in sales and trading, and are generally in charge of either making markets (trading) in particular products (such as U.S. Treasury bonds), or pitching products to institutional investors (selling). Traders are assigned to "desks," such as those focused on distressed fixed income or mortgage-backed securities. As with the move from analyst-level to associate-level positions, advancement from associate to vice president and beyond is usually less structured and potentially quicker in sales and trading than in investment banking.

VAULT REPORTS™
www.vaultreports.com

Arbitrage: The trading of securities (stocks, bonds, derivatives, currencies, and other securities) to profit from a temporary difference between the price of security in one market and the price in another (also called "risk-free arbitrage"). Distinguish from "risk arbitrage" (see below).

Asset Management: Investment banks take money given to them by pension funds and individual investors, and invest and otherwise manage it. For wealthy individuals ("private clients"), the investment bank will set up an individual account and manage the account; for the less well-endowed, the bank will offer mutual funds. Investment banks are compensated for asset management primarily by taking a percentage each year from the total assets managed. (They may also charge an up-front "load," or commission, usually a small percentage of the initial money invested.) Asset management is considered a less volatile business than trading, providing a steadier source of revenues.

Beauty Contest: When investment banks want to land a deal, they usually need to work for it. This means the bank must compete with its rivals in what's called a "beauty contest." For these contests, a bank must explain why a company should choose it, with lines like: "Look how strong our research department is in this industry. Our analyst in the industry is a real market mover, so if you go public with us, you'll be sure to get a lot of attention from her." Or: "We are the top-ranking firm in this type of issuance, as you will see by these league tables."

Bloomberg: Computer terminals providing real time quotes, news, and analytical tools, often used by traders and investment bankers.

Bulge-Bracket: The top firms on Wall Street (including Goldman Sachs, Morgan Stanley Dean Witter, DLJ, Merrill Lynch, Salomon Smith Barney, Lehman Brothers and Merrill Lynch).

Buy side: The clients of investment banks (mutual funds, pension funds) that buy the stocks, bonds and securities sold by the investment banks. (The investment banks which sell these products to investors are known as the "sell side.")

Commercial bank: A bank that lends, rather than raises money. For example, if a company wants $30 million to open a new production plant, it can approach a commercial bank like Chase Manhattan or Citibank for a loan. (Increasingly, commercial banks are also providing some investment banking services to clients.)

Commercial paper: Short-term corporate debt, typically maturing in nine months or less.

Commodities: Assets (usually agricultural products or metals) that are interchangeable with one another and therefore share a common price. (For example, corn, wheat or rubber generally trades at one price on commodity markets worldwide.)

Convertible bonds: Bonds that can be converted into a specified number of shares of stock.

Derivatives: An asset whose value is derived from the price of another asset, like call options, put options, futures, and interest-rate "swaps."

Discount rate: A widely followed short-term interest rate, set by the Federal Reserve to cause market interest rates to rise or fall, thereby causing the U.S. economy to grow more or less quickly. (More technically, the discount rate is the rate at which federal banks lend money to each other on overnight loans.)

Dividend: A payment by a company to shareholders of its stock, usually as a way to distribute some or all of the profits to shareholders.

Equity: In short, stock. Equity means ownership in a company that is usually represented by stock.

The Fed: The Federal Reserve, currently run by guru Alan Greenspan which gently (or sometimes roughly) manages the country's economy by setting interest rates.

Fixed income: In short, bonds and other securities that earn a fixed rate of return. Bonds typically are issued by governments, corporations and municipalities.

Floating rate: An interest rate that is benchmarked to other rates (such as the rate paid on U.S. Treasuries), allowing the interest rate to change as market conditions change.

Floor traders: Traders for an investment bank located in the firm's offices. Floor traders spend most of the day seated at their desks observing market action on their computer screens.

Glass-Steagall Act: Part of the legislation passed during the Depression (Glass-Steagall was passed in 1933) designed to help prevent future bank failures – the establishment of the F.D.I.C. was also part of this movement. The Glass-Steagall Act split America's investment banking (issuing and trading securities) operations from commercial banking (lending). For example, J.P. Morgan was forced to spin off its securities unit as Morgan Stanley. Since the late 1980s, the Federal Reserve has steadily chipped away the act, allowing commercial banks, such as NationsBank and Bank of America, to buy investment banks like Montgomery Securities.

Hedge: To balance a position in the market in order to reduce risk. Hedges work like insurance: a small position pays off large amounts with a slight move in the market.

High-yield debt: Corporate bonds which pay high interest rates (to compensate investors for high risk of default). Also called "junk bonds." Credit rating agencies such as Standard & Poor's rate a company's (or a municipality's) bonds based on default risk. (Bonds with lower default risk and which pay lower interest rates are called "investment grade" debt.)

Market Cap(italization): The total value of a company in the stock market (total shares outstanding multiplied by price per share).

Initial Public Offering (IPO): The dream of every entrepreneur, the IPO is the first time a company issues stock to the public. "Going public" means more than raising money for the company: by agreeing to take on public shareholders, a company enters a whole world of required SEC filings and quarterly revenue and earnings reports, not to mention possible shareholder lawsuits.

I-Banking Job Seekers: Receive free e-mailed job postings matching your interests & qualifications! Register at www.VaultReports.com

VAULT REPORTS™ 11
www.vaultreports.com

Institutional clients: Large investors, such as pension funds or municipalities (as opposed to "retail investors" or "individual investors").

Investment grade bonds: Debt with low risk of default, generally bearing a rating of BBB or above from credit agencies. (Non-investment grade debt is known as "junk." Debt that is rated above BBB by some agencies and below by others is called "split-rated.")

Lead manager: The primary investment banking managing a particular securities offering. (An investment bank may share this responsibility with one or more "co-managers.")

League tables: Tables which rank investment banks based on underwriting volume in numerous categories, such as stocks, bonds, high yield debt, convertible debt, etc. High rankings in league tables are key selling points used by investment banks when trying to land a client engagement.

Leveraged Buyout (LBO): The buyout of a company utilizing borrowed money, often using that company's own assets as collateral. LBOs were the order of the day in the heady 1980s, when successful LBO firms such as Kohlberg Kravis Roberts made a practice of buying up companies, restructuring them, and reselling them or taking them public at a significant profit.

LIBOR: The "London Inter-bank Offer Rate." A widely used short-term interest rate. Many interest rates are set as a spread over LIBOR.

The long bond: The thirty-year U.S. Treasury bond. Treasury bonds are used as the starting point for pricing many other bonds, because Treasury bonds are assumed to have zero credit risk after taking into account factors such as inflation. For example, a company will issue a bond that trades "40 over treasuries." The 40 refers to 40 basis points (100 basis points = 1 percentage point).

Making markets: A function performed by investment banks to providing liquidity for their clients in a particular security, usually for a security that the investment bank has underwritten. (In others words, the investment bank stands willing to buy the security, if necessary, when the investor later decides to sell it.)

VAULT REPORTS™
www.vaultreports.com

Merchant banking: The department within an investment bank which invests the firm's own money in other companies. Analogous to venture capital investments.

Pitchbook: The book of exhibits, graphs, and initial recommendations presented by bankers to a prospective clients when trying to land an engagement during a beauty contest.

Pit traders: Traders who are positioned on the floor of stock and commodity exchanges (as opposed to "desk traders," situated at investment banks' offices).

P/E ratio: The price to earnings ratio. This is the ratio of a company's stock price to its earnings-per-share. The higher the P/E ratio, the more "expensive" a stock is (and also the faster investors believe the company will grow). Stocks in fast-growing industries tend to have higher P/E ratios.

Proprietary trading: Trading of the firm's own assets (as opposed to trading client assets).

Prospectus: A report issued by a company (filed with, and approved by, the SEC) that wishes to sell securities to investors. Distributed to prospective investors, the prospectus discloses the company's financial position, business description, and risk factors.

Red herring: Also known as a "preliminary prospectus." A financial report printed by the issuer of a security that can be used to generate interest from prospective investors before the securities are legally available to be sold. Based on final SEC comments, the information reported in a red herring may change slightly by the time the securities are actually issued.

Retail clients: Individual investors (as opposed to "institutional clients").

Return on equity: The ratio of a firm's profits to the value of its equity. A commonly-used measure of how well an investment bank is doing, since it measures how efficiently and profitably the firm is using its capital.

I-Banking Job Seekers: Receive free e-mailed job postings matching your interests & qualifications! Register at www.VaultReports.com

VAULT REPORTS™

www.vaultreports.com

13

Risk arbitrage: When an investment bank invests in the stock of a company it believes will be purchased in a merger or acquisition. (Distinguish from "risk-free arbitrage.")

Road show: The series of presentations to investors that a company undergoing an IPO usually gives in the weeks preceding the offering. Here's how it works: several weeks before the IPO is issued, the company and its investment bank will travel to major cities throughout the country. In each city, the company's top executives make a presentation to analysts, mutual fund managers, and others attendees. These presentations also include question answering segments.

Sales memo: Short reports written by corporate finance bankers, distributed to the bank's salespeople. The sales memo provides salesmen with points to emphasize when hawking the stocks and bonds the firm is underwriting.

Securities and Exchange Commission (SEC): A federal agency that, like the Glass-Steagall Act, was established as a result of the stock market crash of 1929 and ensuing bank failure. The SEC monitors disclosure of financial information to stockholders, and protects against fraud.

Securitize: To convert an asset into a security, which can then be sold to investors. Nearly any income-generating asset can be turned into a security. For example a 20-year mortgage on a home can be packaged with other mortgages just like it, and then shares in this pool of mortgages can be sold to investors.

Short-term debt: A bond that matures in nine months or less, also called commercial paper.

Syndicate: A group of investment banks that will together underwrite a particular stock or debt offering. Usually the "lead manager" will underwrite the bulk of a deal, while other members of the syndicate will each underwrite a small portion.

Tax-exempt bonds: Municipal bonds (also known as "munis"). Munis are free from state and federal taxes.

Tombstone: The advertisements which appear in publications like the *Financial Times* or *The Wall Street Journal* announcing the issuance of a new security. The tombstone ad is placed by the investment bank to boast to the world that it has completed a major deal.

Underwrite: The function performed by investment banks when they help companies issue securities to investors. Technically, the investment bank buys the securities from the company and immediately resells the securities to investors for a slightly higher price, making money on the spread.

Yield: The annual return on investment. A high-yield bond, for example, pays a high percent of interest.

I-Banking Job Seekers: Receive free e-mailed job postings matching your interests & qualifications! Register at www.VaultReports.com

VAULT REPORTS™

www.vaultreports.com

15

The Vault Reports

TOP 10

Goldman Sachs & Co.

85 Broad Street
22nd Floor
New York, NY 10004
(212) 902-1000
www.goldmansachs.com

Goldman Sachs

LOCATIONS

New York, NY (HQ)
Boston, MA • Chicago, IL • Dallas, TX • Houston, TX • Los Angeles, CA • Memphis, TN • Miami, FL • Philadelphia, PA • San Francisco, CA • Washington, D.C.

Bangkok, Thailand • Beijing, China • Cayman Islands • Frankfurt, Germany • Hong Kong • London, England • Madrid, Spain • Mexico City, Mexico • Milan, Italy • Montreal, Canada • Osaka, Japan • Paris, France • Sao Paulo, Brazil • Seoul, South Korea • Shanghai, China • Singapore • Sydney, Australia • Tokyo, Japan • Toronto, Canada • Vancouver, British Columbia • Zurich, Switzerland

DEPARTMENTS

Asset Management • Controllers • Credit • Equities • Fixed-Income • General Services • Investment Banking • Principal Investments • Global Investment Research • Global Operations and Technology • Information Technology • J. Aron Currency and Commodity • Management Controls • Personnel • Training and Development • Treasury

THE STATS

Annual Revenues: $17.2 billion (1997)
No. of Employees: 12,500 (worldwide)
No. of Offices: 39 (worldwide), 13 (U.S.)
A privately-owned company
Co-Chairmen and Co-CEOs:
Jon S. Corzine and Henry M. Paulson Jr.

KEY COMPETITORS

◆ Credit Suisse First Boston
◆ J.P. Morgan
◆ Merrill Lynch
◆ Morgan Stanley Dean Witter
◆ Salomon Smith Barney

THE BUZZ
What bankers at other firms
are saying about Goldman

◆ "Elite, snobby"
◆ "Clubby and aggressive"
◆ "Brainwash employees"
◆ "The bank that banks admire"

Goldman Sachs & Co.

UPPERS

- High pay and prestige
- Great support services
- Free car service after 8 p.m.

DOWNERS

- Marathon workdays
- Uneven treatment by superiors
- Little job training

EMPLOYMENT CONTACT

Advanced Degree:
Jacqueline Bowman

College Degree:
Alissa D. Burstein

Goldman, Sachs & Co.
22nd Floor
85 Broad Street
New York, NY 10004

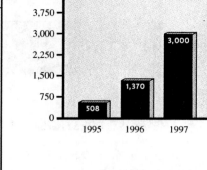

Pretax Profits (in millions)
- 1995: 508
- 1996: 1,370
- 1997: 3,000

Partner Capitalization (in billions)
- 1995: 4.1
- 1996: 5.3
- 1997: 6.1

Employees
- 1996: 8,200
- 1997: 9,100
- 1998: 12,500

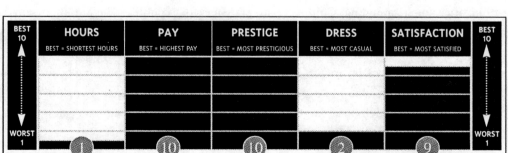

	HOURS BEST = SHORTEST HOURS	PAY BEST = HIGHEST PAY	PRESTIGE BEST = MOST PRESTIGIOUS	DRESS BEST = MOST CASUAL	SATISFACTION BEST = MOST SATISFIED	
BEST 10 ↑ WORST 1	1	10	10	2	9	BEST 10 ↑ WORST 1

I-Banking Job Seekers: Receive free e-mailed job postings matching your interests & qualifications! Register at www.VaultReports.com

VAULT REPORTS™
www.vaultreports.com

19

THE SCOOP

THE MOST PRESTIGIOUS

Founded in 1869 by Marcus Goldman, a European immigrant, Goldman Sachs is one of the nation's oldest and most prestigious investment banking firms. The firm provides a wide array of investment banking and research services to its corporate clients. Goldman is especially renowned for its stock research department and its ability to raise money in the public capital markets by helping companies issue stocks and bonds.

WELL-CONNECTED

The company has made an impressive comeback since 1994, when it posted one of its worst results in its entire 127 years in business. After restructuring its management and refocusing on client service, Goldman is once again posting impressive profits. Most of Goldman's clients are the nation's largest and most established corporations, such as H&R Block, Kroger supermarkets, and Times Mirror. Recently, however, Goldman has made an effort to attract businesses from more entrepreneurial companies, including Internet companies such as Yahoo! In recent years it has taken public tech stars like RealNetworks and DoubleClick. Goldman is also politically well-connected, and is one of the nation's largest campaign contributors; former Goldman co-chairman Robert Rubin serves as U.S. Treasury Secretary.

THE OFF AND ON IPO

In 1998, after much wrangling, Goldman partners voted to go public. The initial offering was expected to be the largest ever for a financial services company, and was expected to value the firm at about $30 billion. Analysts believe the decision was driven by two major factors. The first was that without stock leverage, Goldman could not acquire other banking businesses, and would eventually not be able to keep pace with competitors like Merrill Lynch and Morgan Stanley Dean Witter which boast large retail brokerage capabilities (and thus can more easily sell the securities they underwrite to individual investors). The second was that Goldman's partners sensed that the market was at its peak, and wanted to cash in their chips.

Goldman may have waited too long. World financial markets lurched into turmoil in the late summer and fall of 1998, and Goldman execs decided to shelve the IPO indefinitely. The bank intends to proceed with an offering when market conditions strengthen. Still, the documents Goldman filed as it prepared for its initial offering gave jealous and curious outsiders a peek at the firm's finances: the firm reported $3 billion in pre-tax income in 1997. In its prospectus, Goldman also stressed that for the five-year period beginning in 1993, it ranked No. 1 worldwide in both IPOs and M&A advisory. However, more than its main rivals Merrill Lynch and Morgan Stanley, Goldman depends on its trading operations, leaving it potentially vulnerable to market volatility.

GETTING HIRED

Goldman's interviewing process is notorious for its grueling intensity. Candidates go through at least three rounds of interviews. The first and second rounds usually consist of two half-hour sessions, where the applicant interviews with two Goldman professionals, typically one associate and a vice president. The third round, the most rigorous, consists of five or six two-on-one interviews, each of which is 45 minutes long and involves one or more of the firm's partners. There is no clear delineation of personal and professional questions during the three rounds; candidates must be prepared to answer any question at any time. Candidates who have claimed on their resume or cover letter to have a strong financial background should be prepare to receive several detailed and probing questions on business and finance issues. All candidates are questioned on their willingness and ability to work hard as team players in an intense and demanding work environment. (Goldman is especially fond of teamwork.)

Interviewers say that they look for "people with smart personalities who aren't afraid to work hard. We especially don't want big egos around the place, so we try and find out how you will be able to work with someone you don't like too much personally." Recent interviewees

I-Banking Job Seekers: Receive free e-mailed job postings matching your interests & qualifications! Register at www.VaultReports.com

VAULT REPORTS™
www.vaultreports.com
21

remark that they were surprised by the number of "detailed questions" that interviewers asked them about their grades at college and graduate school, even where school policy prohibited such questions.

When hiring MBAs as associates, Goldman Sachs departments expect work experience that demonstrates an interest in the financial markets. Goldman is unusual among investment banks in that it also recruits at several law schools (Harvard, Yale, NYU, and the University of Pennsylvania) for both associate and summer associate positions. Several Goldman recruiters acknowledge that getting an offer at Goldman is easier for law students than for MBAs because the applicant pool is far smaller.

OUR SURVEY SAYS

TEAM GOLDMAN

Goldman Sachs' workplace is legendary for its "intense, goal-driven" ethic, where "success is taken for granted and teamwork is the highest priority." While the rest of the world may exalt Goldman employees as the "Masters of the Universe," insiders themselves note that the firm "cuts their egos down to size." Goldman Sachs makes it clear from the beginning that "individual personalities are insignificant," and that "the firm comes first, second, and last." New hires take some time to get used to the careful scrutiny to which they are subjected, and sometimes feel as if they're "under constant surveillance." Analysts and associates praise their fellow employees for being "intelligent and perceptive" while also being "prepared to make the sacrifices that have to be made for the team to succeed." However, working as part of a team of Goldman Sachs employees "can also be challenging, because you have to hold up your end, and there's always pressure to measure up to your co-workers' high standards."

Some employees also feel that Goldman's emphasis on teamwork comes at a cost – "individuality and creativity are usually considered much less important than being a good team player." It's not easy working in formation. Even the most successful Goldman employees confess that "occasionally the stress of work can get to be too much, and you come close to cracking."

HAND YOUR LIFE TO GOLDMAN

Goldman Sachs employees work "extremely long hours," but that comes as no surprise. After all, one of the most commonly asked questions in a Goldman interview is, "How will you cope with working 90-hour weeks, or longer, for three years?" For the first few years, analysts usually work between 80 and 110 hours a week, and generally come in to the office "at least six days a week, though you're usually there every day of the week." Working until 10 at night is virtually a daily affair, and "all-nighters are pretty frequent" as project deadlines draw near. Even those employees who say that they love working for Goldman concede that the hours "just get a bit too much at times." One trader notes exasperatedly that "sometimes I don't have enough time to take lunch – or even to go to the bathroom." New hires, however, should take heart from the fact that "the hours loosen up as you get promoted." Vice presidents rarely work all day on weekends; they reportedly usually "just drop in for a couple of hours on Saturday mornings, tell the analysts and associates what to do, and then leave."

FULL SUPPORT

Goldman's support staff wins high marks from employees for being "thoroughly efficient and professional." According to our surveys and sources, Goldman bankers enjoy better support services than anywhere else on the Street. Even analysts have secretaries to answer their calls, although they have to share secretaries – usually one secretary is assigned to four or five analysts or associates. Goldman's support staff infrastructure ensures that back-up secretaries are always available to fill in any gaps caused by illness or absence among the regular support staff. The highly-paid support staff (like other Goldman employees, support staff receive year-end bonuses) not only perform standard administrative and clerical duties such as faxing and filing, but also help associates and analysts with making graphs, setting up databases, and creating charts and tables. Every floor at Goldman's New York headquarters has a word processing room staffed with "friendly, knowledgeable" people. Goldman's Data Resources and Library staff are also "superb" but tend to "grumble about last-minute requests." Overall,

I-Banking Job Seekers: Receive free e-mailed job postings matching your interests & qualifications! Register at www.VaultReports.com

VAULT REPORTS™

23

www.vaultreports.com

Goldman employees remark that their top-notch support staff plays an "integral" role in ensuring the smooth execution of pitch books and presentations.

To order a 50- to 70-page Vault Reports Employer Profile on Goldman Sachs & Co. call 1-888-JOB-VAULT or visit www.VaultReports.com

The full Employer Profile includes detailed information on Goldman's departments, recent developments and transactions, hiring and interview process, plus what employees really think about culture, pay, work hours and more.

"Sometimes I don't have enough time to take lunch – or even go to the bathroom."

– Goldman insider

I-Banking Job Seekers: Receive free e-mailed job postings matching your interests & qualifications! Register at www.VaultReports.com

VAULT REPORTS™
25
www.vaultreports.com

Morgan Stanley Dean Witter

RANKING 2

1585 Broadway
New York, NY 10036
(212) 761-4000
www.msdw.com

MORGAN STANLEY DEAN WITTER

LOCATIONS

New York, NY (HQ)
Atlanta • Austin • Boston • Chicago • Denver • Houston • Los Angeles • Menlo Park • Orlando • San Francisco • Amsterdam • Bangkok • Beijing • Frankfurt • Geneva • Hong Kong • Johannesburg • London • Luxembourg • Madrid • Melbourne • Mexico City • Milan • Montreal • Moscow • Mumbai • Paris • Sao Paolo • Seoul • Shanghai • Sydney • Taipei • Tokyo • Toronto • Zurich

DEPARTMENTS

Corporate Financial Management • Corporate Treasury • Credit • Fixed Income Sales & Trading • Information Technology • Investment Banking • Private Client Services • Public Finance • Reengineering Services

THE STATS

Annual Revenues: $27.1 billion (1997)
No. of Employees: 47,277 (worldwide)
No. of Offices: 435
Stock Symbol: MWD (NYSE)
CEO: Philip J. Purcell

KEY COMPETITORS

- Credit Suisse First Boston
- Donaldson, Lufkin & Jenrette
- Goldman Sachs & Co.
- J.P. Morgan
- Merrill Lynch
- Salomon Smith Barney

THE BUZZ

What bankers at other firms are saying about MSDW

- "White-shoe, top performer"
- "Merrill Lynch meets Goldman Sachs"
- "Second only to Goldman"
- "Powerhouse"

Morgan Stanley Dean Witter

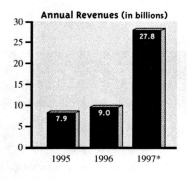

Annual Revenues (in billions)

UPPERS

- Very prestigious
- Evaluation process permits vengeance
- Extensive exposure to upper management

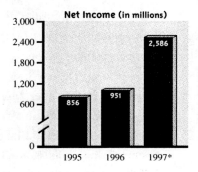

Net Income (in millions)

DOWNERS

- Long workdays
- Beepers worn by all

EMPLOYMENT CONTACT

Recruiting Manager
1585 Broadway
29th Floor
New York, NY 10036
(212) 761-0053

Employees

*reflects Morgan Stanley, Dean Witter merger

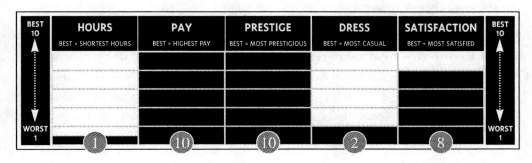

	HOURS	PAY	PRESTIGE	DRESS	SATISFACTION	
BEST 10 → WORST 1	BEST = SHORTEST HOURS	BEST = HIGHEST PAY	BEST = MOST PRESTIGIOUS	BEST = MOST CASUAL	BEST = MOST SATISFIED	BEST 10 → WORST 1
	1	10	10	2	8	

THE SCOOP

In 1997, Morgan Stanley, long considered one of Wall Street's most prestigious investment banking firms, completed its multi-billion dollar merger with the retail brokerage firm of Dean Witter, Discover. The union resulted in a firm dubbed Morgan Stanley Dean Witter, the world's largest securities firm in terms of assets managed and revenues. Before the merger, both companies were near the top of their respective fields. As an investment banking house, Morgan Stanley is one of the leading investment banks in M&A and debt and equity underwriting; Dean Witter, Discover has established itself as the nation's third-largest retail brokerage house (after Merrill Lynch and Smith Barney) and as the third-largest issuer of consumer credit. The marriage is one of misfits, culturally. Morgan Stanley has a reputation as blue-blooded as the Morgan name suggests; Dean Witter was, until 1993, owned by Sears. Economic historian Ron Chernow said of the merger: "This is as shocking as the duchess suddenly announcing that she's marrying the footman."

HAPPILY EVER AFTER?

Thus far, the marriage has been an unconventional fairy tale. Cognizant of cultural clashes that often result from mergers between investment banks and retail brokerage houses usually because high-flying investment brokers bristle at the more austere culture of commercial banks – Morgan Stanley and Dean Witter have decided to consummate their brokered marriage slowly, promising autonomy for both companies. Although Morgan Stanley and Dean Witter have remained separate entities, culturally and legally, their businesses have complemented each other well. As of June 1998, the firm's stock had doubled, and new accounts and mutual-fund sales had risen 40 percent since the merger.

Morgan Stanley has benefited from the added distribution strength. Even before the merger was finalized, the two units were helping each other. In May 1997, Dean Witter brokers sold all of the shares Morgan Stanley released as part of a $150 million issue of United Dominion Realty. Dean Witter brokers played an important role in Morgan Stanley's $2.5 billion secondary issue of First Union common shares; the brokers sold $500 million of that issue to more than 20,000 individual clients in the largest secondary issue ever. The firm reports that only 300 employees out of 48,000 were laid off as the result of the merger. Combined, the firm has more than 400 offices, with a presence in 28 countries. In 1997, Morgan Stanley Dean Witter's return on equity, a commonly used indicator of a bank's performance, was a healthy 22 percent

MONEY — AND CREDIT — TALKS

Those who thought Dean Witter's Sears pedigree was too pedestrian for blueblood Morgan Stanley also probably weren't too thrilled with Dean Witter's declasse Discover credit card and its 1 percent cash back promise. Yet Morgan Stanley Dean Witter is now one of the country's top credit card issuers (behind Citicorp and MBNA) with over 40 million accounts. The Discover card is currently ranked as the third-largest credit card company (behind Visa and Mastercard) in terms of charge volume and outstanding credit-card balances. However, in recent years, the Discover card's performance has stagnated, as the company has developed new products such as Bravo, only to discontinue them. Morgan Stanley, however, says it has no plans to sell the card, viewing the card as a potentially untapped cross-marketing gold mine. The firm has also hinted strongly that it may take the Discover card international by 2003.

GETTING HIRED

Morgan Stanley's interviews are, according to current employees, "quite formal, even for the investment banking industry." Technical questions are common; one business school student interviewing for a trading job reports that for his final round he was asked to sit in a chair while a senior director peppered him with macroeconomic questions. "All he did was pace around and throw questions at me – if I was wrong he'd correct me, and then just go to the next one. I remember thinking, 'God, I'm glad I know some of this stuff.' It was a lot of macroeconomics: inflation, interest rates, currencies." Says that contact: "They had me interview with pretty senior people, the head of all treasury trading, and the second in charge

I-Banking Job Seekers: Receive free e-mailed job postings matching your interests & qualifications! Register at www.VaultReports.com

VAULT REPORTS™
www.vaultreports.com

29

of all fixed income." Some recent associate-level hires report undergoing more than one call-back round while going through the business school recruiting process. "I had three more rounds, all in New York (after the on-campus round)," reports one contact.

OUR SURVEY SAYS

As one of Wall Street's preeminent "white-shoe" firms, Morgan Stanley cultivates an "extremely professional environment" geared toward the "bright, motivated individuals that fill the halls." Insiders say that "everyone seems to have an MBA from a top business school" and state that "no other firm matches Morgan Stanley in terms of education and attitude." Not everyone appreciates this atmosphere, however. One former analyst calls "the people at Morgan Stanley" his "biggest disappointment." He explains: "They are boorish, aggressive, and elitist – even more so than the rest of Wall Street." Another who left the firm recalls that he found his supervisors to be "shallow, uninspiring and heartless."

BEEP!

One of the famed aspects of Morgan Stanley's culture is that bankers are required to wear beepers, which some other banks enjoy pointing out as a MSDW shortcoming during MBA recruiting season. "Depending on how you think about that, [omnipresent beepers are] a good thing or a bad thing," reveals one associate. "The bad thing is, everyone's got access to your number. But the good side is that if you ever want to take a two-hour lunch, you can, because they can page you. If anyone ever complains that you weren't in the office, you can just say 'Why didn't you page me?'" Continues that contact: "And at night, it becomes a terrific social resource. People start paging people, next thing you know, you've got 50 people together."

VAULT
REPORTS™
www.vaultreports.com

ON THE SPOT

Morgan Stanley is also famed for its innovative evaluation system. "You get evaluated every six months and it leads directly into your compensation. You have a 360-degree performance evaluation," explains one insider. "So everyone you work with you put on your list, and that list goes to the HR department. The HR department sends an evaluation form to everyone you work with. [Morgan Stanley] takes this very seriously. Everyone you work with will give you a formal evaluation."

"All the evaluations are collected, and a VP or Principal who's in your group is assigned to collate all the information and pull together what the overall evaluation should be. This happens once in winter, and summer." Although the firm works on a three-tier evaluation system, "there's infinite room in all the tiers, it's not like a forced curve." Morgan Stanley awards its bonuses in July; each tier is awarded a bonus that represents a different portion of base salary.

"You not only get feedback from people above you, but you give them evaluations. The downward evaluations are named, upward are anonymous," says one former analyst. "So if your associate is being a total pain in the ass, you slam them in the reviews. They take very seriously the opinions of the junior people when evaluating for bonuses – so associates go out of the way to be helpful." "I'd say that is a very unique thing about Morgan," says that contact, who points out that the Morgan Stanley evaluation model was actually a case study at his business school.

To order a 50- to 70-page Vault Reports Employer Profile on Morgan Stanley Dean Witter call 1-888-JOB-VAULT or visit www.VaultReports.com

The full Employer Profile includes detailed information on MSDW's departments, recent developments and transactions, hiring and interview process, plus what employees really think about culture, pay, work hours and more.

I-Banking Job Seekers: Receive free e-mailed job postings matching your interests & qualifications! Register at www.VaultReports.com

VAULT REPORTS™

31

www.vaultreports.com

Merrill Lynch

World Financial Center
North Tower
250 Vesey Street
New York, NY 10281
(212) 449-1000
www.ml.com

LOCATIONS

New York, NY (HQ)
Atlanta • Los Angeles • Louisville, KY • New
Orleans, LA • Princeton, NJ • San Francisco •
Washington, DC • Tokyo, Japan • Toronto,
Canada • London, United Kingdom • As well
as locations around the nation and worldwide

DEPARTMENTS

Capital Management
Corporate Finance
Investment Banking
Mergers & Acquisitions
Private Client Services
Sales & Trading

THE STATS

Annual Revenues: $31.7 billion (1997)
No. of Employees: 56,600 (worldwide)
No. of Offices: 550+ (worldwide)
Stock Symbol: MER (NYSE)
CEO: David H. Komansky

KEY COMPETITORS

- Charles Schwab
- E*Trade
- Goldman Sachs & Co.
- J.P. Morgan
- Morgan Stanley Dean Witter
- PaineWebber
- Salomon Smith Barney

THE BUZZ
What bankers at other firms
are saying about Merrill

- "Gargantuan, bureaucratic"
- "They do everything"
- "Normal people"
- "Cultureless"

UPPERS

- Good social life
- Not as stuffy as some other investment banks

DOWNERS

- No company gym
- Can be extremely bureaucratic and political
- Recent layoffs

EMPLOYMENT CONTACT

Undergraduate:
Carrie Higginbotham
Assistant Vice President

Graduate:
Denise Patton
Vice President

Investment Banking Recruiting
Merrill Lynch
World Financial Center
250 Vesey Street, 2nd Fl.
New York, NY 10281

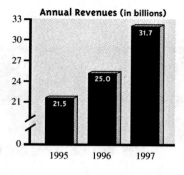

Annual Revenues (in billions)

1995	1996	1997
21.5	25.0	31.7

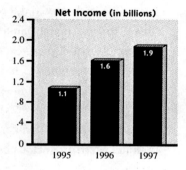

Net Income (in billions)

1995	1996	1997
1.1	1.6	1.9

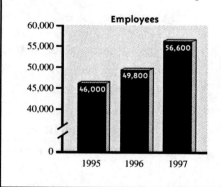

Employees

1995	1996	1997
46,000	49,800	56,600

© Copyright 1999 Vault Reports, Inc. Photocopying is illegal and is expressly forbidden.

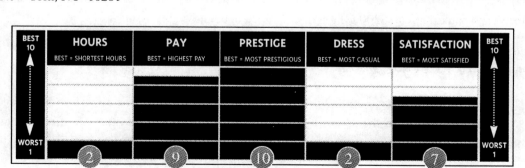

	HOURS	PAY	PRESTIGE	DRESS	SATISFACTION	
BEST 10 ... WORST 1	BEST = SHORTEST HOURS	BEST = HIGHEST PAY	BEST = MOST PRESTIGIOUS	BEST = MOST CASUAL	BEST = MOST SATISFIED	BEST 10 ... WORST 1
	2	9	10	2	7	

I-Banking Job Seekers: Receive free e-mailed job postings matching your interests & qualifications! Register at www.VaultReports.com

VAULT REPORTS™
www.vaultreports.com

33

THE SCOOP

THE BIG GENERALIST BANK

Founded in 1914 as an underwriting firm by Charles Merrill and his friend Edmund Lynch, Merrill Lynch survived the Great Depression by cutting loose its retail customers and limiting itself to investment banking services. Through a 1940 merger with Wall Street firm E.A. Pierce, Merrill Lynch reacquired its retail business, and in 1971 the company became the first Big Board member to have its shares listed on the New York Stock Exchange. For years, Merrill Lynch was unique among major Wall Street firms. Unlike most investment banks, which specialize in serving institutional clients like corporations, governments and big investors, or retail brokerages, which sell stocks, bonds, and mutual funds to the general public, Merrill Lynch caters to both markets.

RANKING HIGH

Merrill's departments are at the top of their respective league tables (the rankings of investment banks) – or, at the very least, hover somewhere in the top five. In 1998, the firm ranked No. 1 in underwriting all domestic issues, No. 1 in domestic investment grade debt, and No. 1 in asset-backed securities. Merrill ranked No. 2 in common stock and IPOs, and No. 2 in worldwide M&A advising. In recent years, Merrill has been at the forefront of a number of major deals in the American market, including the $8.8 billion acquisition of U.S. Healthcare by Aetna and Bell Atlantic's $33 billion merger with Nynex Corporation. In 1998, the firm advised NationsBank in its $61 billion merger with BankAmerica. Also in 1998, the firm came the first I-bank to break $300 billion in combined debt and equity issues.

AN ARMY OF BROKERS

Not only does Merrill have top-notch I-banking capabilities, it also has a massive brokerage army eager to distribute the stocks and bonds the firm helps underwrite. The firm's retail brokerage unit, which has more than 13,000 financial consultants and serves more than 7 million accounts worldwide, is the world's largest. The firm's retail business is based in Princeton, New Jersey, and has more than 600 branch offices. Merrill's mutual funds and other asset management businesses (such as managing pension funds for institutional clients) are also wildly popular – the firm has $1.3 trillion of assets under management, more than double its $557 billion mark in 1993. Because of its historical willingness to cater to retail investors, Merrill has the reputation of a "down-market" firm, at least when compared to blue-blooded competitors like Goldman Sachs and Morgan Stanley. But now, many of Merrill's competitors are following in the giant's money-making footsteps. In 1997, Morgan Stanley merged with retail brokerage Dean Witter (which until recently hawked its wares from Sears department stores). That year, famed Wall Street bank Salomon Brothers merged with retail-heavy Smith Barney. And when in 1998, the crème de la crème of investment banks, privately-owned Goldman Sachs, announced that it would make an initial public offering, industry observers speculated that the firm was attempting to free up capital in order to finance acquisitions.

But Mr. Dow had something to say about all these grandiose banking plans. Goldman shelved its IPO indefinitely in summer 1998 as global market conditions tightened, hurt by the collapse of emerging markets in Asia and Russia. Merrill took major trading losses and announced its first quarterly loss since 1989 for the third quarter of 1998. The firm announced that it would lay off 3400 employees in its hardest-hit departments in October 1998.

GETTING HIRED

Merrill Lynch accepts resumes by regular mail, fax, and e-mail. Resumes should be accompanied by a cover letter detailing the applicant's interests, abilities, and geographical preferences. Applicants can consult Merrill Lynch's employment web page, located at www.ml.com/careers, in order to find out about job openings and contact information for the various groups within the company.

Resumes submitted to Merrill via either mail or through their school are sorted out by Merrill's recruiting personnel, and qualified applicants are invited for an interview. The first round of

I-Banking Job Seekers: Receive free e-mailed job postings matching your interests & qualifications! Register at www.VaultReports.com

VAULT REPORTS™
www.vaultreports.com

35

interviews is held on the applicant's campus, and those applicants who make the cut are invited to further rounds at the New York office. Merrill Lynch, like many other firms, gives preference to those applicants who worked as summer associates or analysts when hiring for full-time positions. However, one Merrill employee confesses that "in recent years, Merrill has overhired for its summer programs, with the result that only 50 percent of the summer class have received offers to work at the company." Insiders also report that Merrill's interviews, even the initial on-campus screening interview "can last a lot longer than the typical half-hour interviews that other firms conduct." Summer hires who are made an offer of employment are generally required to respond within 30 days.

OUR SURVEY SAYS

NO MORE ELEPHANTS

Gigantic Merrill is known for having many subcultures; insiders agree that Merrill's culture is "different from department to department." The investment banking division, according to one analyst, "is more laid back than most bulge-bracket investment banks, primarily because investment banking at Merrill is relatively new." Says that contact: "Historically, you must remember, Merrill was a 'huge lumbering elephant' because that was the culture in the dominant retail side of business. However, things are changing as Merrill becomes one of the top three investment banks, and we're becoming more like Goldman or Morgan Stanley day by day. But we're still different from those places. The people are nicer and there's a much lower asshole factor than at other banks." The contact says, however, that "as with any big company, there will be people who are nasty for no particular reason. There will be assholes in any place. But there are fewer at Merrill." A former trader at Merrill says that Merrill gave him the chance "to work with very talented people with whom you'll keep in touch for the rest of your life." Reports another insider: "No one breathes down your neck here."

EXCELLENT ACCESS

Most insiders feel that the best aspect of working with Merrill is "gaining exposure to the very best firms as your clients, and seeing how they run." "I worked on one fancy project for a large sports company," reports one associate. "The project was great because I was involved with it from start to finish, and I learned a lot about the company and also got a feel for how management at a large, professionally managed company operates. The work environment at Merrill provides a top learning experience."

The major drawback of working for Merrill, most agree, is the "horrendous" bureaucracy, which "can sometimes combine with office politics to make life miserable and incomprehensible. Sometimes, for no apparent reason, you get blamed for things you didn't do, and get assignments you're not supposed to have, and there's no one to complain to – life becomes like a page from a Kafka novel." According to one financial consultant: "While I'm in the world outside, I'm proud to be working for Merrill. But on the inside, I know that bureaucracy and politics can make life pretty miserable." Perhaps the booze-enhanced social life is a compensation. One insider raves that "every Friday, there's a happy hour where everyone goes. It's a great meat market. Everyone's looking to pick someone up. Secretaries are looking for investment bankers to marry, and investment bankers are looking for secretaries for the weekend. It's fantastic."

LUSH, FATTENING SURROUNDING

Merrill Lynch's headquarter offices are "impressive and large." While "they're not furnished in a particularly lavish fashion, they're always tastefully decorated." Employees at the New York office state that "the most impressive feature of Merrill's offices is that they're located in the World Financial Center – Merrill has an entire building to itself. The views from that office are spectacular. The analysts are actually housed in a bullpen and you have a corner view of the Statue of Liberty in that office." Another employee says, "The World Financial Center neighborhood has great bars and shops – though everything is priced exorbitantly." Unfortunately, reports one insider, Merrill's environment isn't the best for staying in shape: "I worked so many hours at the office that I gained a substantial amount of weight. I got fat, to

I-Banking Job Seekers: Receive free e-mailed job postings matching your interests & qualifications! Register at www.VaultReports.com

VAULT REPORTS™

37

www.vaultreports.com

avoid euphemisms. The problem is, you spend so much time sitting at your desk, with no time to exercise, and you're always eating a lot at meetings at night or ordering food from different restaurants." Alas, that associate laments, "there's no company gym for easy, during-the-day access to weights or jogging."

To order a 50- to 70-page Vault Reports Employer Profile on Merrill Lynch call 1-888-JOB-VAULT or visit www.VaultReports.com

The full Employer Profile includes detailed information on Merrill's departments, recent developments and transactions, hiring and interview process, plus what employees really think about culture, pay, work hours and more.

"Sometimes, for no apparent reason, you get blamed for things you didn't do, and get assignments you're not supposed to have... life becomes like a page from a Kafka novel."

– *Merrill insider*

Donaldson, Lufkin & Jenrette

277 Park Avenue
New York, NY 10172
(212) 892-3000
www.dlj.com

Donaldson, Lufkin & Jenrette

LOCATIONS

New York, NY (HQ)
Atlanta, GA • Bala Cynwyd, PA • Boston, MA • Dallas, TX • Houston, TX • Menlo Park, NJ • Miami, FL • San Francisco, CA • Los Angeles, CA • Bangalore, India • Buenos Aires, Argentina • Geneva, Switzerland • Hong Kong • London, England • Lugano, Switzerland • Mexico City, Mexico • Paris, France • Sao Paulo, Brazil • Tokyo, Japan

DEPARTMENTS

Investment Banking
Institutional Equity Research
Institutional Equity Sales
Investment Services Group
Taxable Fixed Income

THE STATS

Annual Revenues: $4.6 billion (1997)
No. of Employees: 7,000
No. of Offices: 22
Stock Symbol: DLJ (NYSE)
CEO: Joe L. Roby

KEY COMPETITORS

◆ Credit Suisse First Boston
◆ Goldman Sachs & Co.
◆ J.P. Morgan
◆ Merrill Lynch
◆ Morgan Stanley Dean Witter
◆ Salomon Smith Barney

THE BUZZ
What bankers at other firms
are saying about DLJ

◆ "Commission-shop culture"
◆ "Hot firm, big bonuses"
◆ "Aggressive, slavery"
◆ "One phrase: DLJail (long hours!)"

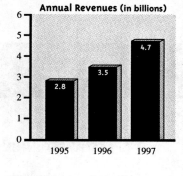

Annual Revenues (in billions)

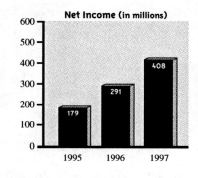

Net Income (in millions)

Employees

UPPERS

- ◆ Early responsibility
- ◆ Strong presence on West Coast
- ◆ Extensive exposure to upper management

DOWNERS

- ◆ Long workdays, even by Wall Street standards
- ◆ Demanding workload

EMPLOYMENT CONTACT

Investment Banking MBAs:
Elizabeth Derby
Manager Recruiting

Investment Banking Undergraduates:
Deborah A. Mc Carroll
Assistant Vice President

Sales, Trading and Research:
Erica DeBenedetto
Manager of Recruiting, Human Resources

Donaldson, Lufkin & Jenrette
277 Park Avenue
New York, NY 10172

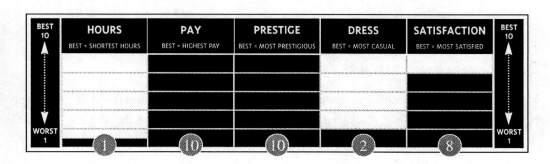

	HOURS	PAY	PRESTIGE	DRESS	SATISFACTION	
BEST 10 ↑ WORST 1	BEST = SHORTEST HOURS	BEST = HIGHEST PAY	BEST = MOST PRESTIGIOUS	BEST = MOST CASUAL	BEST = MOST SATISFIED	BEST 10 ↑ WORST 1
	1	10	10	2	8	

I-Banking Job Seekers: Receive free e-mailed job postings matching
your interests & qualifications! Register at www.VaultReports.com

VAULT REPORTS™
www.vaultreports.com

41

THE SCOOP

A SPLASHY BEGINNING

Founded in 1959 by three Harvard MBAs, Donaldson, Lufkin & Jenrette (DLJ) has grown into one of Wall Street's most influential investment banks. DLJ was first known on Wall Street as a research firm. Its reputation soon expanded – in 1970, DLJ created a media sensation by becoming the first New York Stock Exchange firm to go public. DLJ leapt whole-heartedly into the hostile takeover market of the 1980s, advising legendary corporate raider T. Boone Pickens on some of his more audacious forays.

HIGH-FLYING RISK TAKERS

DLJ probably won't be offended if you call it junky – the firm has profited enormously from underwriting junk bonds (high-yield debt) at a time when other banks thought the category was dead for good. In fact, when the fiefdom of junk bond czar Michael Milken, Drexel Burnham Lambert, imploded in 1991, DLJ zoomed in and scooped up Drexel's best and brightest , unlike other firms, who shied away from the stench of scandal. Today, DLJ is the perennial leader in junk bond underwriting. DLJ showed its long-term savvy again in 1995 – while other banks cringed at the onset of the peso crisis, DLJ recognized the future potential of the region remained unchained and hired away several of Bankers Trust's Latin American analysts.

Rivals believe that DLJ will not be able to transfer its market-leading position in the international market. DLJ's betting they're wrong. DLJ is betting that with the establishment of the pan-European Euro currency – which will reduce fluctuating currency risks that make fixed income products chancy – the junk bond market in the Old World will flourish.

DARING MERCHANT BANKERS

Majority-owned by the Equitable insurance company, DLJ provides a full range of investment banking services, including stock and debt offerings, equity and fixed income research, and sales and trading. In addition, the firm has an immensely successful merchant banking operation, through which the firm invests its own money in venture capital, leveraged buyouts, and other deals. DLJ tends to target small to medium-sized banks to pump up its growth. Its Los Angeles branch office commands enormous respect through the West Coast as a leader in high-yield debt offerings and entertainment and media initial public offerings. DLJ has also developed especially strong franchises in Asia and Latin America. DLJ has been aided by the high degree of autonomy the firm grants to its branches and departments.

Hello Roby

In February 1998, longtime CEO John Chalsty stepped down to turn the firm over to then-president and COO Joe Roby. Roby has pursued several immediate expansion initiatives – opening a London office to specialize in junk bonds, as well as trading and underwriting European securities. The firm also planned to more than double its I-banking operations in London. The firm also has been looking to boost its performance in investment-grade bond underwriting, hiring away several senior-level bankers focused on the "non-junk" bonds in the summer of 1998.

GETTING HIRED

DLJ manages its recruiting process from New York in coordination with its regional offices. For a comprehensive list of the dates and locations of DLJ's on-campus recruiting, visit the firm's "Career Opportunities" Web page, located at www.dlj.com.

The number of rounds and interview process for analysts depends on the size of the school. The process generally ends, however with a "Super Day." This super day involves a trip to the firm's NY headquarters, usually on a Saturday, but sometimes a Friday or another day. On these days, the firm brings in many candidates, maybe 5 to 8, on the same day. "At the end of day, all of the interviewers get together in a room and debate for several hours until they reach consensus on all candidates," explains one recruiter. "They also have before them all written

I-Banking Job Seekers: Receive free e-mailed job postings matching your interests & qualifications! Register at www.VaultReports.com

VAULT REPORTS™
www.vaultreports.com

43

feedback from earlier rounds. They start with the candidates being considered most seriously. In rare cases if they can't agree, they'll have to call in some of the interviewers from the earlier rounds to discuss."

For analysts, the super day is actually a half-day: The analysts arrive in the morning, and have five to six half-hour interviews. Most interviews are one-on-one, though some are two-on-one (two interviewers, not two candidates). At lunch, all the candidates and interviewers eat together, an event that no doubt decreases the appetite of some anxious interviewees. (Sometimes, the super day starts in the afternoon, and begins with this lunch.)

DLJ's core business schools for investment banking are Columbia, Wharton and Harvard. The firm makes presentations at these key schools, sending bigwigs such as the CEO or head of investment banking. I-Banking now recruits at 18 different schools.

DLJ has a three-round interview process for MBAs. The first round is held on campus, the second at a hotel near the school, and the third "super day" round at the firm's NY headquarters. Both of the first two rounds involve two-on-one interviews. During the second round, held at local hotels, candidates undergo two half-hour two-on-ones. "We like to do two-on-ones," notes a recruiter. The final round is held at DLJ's New York headquarters. The MBA super day process is similar, if a little more taxing, than the final round for analysts – expect five to six hours, including a lunch with all of the candidates and interviewers. Insiders tell us that DLJ will call candidates for a fourth round of interviews at the company's headquarters as a "tie-breaker."

The firm recruits at 15 schools for its investment services division (the division that covers high net worth and small institutions). For equities trading, the firm holds a first round interview on campus, and a second round in New York. For investment services, the first round is on campus, the second round at the local office the candidate is being considered for, with a third round in NY. For each of these, the first round is a two-on-one interview.

OUR SURVEY SAYS

FIERCELY ENTREPRENEURIAL

DLJ has a "fiercely entrepreneurial" culture that is "individualistic and exciting," employees say. One insider suggests that "to understand DLJ's culture, think of DLJ and Goldman as being the two opposite poles of the world of investment banking. Goldman is solidly conservative, and extremely team-oriented. DLJ is daring and individualistic." An associate in the New York office comments that because of DLJ's aggressive attitude "people are better rewarded here for their performance than in other banks. DLJ is more of a meritocracy than other firms. If you work hard, you move through the whole spectrum of jobs really rapidly. Everything that goes on is really based on performance. So there's nothing in the way of people getting moved up more quickly or getting higher compensation if they're doing something good. DLJ keeps the politics away." Investment banking employees praise the company for being "bold enough" to permit them to invest their own money in company transactions – "something that Goldman would never agree to do." Says another insider: "The environment is collegial, aggressive and hard-working."

HIGH MARKS FOR WOMEN

Despite this reputed gung-ho culture, DLJ now wears the honor of being named one of the top 100 best places to work by *Working Mother Magazine*, and offers flex-time, job sharing, a unisex three-month parental leave policy, and other family-friendly measures. DLJ states that 19 percent of its vice presidents are women and 7 percent of senior executives are female. "DLJ is more of a meritocracy than other firms," says one insider. "If you work hard, you move through the spectrum of jobs really rapidly... there's nothing in the way of people getting moved up more quickly or getting higher compensation if they're doing something good."

I-Banking Job Seekers: Receive free e-mailed job postings matching your interests & qualifications! Register at www.VaultReports.com

VAULT REPORTS™
www.vaultreports.com

45

WORK HARD

It's a good thing your co-workers will be nice and fair, because you'll be spending a lot of time with them. DLJ's hours "may be worse than at other investment firms." Analysts "easily work 90 or 100 hours every week," with associates putting in "80- or 90-hour weeks." Even one vice president says that while "the longer you stay, the less you work," it's still "a lot. I work 70 or 80 hours a week – at least 8 a.m. to 8 p.m. every day." Still, say employees, "people here are happier here than elsewhere," since the "sink or swim environment" leads "those who don't like the work to get out early – which is better for them and the firm."

Putting in those hours and contending with the tough environment also brings pay that's "a little better" than other investment banks, and unusual benefits – like the opportunity to invest your own money in DLJ deals. Dress at DLJ is formal except for "casual Fridays in the summer in some offices." The firm's NY headquarters also has a subsidized cafeteria. The cafeteria is closed for dinner, but employees can order food – there's a $25 limit in I-banking. There's also "free flowing Starbucks coffee in investment banking."

To order a 50- to 70-page Vault Reports Employer Profile on Donaldson, Lufkin & Jenrette call 1-888-JOB-VAULT or visit www.VaultReports.com

The full Employer Profile includes detailed information on DLJ's departments, recent developments and transactions, hiring and interview process, plus what employees really think about culture, pay, work hours and more.

VAULT REPORTS™
www.vaultreports.com

"DLJ is more of a meritocracy than other firms. If you work hard, you move through the whole spectrum of jobs really rapidly."

— *DLJ insider*

J.P. Morgan

60 Wall Street
New York, NY 10260
(212) 483-2323
www.jpmorgan.com

JPMorgan

LOCATIONS

New York City, NY (HQ)
Boston, MA • Chicago, IL • Dallas, TX• Houston, TX • Los Angeles, CA • Newark, DE • Palm Beach, FL • Philadelphia, PA • San Francisco, CA • Washington, DC

Numerous international locations including ones in Buenos Aires • Brussels • London • Paris • Singapore • Tokyo

BUSINESS LINES

Investment Banking • Equities • Fixed Income • Emerging Markets • Foreign Exchange • Commodities • Private Client Group • Investment Management

THE STATS

Annual Revenues: $7.22 billion (1997)
No. of Employees: 16,000 (worldwide)
No. of Offices: 50 (worldwide), 11 (U.S.)
Stock Symbol: JPM (NYSE)
CEO: Douglas ("Sandy") A. Warner III

KEY COMPETITORS

- Chase Manhattan
- Credit Suisse First Boston
- Donaldson, Lufkin & Jenrette
- Goldman Sachs & Co.
- Lehman Brothers
- Merrill Lynch
- Morgan Stanley Dean Witter
- Salomon Smith Barney

THE BUZZ

What bankers at other firms
are saying about J.P. Morgan

- "Competitive, classic Wall Street firm"
- "Friendly"
- "Top-notch but with growing pains"
- "Great name but always second rate"

J.P. Morgan

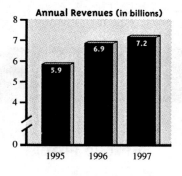

Annual Revenues (in billions)

UPPERS

- ◆ Emphasis on job training
- ◆ Subsidized gym memberships
- ◆ Generous vacation policies
- ◆ Great diversity for Wall Street

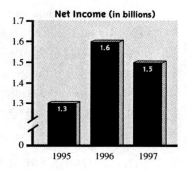

Net Income (in billions)

DOWNERS

- ◆ Struggling firm
- ◆ No more free lunch
- ◆ Somewhat stuffy

EMPLOYMENT CONTACT

JP Morgan
60 Wall Street
New York, NY 10260

Check out the web site at
www.jpmorgan.com for addresses
of recruiting in principal locations.

Employees

	BEST 10 ↕ WORST 1	HOURS BEST = SHORTEST HOURS	PAY BEST = HIGHEST PAY	PRESTIGE BEST = MOST PRESTIGIOUS	DRESS BEST = MOST CASUAL	SATISFACTION BEST = MOST SATISFIED	BEST 10 ↕ WORST 1
		2	9	10	1	9	

I-Banking Job Seekers: Receive free e-mailed job postings matching
your interests & qualifications! Register at www.VaultReports.com

VAULT REPORTS™
www.vaultreports.com

49

THE SCOOP

A PROUD HISTORY

The financiers of household names such as U.S. Steel, General Electric, and AT&T, J.P. Morgan is more than an investment bank – it's an American institution. The firm's founders, father Junius Spencer Morgan and son J. Pierpont, rose to fame as a powerful banking team in the second half of the 19th century. Working on both sides of the Atlantic, the Morgans were responsible for bringing capital from Europe to the U.S. that was crucial to the new nation's growth. After Junius died in 1890, J. Pierpont consolidated the family businesses under th name J.P. Morgan and Company and commenced a reign as a symbol of Wall Street's power.

STILL OUTSIDE THE INNER SANCTUM

Despite its hallowed name, J.P. Morgan still hasn't made it into the coveted investment banking elite. The firm has for years attempted to transform itself from a commercial bank into an investment bank. Unlike other large commercial banks, such as NationsBank and Deutsche Bank, which have built its I-banking practices by acquiring firms, traditional Morgan has decided to grow its business from within.

Firm officials and Wall Street analysts cite Morgan's ability thus far to transform itself – the firm ranks respectably in league tables – as an astounding story of successful restructuring. In 1980, about 50 percent of the bank's revenue came from traditional commercial banking businesses such as corporate lending; nowadays, 75 percent comes from investment banking business such as trading and underwriting. Industry observers point to the firm's folding its lending operation into its fixed-income trading business in December 1997 as symbolic of this change.

WHERE'S THE PERFORMANCE

But while Morgan has been successful in its transformation, the bank hasn't been utterly triumphant. In comparison to already established investment banks like Goldman Sachs and Merrill Lynch, the firm's actual performance is much less impressive than its hallowed name.

In 1997, the firm's 13.4 percent return on equity fell behind the 17.5 percent average of money-center banks and the 21 percent average of investment banks. J.P. Morgan has pursued a strategy of growing its investment banking business organically, through leveraging its corporate lending relationships. This has worked well in M&A and bond underwriting, but not as well in areas such as stock underwriting, since many of Mogan's prime customers – blue-chip, established companies – have little need for stock offerings.

No, THERE ISN'T SUCH A THING AS A FREE LUNCH

J.P. Morgan has taken huge financial hits recently, especially in the fourth quarter of 1997 and the first quarter of 1998, when earnings fell 35 and 48 percent, respectively. Part of the reason for the faltering profits is that Morgan had invested heavily in Asia, where financial crisis eviscerated local banks. In response, the firm has looked for ways to cut spending. It announced a 5 percent cut in staff in February 1998, and also began to trim fat elsewhere, most notably by axing the firm's free-lunch policy. In May 1998, the firm announced that it planned to slash between $300 to $500 million in costs annually.

GETTING HIRED

Like the bank itself, Morgan's recruiting process has changed dramatically in the past decade or so. The firm's different divisions recruit separately (rather than relying on a cumbersome and less focused unified recruiting effort). Also, although the firm doesn't generally shell out huge signing bonuses to attract name-brand Wall Street talent, the firm no longer limits its hiring to recent graduates. Clayton Rose, who heads Morgan's diversity effort, told *The Wall Street Journal* recently: "When I joined this firm, you could shoot a gun and not hit a midcareer hire. (Now) we have become comfortable with the notion that loyalty doesn't only come from being born and bred here."

I-Banking Job Seekers: Receive free e-mailed job postings matching your interests & qualifications! Register at www.VaultReports.com

VAULT REPORTS™
www.vaultreports.com

51

J.P. Morgan has extensive recruiting literature on its web site, located at www.jpmorgan.com. The site includes a nifty cross-referencing chart that allows a candidate who knows his or her function (accounting, auditing, etc.) and what Morgan business group he or she is interested in, to find the perfect job in the firm.

J.P. Morgan recruits at 50 undergraduate schools and 15 MBA schools. For business schools, there is typically one big presentation. After that initial presentation, Morgan's individual business groups often go back to the campus to make smaller presentations. These are generally club sponsored; the firm's assent management division, for example, will be sponsored by a school's investment management club. Sometimes the firm holds brown bag lunches or cocktail presentations. For lucky schools, such as UCLA, there are Morgan beer busts. The firm does not conduct on-campus recruiting at law schools, but they do accept resumes from law students and do hire JDs.

Morgan also hosts dinners at the major business schools. "The goal is to get to know you," explains one recruiter. These dinners are usually held one to two months before interviewing begins. There's also an "after offer" dinner for offerees. At undergraduate colleges, the dinner is usually held for invited interviewees at the firm's target schools. This policy varies by business (sometimes dinners are only for candidates who have received an offer.

Candidates applying to Morgan through the firm's on-campus recruiting efforts go through the process of a lengthy on-campus interview and then a full day of callbacks at the firm's New York headquarters. (For summer hires, the second round is held locally.) The firm's investment banking department does a "Super Saturday," when many candidates are brought to the headquarters to run the gantlet of interviewing. A candidate usually interviews with five to eight people during the second round.

MBAs who get offers are asked back for sell days, when they meet members of the group who schmooze with them in hopes of getting them to sign up. Most new hires are brought aboard at New York City, London, Brussels, Singapore, and Tokyo. Analysts are not hired into specific groups, which some insiders note as a drawback.

OUR SURVEY SAYS

FIRST-CLASS PEOPLE

J.P. Morgan's mantra, bankers tell us, is "first-class people doing business in a first-class way." Translation: an emphasis on civility and teamwork, with a touch of old-school elitism and bureaucracy. One analyst in the firm's equity research department describes the firm as "very corporate" and "white collar." Another insider comments on the firm's "notably high ethical standards." Says another insider, in the firm's fixed-income department: "It's somewhat conservative, extremely politically correct, and very elite." However, one associate says this reputation is overstated: "It's professional, but not as haughty as is sometimes thought."

Insiders agree that J.P. Morgan is "on the friendly end of the Wall Street spectrum." There's "very little petty office politics." Comments an associate in investment banking: "It's generally very inclusive and team-oriented. There's not much backstabbing. Managing directors and vice presidents are concerned about developing junior people."

But in this imperfect world, even Morgan's emphasis on teamwork is considered an outmoded drawback by some. Says one analyst: "The team environment sometimes leads to failure to recognize those working harder or on more advanced assignments." An associate in investment management agrees: "The consensus-driven approach makes accountability and contrarian thinking difficult to achieve." Says one I-banking analyst: "[J.P. Morgan] is friendly and cooperative, but it can become too entrenched in its own history at times and not aggressive enough." And, says one associate in sales: "The only think that really bugs me is that we tend to keep weak people circulating in-house rather than aggressively firing those not up to par."

DIVERSE BY WALL STREET STANDARDS

The opportunities for both women and other minorities at Morgan is "surprisingly good for this business," employees say, emphasizing J.P. Morgan's "excellent gender diversity." Reports one I-banking analyst: "I work in a very diverse group – several different races and good representation of women."

I-Banking Job Seekers: Receive free e-mailed job postings matching your interests & qualifications! Register at www.VaultReports.com

VAULT REPORTS™
53
www.vaultreports.com

One insider comments that "there certainly are more women here than at any other Wall Street firm – Morgan puts a big effort forward in this area, and it's definitely paying off for them." Reports one supervisor: "I supervise a group of all women." Says an associate in investment banking: "The head of my group is a woman and almost half of all junior personnel are women." But Morgan is still on Wall Street, and some women believe their opportunities could be improved. "The firm appears to try and reach out to women in hiring for junior positions, but there are very few women in leadership positions, or in positions to mentor or support young women," reports one woman analyst. One woman associate says that while receptivity to women is "very good," "it becomes increasingly difficult to rise to the 'next level' with each promotion. While this is true of men, too, I think it is more pronounced for women."

As for ethnic and other minorities, "J.P. Morgan's diversity efforts are known by all employees," says one vice president. Every business area is overseen by the 'Diversity Steering Committee,' a group of senior managers brought together to discuss diversity issues affecting the firm on a global basis. Regarding Morgan's minority recruitment efforts, one employee tells Vault Reports, "If you're black or Hispanic, Morgan definitely wants to hire you. Another employee reports: "If you're a minority and you want to leave the job, they'll sit you down for an interview to try to find out what it was that made you want to leave this place." Two of Morgan's three vice chairmen are foreign born. In August 1997, Morgan announced same-sex domestic partner benefits, the first Wall Street firm to do so. The firm has brought in speakers like Allen Gilmour, a retired vice chairman of Ford Motor, to speak to employees about being openly gay in the workplace. One analyst puts it simply: "Morgan has a huge diversity initiative."

ON THE LOW-END FOR THE STREET, BUT C'MON...

Morgan is known for being on the low end of pay on the Street; insiders suggest that the firm's prestige and job satisfaction allow it to get away with paying salaries below those of competitors. One employee comments: "There's a rumor going around that so far has proven to be pretty true, that if you take a job at, say, Salomon Smith Barney, you'll get paid more than at J.P. Morgan because Morgan has a better reputation. So with Salomon, it's more of a recruiting effort than anything else." Says one associate in investment management: "Morgan is on the low end, and buy-side is lower than sell-side, but there's a fair amount of predictability and stability." Says one young VP: "I was worried that at J.P. Morgan I would not be paid as much, and I believe I am underpaid compared to my peers at other firms, but I love my job and don't want to work anywhere else."

Still, it's not as if bankers at Morgan are going hungry. Although first-year salaries are sometimes called "a bit low," insiders say they are on par with "industry averages, if you consider your signing bonus." Says one second-year analyst in investment banking, earning nearing $90,000 in total compensation: "I'm not sure how this compares to other Wall Street firms, but straight out of college, I couldn't expect much more." And the third year of working with J.P. Morgan is "the payoff, because that's when profit sharing kicks in." Afterwards, analysts say, "increases depend on whether or not you make associate." If you do, "expect to be pushed way up the pay scale." One associate in sales and trading reports expecting to make $120,000 in his first year, describing his compensation as the "standard top-tier Wall Street package." One associate just beginning his third year in the firm's M&A group reports expecting to make $280,000. Another in the same group expects to make $300,000. (That associate remarks: "Although it is a lot of money, you earn it.")

To order a 50- to 70-page Vault Reports Employer Profile on J.P. Morgan call 1-888-JOB-VAULT or visit www.VaultReports.com

The full Employer Profile includes detailed information on J.P. Morgan's departments, recent developments and transactions, hiring and interview process, plus what employees really think about culture, pay, work hours and more.

I-Banking Job Seekers: Receive free e-mailed job postings matching your interests & qualifications! Register at www.VaultReports.com

VAULT REPORTS™

55

www.vaultreports.com

Lazard Freres & Co.

30 Rockefeller Plaza
New York, NY 10020
(212) 632-6000
Fax: (212) 632-6060
www.lazard.com

LAZARD FRÈRES & CO. LLC

LOCATIONS

New York, NY (U.S. HQ)
Paris, France
London, U.K.

DEPARTMENTS

Asset Management
Capital Markets
Corporate Advisory Services
Principal Investing

THE STATS

Worldwide Profits: $400 million (1997)
A privately-held company
CEO: Michel David-Weill

KEY COMPETITORS

- Allen & Co.
- Goldman Sachs & Co.
- Morgan Stanley Dean Witter
- Merrill Lynch
- Salomon Smith Barney
- Wasserstein Perella

THE BUZZ

What bankers at other firms
are saying about Lazard

- "Rich, schmoozy"
- "The lizards"
- "Old boys network to the extreme"
- "Excellent cachet but small"

UPPERS

- Super-high pay
- Dynamic working environment
- Great finance training

DOWNERS

- Health-impairing workload
- Political infighting among partners
- Bad company infrastructure

EMPLOYMENT CONTACT

Human Resources
Ms. Suzanne Zywicki
Lazard Freres & Co.
30 Rockefeller Plaza
New York, NY 10020

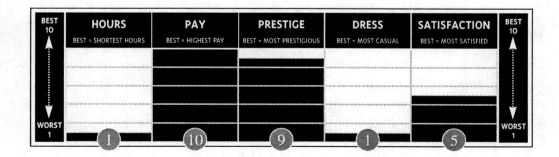

	HOURS	PAY	PRESTIGE	DRESS	SATISFACTION	
BEST 10 / WORST 1	BEST = SHORTEST HOURS	BEST = HIGHEST PAY	BEST = MOST PRESTIGIOUS	BEST = MOST CASUAL	BEST = MOST SATISFIED	BEST 10 / WORST 1
	1	10	9	1	5	

I-Banking Job Seekers: Receive free e-mailed job postings matching your interests & qualifications! Register at www.VaultReports.com

VAULT REPORTS™
www.vaultreports.com

57

THE SCOOP

FRENCH ROOTS

In 1848, brothers from the Lazard family in France emigrated to New Orleans, where they started-up a dry-goods business. Following the destruction of the business by fire, the Lazard brothers moved to San Francisco in 1848, just in time to cash in on that city's explosive Gold Rush growth. The real growth started, however, after the Lazards turned their business over to cousin Alexandre Weill. By 1883, Weill had transformed Lazard Freres into a thriving banking concern, with offices in London, New York, San Francisco and Paris. The company has since remained in the hands of Weill's descendants (who hyphenated the family name David-Weill in the 1920s to add aristocratic luster). The current CEO, Michel David-Weill, took the helm of the company in 1977, reacquiring the long-lost London branch, revamping the New York office and increasing coordination between the three branches of Lazard Freres.

THE CLASSIC, CHIC M&A BOUTIQUE

Today, Lazard Freres might be called the classic advisory boutique, specializing primarily in providing mergers and acquisitions advice. The firm also has a small underwriting and trading business and an asset management arm that has $65 billion dollars under management as of the summer of 1998. Despite the firm's specialization, Lazard's Freres profits and influence are hardly limited. The firm has been tapped for such high profile mergers as Viacom/Paramount, Bertelsmann/Random House and IBM/Lotus. Lazard is known for a superstar culture: its elite, connected bankers are known as the trusted advisers of the princes of business.

IN THE NEWS (DARN)

However, changes may be in store for Lazard's manner of operation. The firm, known for its avoidance of publicity, has been in the news in recent years. In 1997, a partner was convicted of failure to disclose a conflict of interest to public clients. After a struggle between David-Weill and his son-in-law and intended successor, Edouard Stern, Stern left the firm in mid-

1997. Also 1997, Felix Rohatyn, the architect of New York City's recovery from bankruptcy in the 1970s, left to become U.S. Ambassador to France.

UNCOMFORTABLE CHANGES

In response, the company is re-evaluating its tripartite structure, its compensation system (under which partner pay is still determined by firm leader Michel David-Weill) and lack of industry specialization. The firm has established a board of directors, which includes presumed heir apparent Steven Rattner, who as deputy CEO of the New York office, runs the entire firm's day-to-day operations. However, speculation that Rattner will leave the firm for a government position, and the departure of Rohaytn, Stern, and several other top bankers have led industry observers to suggest that the firm's old-school style of banking is endangered in the world of giant financial services firms like Morgan Stanley Dean Witter and Salomon Smith Barney.

GETTING HIRED

Lazard's investment banking division recruits at undergraduate colleges and business schools, but other departments, such as asset management, fill their open slots primarily through word-of-mouth, insiders say. A recruiting schedule for investment banking and contact information for other departments are available at the firm's web site, located at www.lazard.com.

In investment banking, Lazard hires its associates largely through its summer program. Explains one insider: "They want the summer people to work out and get a look at them, rather than take a crapshot with someone you met at a Super Saturdays."

B-school insiders report mostly two-on-one interviews. At some schools, after the initial screening round, "they call you later on that night and have you come back and do some more interviews, and they will give you the offer then," but at others "they fly people to New York." "They don't interview many people," says one insider. While it is not an explicit requirement, "you need to have M&A experience to work at Lazard [as an associate]."

I-Banking Job Seekers: Receive free e-mailed job postings matching your interests & qualifications! Register at www.VaultReports.com

VAULT REPORTS™

59

www.vaultreports.com

Insiders advise showing up for your interview with a "nice expensive suit." "The people that they hire – there's no way to say this really – but they tend to be attractive people," says one Lazard insider. "They're not looking for the nerdy number cruncher that you get at some of the banks like Goldman. They want it so when there's a meeting, you can tell Lazard walked in the door."

Reports one recent interviewee: "One question they like to ask is 'What was the hardest thing you did – what was the most complicated deal?' If you brought up an M&A deal, then from talking to you about that deal, they can tell where you are." Says that insider: "I strongly stress for anyone who wants to work there as an associate – you've got to be a banker. They expect you to walk in the first day and be ready. My first day, my phone rang, and they said you're late. I said, 'I'm late? I just walked in the door' It was a secretary of one of the senior people, and she tells me that 'there's a meeting up on 62 and you've got to get up there.' I get up there and There's the CEO and he's talking about what type of company he wants to acquire. I start taking notes. That evening and the rest of the night I crank out merger models."

OUR SURVEY SAYS

YOU HAVE NO LIFE

To say Lazard "demands total commitment," is an understatement. "Working hours are just crazy," says one insider, who sometimes wishes for "more time for family, friends, and non-professional areas of interest." Says another: "You will definitely work over one hundred hours during an average workweek;" another worker puts the figure at "110 to 130" hours weekly. One employee criticizes the "superhuman expectations" at the firm. "You can't work any harder than they work," one former Lazard banker says. "There were people carried out by ambulance – they had collapsed from exhaustion."

How bad it is for Lazard bankers depends almost entirely on where one is on the totem pole, insiders say. Contacts concur that "analysts have no life." Explains one insider: "The attitude is that the analysts are not bankers. It's 'I want to work you for two years and then spit you out, and you're lucky to be here.'" That contact continues: "The analysts do not exercise, they do not leave, they are there all the time. They're basically treated like support staff." Because of the poor lifestyle, insiders say, the firm suffers from extremely high turnover in its analyst ranks. "The analysts for the most part are extremely bitter," says one associate. One insider reports that from a class of 30 analysts hired in 1997, only three were still with the firm by mid-1998. "I think they're going to do better in the future, because they're starting to realize that it's not good," says that contact. Associates don't have it much better, insiders say, but "they know what they're getting into" and morale is pretty high. "The first three years as an associate – you're throwing those years away," says insider. "You're just trying to survive."

Why do associates put up with the intense work? For the promotion to VP that happens in maybe four or five years. "If you can survive the four years, you're looking at a pretty good lifestyle," explains one insider. "A VP at Lazard is very different from a VP at other places. At other places, the VP gets dragged down to do associate work, and still gets dragged into the office on weekends. A VP at Lazard – they really know they're shit, and if they want to, which pretty much everyone wants to, they refuse to do associate-level work. They want to be working on getting clients and things like that." Although during the week, VPs are there "till 9 o'clock – even MDs put in long hours at Lazard," on the weekends "they'll be at the Hamptons with a fax machine."

I'VE NEVER SEEN SO MUCH DECADENCE

"Lazard is like Wall Street was in the early 1980s," says one insider. "Cigar smoke is thick on the floor by 10 in the morning, they're all smoking. They play Polo, they've got their polo gear in the office. I've never seen so much decadence in a firm. They all had huge houses in the Hamptons, and they didn't mind talking about it – 'Oh, the roof in my Hampton's house is leaking, and now I can only sell it for $3 million.'"

The amazing luxury that the Lazard lifestyle affords is the reason the firm's bankers endure the almost unconscionable hours. "Bankers at Lazard are usually paid 25 to 50 percent more than

I-Banking Job Seekers: Receive free e-mailed job postings matching your interests & qualifications! Register at www.VaultReports.com

VAULT REPORTS™

61

www.vaultreports.com

the market salary, compared to comparable positions at other banks," says an analyst. Says one associate: "Your first full year, you can get close to $200,000 by the end." For summer associates going back for their second year of B-school, "they offer to pay for your second year [of business school], and no one else does that." "They basically tell you that their goal is to be the highest paying firm, and they're looking to start private equity stuff up in order to expand what they can do as far as compensation."

THIS IS SERIOUS STUFF

"If you consolidate all the worldwide M&A transactions completed between 1987 and 1997, Lazard ranks number one," says a former Lazard banker. Insiders agree that Lazard is at the top of the list when it comes to prestige. "It's an amazing place," says one insider. "They really do have great relationships with the CEOs of major companies." Says another: "We're the cutting edge of management and finance theory. The culture is very focused on production, merit and profits." Says a former banker: "They're not spinning they're wheels working their hours. They really put in some time and thought into the work they're doing."

NOT GREAT DIVERSITY

One employee maintains that the firm is "relatively progressive, with active recruitment of women and minorities," but notes that "there are very few women investment bankers at Lazard, not because we do not hire them, but because many of them leave due to the inhumane working environment." Another I-banking insider is more caustic: "There's one female managing director, and then there's some among the associates, but basically it's men. And it's not very diverse at all, it's a bunch of white guys." Says that contact: "It's a lot more of the old boy Waspy network rather than the Jewish network at other banks."

One employee criticizes Lazard's "limited resources," noting the firm's lack of consolidated databases forces employees to "fish for information using highly unorthodox methods, sometimes making life miserable. If you were working at a bulge bracket firm, most of the information would be a telephone call or a click of the mouse away."

"I've never seen so much decadence in a firm."

– *Lazard insider*

Salomon Smith Barney

388 Greenwich Street
New York, NY 10013
(212) 783-7000
Fax: (212) 940-4299
www.salomonsmithbarney.com

SALOMON SMITH BARNEY

LOCATIONS

New York, NY (HQ)
As well as offices in CA • CT • DC • FL • GA • IL • MA • NJ • PA • TX • International offices worldwide

DEPARTMENTS

Compliance • Credit Review • Domestic Corporate Finance • Equity • Fixed Income • Investment Banking • Legal • Sales & Trading • Asset Management • Capital Markets • Finance and Administration • Information Systems • Investment Banking • Public Finance • Research • Sales

THE STATS

Assets: $115+ billion
No. of Employees: 36,250 (worldwide), 5,000 (U.S.)
No. of Offices: 541 (worldwide)
A subsidiary of the Travelers Group
Chairmen and CEO: Deryck C. Maughan

KEY COMPETITORS

- ◆ Donaldson, Lufkin & Jenrette
- ◆ Goldman Sachs & Co.
- ◆ J.P. Morgan
- ◆ Lehman Brothers
- ◆ Merrill Lynch
- ◆ Morgan Stanley Dean Witter
- ◆ PaineWebber

THE BUZZ

What bankers at other firms are saying about Salomon SB

- ◆ "New, no culture"
- ◆ "Too many fiefdoms"
- ◆ "Scandal-prone"
- ◆ "Rudderless"

Salomon Smith Barney

UPPERS

- Still prestigious
- Company gym
- Free bank account
- Free late night dinners

DOWNERS

- Culture clash
- High pressure
- Merger uncertainty

EMPLOYMENT CONTACT

Ms. Lea Varelas
MBA Recruiting Manager

Ms. Patti Harley
Undergraduate Recruiting manager

Salomon Smith Barney
388 Greenwich Street
New York, New York 10013

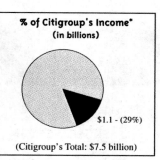

% of Citigroup's Income* (in billions)

$1.1 - (29%)

(Citigroup's Total: $7.5 billion)

% of SSB Employees that are Retail Brokers

10,500 - (29%)

(Citigroup's Total: 36,000)

* Citigroup's 1997 pro forma figures

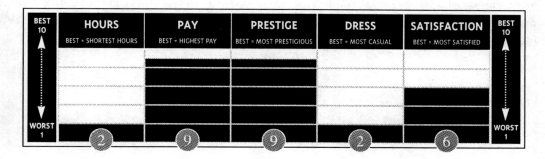

	HOURS	PAY	PRESTIGE	DRESS	SATISFACTION	
BEST 10 ↕ WORST 1	BEST = SHORTEST HOURS	BEST = HIGHEST PAY	BEST = MOST PRESTIGIOUS	BEST = MOST CASUAL	BEST = MOST SATISFIED	BEST 10 ↕ WORST 1
	2	9	9	2	6	

THE SCOOP

MERGER HEAVEN

When word hit Wall Street that Travelers Group chairman Sanford Weill was looking for an investment bank to add to his insurance giant, Salomon Brothers didn't wait for Weill to come a'courtin. Instead, the famed investment bank, immortalized in Michael Lewis' *Liar's Poker*, took the initiative to call Weill. In December 1997, Travelers bought Salomon for more than $9 billion. Salomon was merged with Travelers' brokerage arm, Smith Barney, to create Salomon Smith Barney. But Weill wasn't finished. In the spring of 1998, Travelers announced plans to merge with commercial banking giant Citicorp, a move that has created a financial services behemoth called Citigroup in a $70 billion merger.

MERGER PURGATORY

So where does this leave Salomon Smith Barney? At the grown-up table, seated next to big boys like Morgan Stanley Dean Witter (also the product of a mega-merger), Merrill Lynch, and Goldman Sachs. Despite a somewhat rocky beginning because of restructuring costs, the merger has proved thus far to be a success. Despite initial concerns about overlapping business and clashing cultures, the merger has allowed Salomon Smith Barney to reach a "critical mass" in certain industries (the combination of clients in the energy industry, for example, has enabled the firm to become a player in that field), and strengthening its position across the board. With the addition of Citicorp's international presence, the firm expects to have increased leverage internationally. However, the Citigroup merger has gotten off to a shaky start, at least as far as Salomon Smith Barney is concerned. In November 1998, Jamie Dimon, the then-CEO of Salomon Smith Barney and Weill's longtime right-hand man, resigned after disagreements about the future autonomy of Salomon Smith Barney.

GETTING HIRED

The 1998 recruiting season is the first in which Salomon and Smith Barney have integrated their hiring. In the past, both firms have interviewed applicants over several rounds. Since most new analysts and associates are recent undergrad or B-school grads, a campus interview usually starts off the process. Says one recent hire: "I had a first round in the morning, a second round in the evening, and then the final round in New York." Several insiders report receiving two-on-one interviews during the on-campus interviews.

The second round, for those who are invited to participate, usually involves a full day of interviews at the firm's headquarters. "It was a few hours, six interviews," reports one recent interviewee. Most applicants participate in a Saturday session referred to as a "Super Saturday." Says one contact: "The interviews start out rather informal and the final round is usually five or more interviews on a Saturday." The firm provides a recruiting calendar for business school students on its web site, at www.salomonsmithbarney.com.

OUR SURVEY SAYS

A STAGGERING BLEND

In January 1998, the Salomon Brothers and Smith Barney operations merged, during a staggered two-week moving period. Some operations consolidated at Smith Barney's Greenwich Avenue headquarters, others consolidated in Salomon Brothers' World Trade Center headquarters. "Industrial groups, transportation, environmental all moved to Salomon," explains one Salomon Smith Barney insider. "It was pretty much a power thing. The health care group, for example, stayed at the Greenwich Avenue location. Telecom stayed at the Salomon side. The energy group moved to Smith Barney location. You moved to where

I-Banking Job Seekers: Receive free e-mailed job postings matching your interests & qualifications! Register at www.VaultReports.com

VAULT REPORTS™
www.vaultreports.com

67

the biggest practice was." The firm's capital markets groups also were organized around power centers: "High-yield moved to Solly, bond trading moved to Solly, equities moved to Smith Barney." "All of a sudden, there was a new group of people," says one I-banking insider from the Salomon side. "We had had some sort of social session beforehand. And now, we're all integrated."

Two cultures

That the Salomon and Smith Barney cultures contrast is not in dispute. "Salomon is much more aggressive, much more individualistic, somewhat Neanderthal-like," explains one insider from the Salomon side. Says one who was hired initially by Smith Barney: "On the investment banking side, you could see it in terms of team players. The Solly people came out more as individual – the 'I don't give a shit what you need to do, I need to get my work done' thing. You get a lot of that in banking, but more so at Solly – it's a little more ruthless. Smith Barney people bent a little over backward to help you." Continues that contact: "You've got to realize that these were two very different cultures – on the Smith Barney side you had a younger bank, younger MDs, who were more gung ho about making money, less concerned about big ticket items. Salomon would go for big names. The Smith Barney guys were concerned about making money. They were like, if it's a high-yield company that is kind of on the edge, but will pay more, hey, we'll do it. The Solly guys wouldn't even touch it."

Driven by power

Says one I-banking insider about the merger: "I think it's gone pretty smoothly, I was impressed with how quickly things got rolling, and we sort of became one firm, it's a tough environment to do it in, because things move really fast. I was impressed." Perhaps that assessment stems from the fact that that analyst was originally hired by Salomon Brothers. As one Smith Barney I-banker puts it: "We bought Solly, but invariably Salomon took over the investment banking operations." Insiders, however, say that the culture of the firm is driven by the firm that had the more powerful group – Smith Barney for health care, Salomon for M&A, etc.

EVENING OUT

Because of turnover in the wake of the merger, insiders expect that the firm's culture will begin to even out between Salomon and Smith Barney, especially because of the pending merger with Citigroup. "I would guess that it's going to come up somewhere in the middle," says one insider. "Although the Salomon culture is still stronger, a lot of people left. Especially when you get a commercial bank in there, things are bound to change."

To order a 50- to 70-page Vault Reports Employer Profile on Salomon Smith Barney call 1-888-JOB-VAULT or visit www.VaultReports.com

The full Employer Profile includes detailed information on SSB's departments, recent developments and transactions, hiring and interview process, plus what employees really think about culture, pay, work hours and more.

I-Banking Job Seekers: Receive free e-mailed job postings matching your interests & qualifications! Register at www.VaultReports.com

VAULT REPORTS™
www.vaultreports.com

69

Credit Suisse First Boston

11 Madison Avenue
New York, NY 10010
(212) 325-2000
www.csfb.com

CREDIT SUISSE | FIRST BOSTON

LOCATIONS

New York, NY (HQ)
Los Angeles, CA • London, UK • Zurich,
Switzerland • 50 other offices in 30 countries

DEPARTMENTS

Corporate & Investment Banking
(including Corporate Finance, M&A
and Public Finance)
Equity
Fixed Income
Derivatives
(Credit Suisse Financial Products)
Private Equity

THE STATS

Annual Revenues: $7.1 billion (1997)
No. of Employees: 13,000+
No. of Offices: 50 (worldwide)
A subsidiary of Credit Suisse Group
CEO: Allen D. Wheat

KEY COMPETITORS

- Deutsche Bank Securities
- Goldman Sachs & Co.
- J.P. Morgan
- Merrill Lynch
- Morgan Stanley Dean Witter
- Salomon Smith Barney
- Warburg Dillon Read

THE BUZZ

What bankers at other firms
are saying about CSFB

- "Seen better days"
- "Nerdy, boring"
- "Great people, poor franchise"
- "Innovative"

UPPERS

- ◆ Relaxed dress for Wall Street
- ◆ Friendly environment
- ◆ Great gym in New York

DOWNERS

- ◆ Recent cutbacks in perks and staff
- ◆ Bad press from Holocaust victims suit

EMPLOYMENT CONTACT

Human Resources
Credit Suisse First Boston
Eleven Madison Avenue
New York, NY 10010

wrecruit@csfb.com

© Copyright 1999 Vault Reports, Inc. Photocopying is illegal and is expressly forbidden.

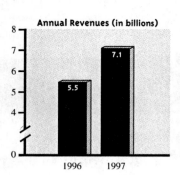

Annual Revenues (in billions)

1996: 5.5
1997: 7.1

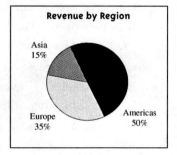

Revenue by Region

Asia 15%
Europe 35%
Americas 50%

Employees by Region

Asia 13%
Europe 39%
Americas 48%

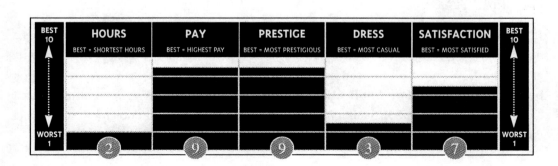

	HOURS	PAY	PRESTIGE	DRESS	SATISFACTION	
BEST 10 ↑ WORST 1	BEST = SHORTEST HOURS	BEST = HIGHEST PAY	BEST = MOST PRESTIGIOUS	BEST = MOST CASUAL	BEST = MOST SATISFIED	BEST 10 ↑ WORST 1
	2	9	9	3	7	

I-Banking Job Seekers: Receive free e-mailed job postings matching
your interests & qualifications! Register at www.VaultReports.com

VAULT REPORTS™   71

www.vaultreports.com

THE SCOOP

A BULGING BRACKET

Credit Suisse First Boston (formerly known as "CS First Boston") is one of New York's most renowned investment banks and a member of Wall Street's prestigious "bulge bracket" of top securities firms. The firm was established as the wholly-owned investment bank unit of the Credit Suisse Group, one of Europe's largest financial institutions. Credit Suisse Group, one of Europe's largest financial institutions. Credit Suisse Group, formerly known as CS Holdings, initially invested in First Boston in 1988, renaming the investment bank CS First Boston. Since that infusion of Swiss cash, the firm itself has changed significantly. Credit Suisse First Boston now has a much larger capital base than First Boston ever had. CSFB's trading division is famously aggressive and profitable, and the investment banking division now has a notable global reach.

DIVISIONS

The firm is divided into five divisions. Corporate and Investment Banking (CIBD) is a leading player in M&A worldwide. The firm's Fixed Income division is one of the world's largest, trading more than $100 billion of fixed income securities each day. Other divisions include the Equity, Credit Suisse Financial Products (the derivatives division, based in London), and Private Equity.

CATCHING FLAK

In recent years, Credit Suisse has caught some unwanted publicity for stonewalling the descendants of Holocaust survivors who demand access to dormant accounts. Credit Suisse, along with UBS, eventually agreed in August 1998 to pay Holocaust survivors $1.25 billion over 3½ years. In May, CSFB also settled with Orange County in its well-publicized bankruptcy lawsuit. The $52.5 million settlement served as partial restitution for the California county's losses, but the bank denied undertaking unsubstantiated risks.

In between the suits, the firm has conducted some big business. In 1998, Credit Suisse First Boston outbid competitors Goldman Sachs and Morgan Stanley in purchasing Garantia S.A., Brazil's top investment bank, for $675 million. The bank also stands to benefit as an advisor to the mega-merger between Daimler-Benz and Chrysler. CS First Boston is advising longtime client Chrysler in the largest industrial deal ever. The latest financial collapse in Russia hit CSFB hard. The most active bank in the Russian market, the firm took major hits, announcing trading losses exceeding $500 million, and slashing its staff in Russia.

GETTING HIRED

Credit Suisse First Boston posts a list of current job openings on its web site, located at www.csfb.com. The firm's on-campus recruiting program is managed on a firm-wide basis, and organized by each of the bank's target schools. Each school is assigned an "ambassador" (who is a member of the firm's operating committee) a "team captain" (who is a managing director). Also, each division has a team leader for a school, who reports to the ambassador and team captain.

At all of the bank's target schools, there is a campus presentation (which provides an overview of the firm and a Q&A session), and in some cases, a dinner. The firm also participates in other get-to-know-you events such as golf tournaments and charity functions. Applicants with bachelor's degrees are hired as analysts. MBAs are hired as associates. At the associate level, the firm also hires JDs into its Corporate and Investment Banking division, and PhDs into Credit Suisse Financial Products (its division devoted to the math-heavy derivatives and risk management products).

CSFB conducts a Summer Associate Program that gives students finishing their first year of business school a chance to learn about the investment banking industry; the program runs for 10 weeks. Summer Associates participate in new business presentations, financial advisory assignments, and the completion of transactions. CSFB also has a sales and trading summer associate program which allows summer associates to be exposed to as many functional areas as possible within Fixed Income and Equities. In their final weeks, summer associates can remain in the product area of their choice.

I-Banking Job Seekers: Receive free e-mailed job postings matching your interests & qualifications! Register at www.VaultReports.com

VAULT REPORTS™   73
www.vaultreports.com

OUR SURVEY SAYS

FRIENDLY FOLK

Credit Suisse First Boston fosters a "collegial" environment in which new employees enjoy a large degree of "interaction with senior management." One former associate reports: "We would go out at least once a week. Anytime there was someone new in our group visiting from one of the other CSFB offices, it was basically their duty to take you to a bar, go out for drinks and dinner, hang out with them, so you got to drink a lot of free beer and eat free meals." CSFB emphasizes "teamwork" and says its employees must possess "quantitative and modeling skills." Support staff are "well qualified" and often "cover up for some analysts' weaknesses with using computers and high-tech equipment."

CSFB employees "regularly" receive free tickets for sporting events and cultural events, and also the opportunity "to go out for nice dinners in nice restaurants like Dawat, River Café, Remi, and Four Seasons." The only problem is that CSFB people spend so much time in the office that "who really has time for anything else?"

HEALTHY OPTIONS

Working at CSFB has more mundane benefits. "They have lots of healthcare options, including one in which you can save money for healthcare expenses tax-free," says one insider. "So say you know that later in the year you'll have $2000 in medical expenses that won't be covered by insurance. You can save for that in a pre-tax account. So if you didn't have that account, you might have to earn $2800 to pay for the $2000 in expenses."

DINNER'S ON US

Professionals who stay past 7 p.m. – which is just about everyone – can have their dinners picked up by the firm. Many go to the firm's cafeteria, where "all you have to do is show your I.D." Tired bankers can also call for car service after 9 p.m. For those looking to re-energize, there's the firm's health club. The monthly fee for the club depends on one's position – "for people below VP it's $30 a month." Perhaps the biggest perk, say New York employees, is that "you get to live in Manhattan – and earn enough money to enjoy it."

LAME PARTIES

Like many of its competitors, CSFB is cutting back on some of its perks because of tight times. "They sent a memo around announcing that there's only a $50 allowance per person for this year's Christmas party. Things don't look good, it's not a fat year," says one insider about the 1998 holiday. "And in the health club, they used to provide free fruit, and it just went away. It's because the gym is run by another company, but the fruit was provided by CSFB."

DON'T SEE ANYONE OVER 30

And like most on Wall Street, CSFB's employees contend with "long," "intense" workdays and "excruciatingly tight deadlines." According to one associate: "Trading is like warfare. It can get very frantic, and then very quiet, and flare again without warning. It's long periods of silence punctuated by fear and terror. That's what makes it stressful." I-bankers are no more relaxed; one analyst says "You burn out by the time you're 30. Most people only last until they're about 35, then go off and do something else." Many employees comment that their jobs "require a high level of energy and dedication." The intensity continues with a "very business-like" dress code that stipulates "suits and ties – no sports coats at all." Since CSFB lacks the marquee name and underwriting franchise that some of its competitors enjoy, the bank maintains an "entrepreneurial" culture in which employees are "encouraged to go out and win business for the firm."

BREAKDOWN IN DISCIPLINE

CSFB is creeping toward an ever more casual environment when it comes to dress. "Fridays are dress-downs all year, and lately, in late summer, we get one week of dress-down, like the last week of August," reports one insider. Also: "Dress-down is for the last day of any week, so if it's a three-day weekend you can dress down on Thursday." And on those occasions when

I-Banking Job Seekers: Receive free e-mailed job postings matching your interests & qualifications! Register at www.VaultReports.com

VAULT REPORTS™

75

www.vaultreports.com

employees are free from the scrutiny of top management and clients, "discipline kind of breaks down. Shirts without ties, that sort of thing – you can take it a bit easier." The moment the boss or a client comes back, though, "the ties come right back on." For traders, however, the dress code is much more relaxed, and "traders in New York don't have to wear a suit during the week. We can dress business casual during the week. On Friday we can wear whatever we want, and some of us wear jeans." One New York trader recalls: "For some time we used to wear jeans even during the week, but we got remarks like, 'You really should wear something smarter.'" Employees at CSFB's foreign offices have to conform to "stricter dress codes." This is especially true in London, which is "a button-up kind of town. Everyone is formal here."

To order a 50- to 70-page Vault Reports Employer Profile on Credit Suisse First Boston call 1-888-JOB-VAULT or visit www.VaultReports.com

The full Employer Profile includes detailed information on CSFB's departments, recent developments and transactions, hiring and interview process, plus what employees really think about culture, pay, work hours and more.

"Most people only last
until they're about 35,
then go off and do
something else."

– CSFB insider

Lehman Brothers

3 World Financial Center
New York, NY 10285
(212) 526-7000
www.lehman.com

LEHMAN BROTHERS

LOCATIONS

New York, NY (HQ)
Other offices in CA • DC • FL • GA • IL • MA
• NJ • PA • TX • WA • Argentina • Bahrain •
Brazil • Canada • Chile • China • Dubai • France
• Germany • Hong Kong • India • Indonesia •
Israel • Italy • Japan • Mexico • Puerto Rico •
Singapore • South Korea • Spain • Switzerland •
Taiwan • Thailand • United Kingdom • Uruguay

Stock Symbol: LEH (NYSE)
CEO: Richard S. Fuld, Jr.

KEY COMPETITORS

- Bankers Trust
- Bear Stearns
- Credit Suisse First Boston
- Donaldson, Lufkin & Jenrette
- Goldman Sachs & Co.
- J.P. Morgan
- Merrill Lynch
- Morgan Stanley Dean Witter
- Salomon Smith Barney

DEPARTMENTS

Corporate Advisory
Equities
Finance
Fixed Income
Human Resources
Investment Banking
Operations
Private Client Services
Technology

THE BUZZ

What bankers at other firms
are saying about Lehman

- "Friendly"
- "No longer deteriorating but not on upswing"
- "Volatile"
- "Perpetually for sale"

THE STATS

Annual Revenues: $16.9 billion (1997)
No. of Employees: 8,340 (worldwide)
No. of Offices: 39 (worldwide)

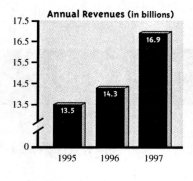

Annual Revenues (in billions)

UPPERS

- ◆ Growing firm
- ◆ Not as stuffy as other Wall Street firms
- ◆ Excellent advancement opportunities

DOWNERS

- ◆ Sometimes fratty atmosphere
- ◆ Intense pressure

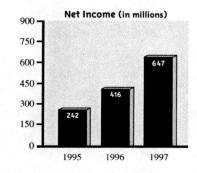

Net Income (in millions)

EMPLOYMENT CONTACT

Investment Banking:

Dorine McManus
Associate Recruiting

Jennifer Murphy
Analyst Recruiting

Capital Markets:

Kristin Williams
Recruiting

Lehman Brothers
3 World Financial Center
New York, NY 10285
Fax: (212) 526-3738

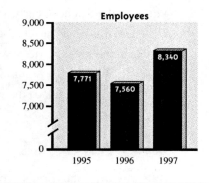

Employees

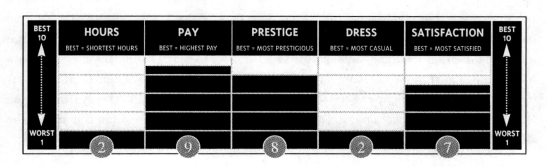

I-Banking Job Seekers: Receive free e-mailed job postings matching
your interests & qualifications! Register at www.VaultReports.com

VAULT REPORTS™
www.vaultreports.com

79

THE SCOOP

ACQUIRED AND DE-ACQUIRED

Founded 150 years ago as a cotton-trading business in the American South, Lehman Brothers offers a wide range of investment banking services, including fixed income and equities sales, trading and research; M&A advisory; public finance; and private client services. American Express acquired the firm in 1984; later, when American Express decided to refocus on its core business, Lehman Brothers was unceremoniously dropped. With a $1 billion kiss-off, Lehman was sold off to American Express stockholders and the public in 1994. Once again a stand-alone firm, Lehman has been fighting hard to regain its position as one of Wall Street's premier investment banks. After some tough decisions, such as major layoffs and cost cutting in 1994 and 1995, the firm has boosted its revenues increased, its profitability and gained market share in high-margin businesses such as equity origination, M&A, and high-yield debt underwriting.

Word on the Street in early 1998 had Lehman re-merging, perhaps with Chase Manhattan or Deutsche Bank. (Deutsche opted for Bankers Trust instead, in December 1998.) The rumors sent Lehman's stock price – and profitability – skyrocketing. In April 1998, the stock reached $84 5/8. But as the overall market began to fall midyear, Lehman sank more than most. The company's stock sank to the mid-$20 range before recovering late in the year.

KING FOR A DAY

But why was the firm's stock so popular before its precipitous decline? The takeover speculation was driven in part by the firm's recent strong performance. After four years as a public company, Lehman has recently been making the case that it again should be considered one of Wall Street's top investment banks. In 1996 and 1997, the trimmer Lehman began rebuilding itself; in 1997 and 1998, profits stood at record levels. As of early 1998, the firm had exceeded analyst estimates for 11 straight quarters. And recently, Lehman Brothers has built its human base back up to 8700 workers. However, Lehman is still the only firm on Wall Street with fewer employees now than it had in 1994. Despite the turmoil in debt markets in

August and September, Lehman said in September 1998 that it wasn't planning any large-scale layoffs – even as competitors such as Merrill Lynch were announcing broad staff cuts.

GETTING HIRED

First impressions are key at Lehman. After meeting students at colleges and business schools, the firm's recruiters will focus on a number of top candidates. Says one recent MBA hire: "I was targeted and was pursued hard." In fact, the firm prefers to have identified its targets by the time campus interviewing starts. The firm focuses on nine business schools (Chicago, Columbia, Wharton, Tuck, Fuqua, Stern, UCLA, Kellogg, and MIT's Sloan).

How does Lehman pick its targets? In part, through on-campus get-to-know you functions. For example, the firm's sales and trading recruiters host a "Trading Game" on campus, where they simulate three to four "pits" similar to those on the Chicago Futures exchanges. The "game" (read: tryout) lasts four to five hours. People from Lehman play one role, while students play another. The trading game allows Lehman to observe students in action, so it can identify strong candidates. Lehman also hosts cocktail parties to identify targets. Despite these ulterior motives, the firm tries to keep the events as informal and social as possible, insiders say. "The focus is on personalities."

As at many banks, Lehman's summer programs act as a feeder system for full-time hires. The firm reports that 75 percent of its incoming full-time class for the fall of 1998 were interns at Lehman. The firm also reports that 90 percent of the summer MBA interns Lehman hosts in its capital markets department get offers (although insiders claim that the number is closer to 80 percent). Summer associates receive their offers within two weeks of the end of the program. MBAs are hired into the firm as associates; undergrads, as analysts. Those interested in Lehman should visit the firm's web site, located at www.lehman.com and chock full of detailed recruiting information. Most associates report an excellent recruitment process. Says one: "There was no bullshit in the recruiting process. They were honest with us."

I-Banking Job Seekers: Receive free e-mailed job postings matching your interests & qualifications! Register at www.VaultReports.com

VAULT REPORTS™
81
www.vaultreports.com

OUR SURVEY SAYS

EFFORT REWARDED

Perhaps the most attractive aspect of working for Lehman, our contacts observe, is that "the firm rewards effort. This place is as close to a meritocracy as it gets." "I've been given more responsibility than I'd ever imagined," says one associate in trading. Says another associate, in Lehman's fixed income group: "It's an aggressive firm that will let you take risk, if you can justify it." "For a young person, the opportunity to develop a career at a place like Lehman is so much greater (than elsewhere)." Says another capital markets associate: "[Lehman gives] lots of responsibility early. They push employees to progress quickly." Says another associate in that area: "The opportunity is fantastic. The firm has focused on a number of growth opportunities and is aggressive about getting people involved." A 1998 summer associate relates that a summer research analyst helped put together some industry research because she had some expertise, and "they put her name on the cover. That's not something that's going to happen if you're at Merrill Lynch." Continues that contact: "You're given responsibility as a trader. If you're interested in equities, you have the opportunity to do it. In other places, you have to wait till somebody dies, or something like that. It's a very young culture here."

SCRAPPY, FRIENDLY SURVIVORS

Lehman's culture is one of "survivors and fighters – people have been through a lot together, and they are very loyal to each other," says one recent hire. Insiders speak enthusiastically about Lehman's "social" corporate offices, where "most employees are extremely nice and friendly, and very down-to-earth, unlike at some other places on the street." As one Lehman newcomer says, Lehman's "culture is open," largely because of the "affable" upper management who "make an effort to be readily approachable." "Culture very much depends on which business and which desk, but overall, it is not at all stuffy," says one associate in trading. "There are fairly honest professional people."

"Lehman has more of a laid-back collegial environment than other firms that I've worked at. I've seen all the other firms, and also over the summer I visited a bunch of firms," says one associate who summered at Lehman. "It's not laid back in that people are easygoing, it just doesn't have the pretension that you might have at other places," continues that associate. "People work hard, but people also are welcoming, no one's putting on airs, that's the feeling that I got. I've been all around the firm, and I never had a situation where someone blew me off or wasn't interested in talking about him." Says one analyst in the firm's research department: "It's warm, and less intense than your typical Wall Street firm." Cozy indeed.

Although Lehman may be less stuffy and aristocratic, that doesn't mean the temperature doesn't make working at Lehman a walk in the park. One ex-employee in New York notes, "There's a lot more yelling at Lehman Brothers than at my current firm." Insiders say that Lehman, like most major investment banks, has a "macho culture" and "many arrogant attitudes." Says one: "Antics are somewhat unprofessional. Many employees have something of a locker-room, fraternity culture." Says another insider: "[Lehman's culture] is meritocratic but can be easily abused by overly aggressive people."

To order a 50- to 70-page Vault Reports Employer Profile on Lehamn Brothers call 1-888-JOB-VAULT or visit www.VaultReports.com

The full Employer Profile includes detailed information on Lehman's departments, recent developments and transactions, hiring and interview process, plus what employees really think about culture, pay, work hours and more.

I-Banking Job Seekers: Receive free e-mailed job postings matching your interests & qualifications! Register at www.VaultReports.com

VAULT REPORTS™   83
www.vaultreports.com

Hambrecht & Quist

One Bush Street
San Francisco, CA 94104
(415) 576-3300
www.hamquist.com

H&Q
HAMBRECHT & QUIST

LOCATIONS

San Francisco, CA (HQ)
Boston, MA • New York, NY • Newport Beach, CA • San Diego, CA • London, England • Paris, France • Tokyo, Japan

DEPARTMENTS

Capital Management
Investment Banking
Research
Sales and Trading
Venture Capital

THE STATS

Annual Revenues: $346 million (1998)
Net Income: $43.2 million (1998)
No. of Employees: 823 (worldwide)
No. of Offices: 8 (worldwide)
Stock Symbol: HMQ (NYSE)
CEO: Daniel H. Case, III

KEY COMPETITORS

- BancBoston Robertson Stephens
- BT Alex. Brown
- Goldman Sachs & Co.
- Merrill Lynch
- Morgan Stanley Dean Witter
- Nationsbanc Montgomery Securities
- SG Cowen

THE BUZZ

What bankers at other firms
are saying about NationsBanc

- "High tech player"
- "Niche, arrogant"
- "One-trick pony"

UPPERS

- ◆ 10 percent company match on IRAs
- ◆ Opportunity to invest in company ventures
- ◆ Proudly independent

DOWNERS

- ◆ 5 a.m. meetings
- ◆ Lower pay than competitors
- ◆ Constant buyout rumors

EMPLOYMENT CONTACT

Sharon Henning
Vice President
Professional Recruiting
Hambrecht & Quist
One Bush Street
San Francisco, CA 94104

Fax (415) 439-3016
recruiting@hamquist.com

Annual Revenues (in millions)

- 1995: 220
- 1996: 390
- 1997: 346

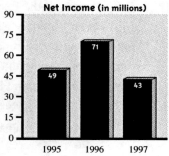

Net Income (in millions)

- 1995: 49
- 1996: 71
- 1997: 43

Employees

- 1995: 500
- 1996: 685
- 1997: 823

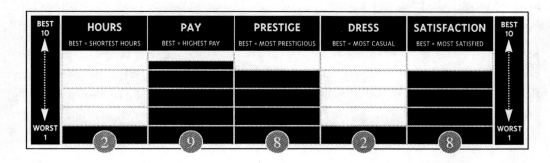

	HOURS	PAY	PRESTIGE	DRESS	SATISFACTION	
BEST 10 ... WORST 1	BEST = SHORTEST HOURS	BEST = HIGHEST PAY	BEST = MOST PRESTIGIOUS	BEST = MOST CASUAL	BEST = MOST SATISFIED	BEST 10 ... WORST 1
	2	9	8	2	8	

I-Banking Job Seekers: Receive free e-mailed job postings matching
your interests & qualifications! Register at www.VaultReports.com

VAULT REPORTS™
www.vaultreports.com

85

THE SCOOP

A TURNAROUND IN THE VALLEY

Founded in 1968 by William Hambrecht and the late George Quist to find and support the best entrepreneurs in the fastest-growing sectors of the economy, Hambrecht & Quist has not always been a glittery Silicon Valley success story. In the early 1990s, the firm was on the verge of bankruptcy, reporting an annual loss of $10 million. Wall Street hadn't yet fallen in love with high tech, and H&Q had underwritten IPOs of several companies that failed. The firm was turned around largely because of the efforts of CEO Daniel Case, who took over in 1992. Case, older brother of America Online CEO Steve Case, beefed up the firm's research, brokerage and M&A businesses.

STICK TO TECH

H&Q is now a full-service investment bank that focuses on high-growth companies in the technology, health care, information services, and branded consumer products industries. CEO Daniel Case concedes that H&Q's core business remains the technology market. "We have chosen, unlike other people, not to go into new areas," he told *The Wall Street Journal*. The firm's distinguished recent history includes management of the initial public offerings (IPOs) for high-tech companies such as Apple, Next, Pixar, Netscape, and Adobe – some of most successful IPOs of all time. Other high-growth companies Hambrecht & Quist counts as clients are U.S. Robotics, Genentech, The North Face (maker of the ubiquitous down jackets), and Starbucks (the coffee masters). In 1997 H&Q helped to manage 94 IPOs, 49 of which were for technology-oriented firms. The bank lead managed 22 of those IPOs, and was co-manager in some of the hottest offerings, including those of Rambus, Amazon.com and @home.

Still, the past few years have not been particularly kind to Hambrech & Quist. As former boutiques merge with bigger firms, and other banks show interest in the booming technology field, H&Q's market share is declining. In 1997, Merrill Lynch opened a technology banking office in Palo Alto, California, and in January 1998 Goldman Sachs opened an office in Menlo

Park, California to beef up its growing San Francisco-based technology banking operation. This increased Left Coast presence was reflected in excellent underwriting numbers posted by these banks in 1997. Merrill Lynch became the No. 2 technology-stock underwriter in that year, with 13.1 percent of the market (an impressive increase over its 1996 market share of 6.1 percent). Goldman Sachs continued in the top tech-stock slot, with 15 percent of the 1997 market, up from 14.1 percent. Meanwhile, H&Q's share of the technology-stock underwriting market, its bread and butter, slumped to 3.5 percent in 1997, down from 6.1 percent in 1996. Tech companies admit that golden names like Goldman and Morgan Stanley boost the chance of a successful IPO. Rambus CEO Geoff Tate explained to *Fortune* in 1998 why the company's board of directors picked Morgan Stanley to lead manage its IPO, leaving H&Q with a role as a co-manager. "We felt that Morgan Stanley has a worldwide reputation," said Tate. "And there's the perception that if Morgan Stanley picked you, then you're really in the top tier."

H&Q FOR SALE?

With H&Q's core competency shaky, the bank itself looks like a buy. Suitors like Merrill Lynch and Deutsche Bank have already taken a strong interest in Hambrecht & Quist. High-level execs like CEO Daniel Case III and Cristina Morgan, co-director of investment banking, however, are putting on a brave face. The company line is that the firm does not need to partner up with a giant in order to maintain its position within the tech I-banking world. However, the firm knows it likely could not expand past that position without more cash. As Daniel Case told CNBC in October 1998: "We have plenty of capital for our existing business, and if we ever tried to change our model dramatically, we wouldn't have nearly enough capital. And if we ever thought we needed a lot more capital, we would then seek a partner."

I-Banking Job Seekers: Receive free e-mailed job postings matching your interests & qualifications! Register at www.VaultReports.com

VAULT REPORTS™

87

www.vaultreports.com

GETTING HIRED

Hambrecht & Quist recruits self-motivated individuals distinguished by their academic accomplishments and extracurricular activities. Recent graduates are hired as analysts in each office. The firm recruits undergrads at Princeton, UPenn, Yale, UC Berkeley, Stanford, Dartmouth and Harvard. The recruiting e-mail address is recruiting@hamquist.com. MBA associates are hired through an interview process on business campuses and at corporate offices in San Francisco, New York and Boston. The firm recruits MBAs at Harvard, Kellogg, Stanford, Wharton, and UCLA. Associates are hired as generalists and work with senior investment banking professionals on public equity and debt offerings, mergers and acquisitions, and private placements.

OUR SURVEY SAYS

A CUTTING EDGE CULTURE

Hambrecht & Quist cultivates a "rapidly changing," "entrepreneurial" culture in which analysts "pour their energies" into staying on top of the current developments in the "hottest fields around," such as technology, information services, and health care. Employees work "long," "hectic" schedules. "The work hours depend on where you work," reports one employee, "from 40 to 50 in sales and trading to 70 or so in research to 80 to 100 in corporate finance." However, contacts say that the office environment is "less formal" and "more social" than the firm's New York-based competitors. "Friday is casual day for some departments, otherwise a suit is required," according to one insider. "The dress is corporate but not stuffy," says another. "Everyone I work with is young and enthusiastic and fun," says another employee. "We do fun stuff as a company: we went on a rafting trip in August, we did Habitat for Humanity, a bunch of us are going skiing in February." Working in "cutting-edge" industries, moreover, enables employees to leave the firm for "high-paying and high-prestige" industry positions "easily."

GREEN LIGHT

Although "the pay relative to other investment banks is said to be slightly lower," H&Q bankers don't struggle for their daily bread. "Our IRA is matched by the company up to 10 percent of your income," reports one insider. "Depending on your position, there is an opportunity to invest in some (company) venture." In conclusion, says one contact: "I give H&Q a green light."

To order a 10- to 20-page Vault Reports Employer Profile on Hambrecht & Quist call 1-888-JOB-VAULT or visit www.VaultReports.com

The full Employer Profile includes detailed information on H&Q's departments, recent developments and transactions, hiring and interview process, plus what employees really think about culture, pay, work hours and more.

I-Banking Job Seekers: Receive free e-mailed job postings matching your interests & qualifications! Register at www.VaultReports.com

VAULT REPORTS™
www.vaultreports.com

89

Leading Investment Banking Firms

A.G. Edwards & Sons

One North Jefferson
St. Louis, MO 63103
(314) 289-3000
Fax: (314) 955-5612
www.agedwards.com

LOCATIONS

St. Louis, MO (HQ)
560 offices in 48 U.S. states

THE STATS

Annual Revenues: $2.0 billion (1998)
Net Income: $269 million (1998)
No. of Employees: 12,967 (U.S.)
No. of Offices: 604 (U.S.)
Stock Symbol: AGE (NYSE)
CEO: Benjamin F. Edwards III

KEY COMPETITORS

Charles Schwab
Edward D. Jones & Co.
Merrill Lynch
Morgan Stanley Dean Witter
PaineWebber
Salomon Smith Barney
U.S. Bancorp Piper Jaffray

UPPERS

- Serious about training
- Low turnover rate
- Stock options
- Great retirement plan
- Family-oriented

DOWNERS

- Somewhat conservative atmosphere
- St. Louis not finance hot spot

EMPLOYMENT CONTACT

Human Resources
One North Jefferson
St. Louis, MO 63103

employment@agedwards.com

HOURS	PAY	PRESTIGE	DRESS	SATISFACTION
BEST = SHORTEST HOURS	BEST = HIGHEST PAY	BEST = MOST PRESTIGIOUS	BEST = MOST CASUAL	BEST = MOST SATISFIED
4	8	6	4	9

THE SCOOP

SPIRIT OF ST. LOUIS

Headquartered in St. Louis, A.G. Edwards & Sons is the nation's largest securities firm based outside of New York. After serving as Abraham Lincoln's Treasurer in the 1860s, A.G. Edwards founded the firm in 1887 to serve St. Louis banks trading on the NYSE. Although the firm suffered some tough times during the Great Depression, the reputation of A.G. Edwards remained unmarred. The company leapt into the computer revolution early on, installing IBM computers at its company headquarters in 1948. Edwards' firm has now grown to include more than 590 offices in 48 states (and the District of Columbia); the company employs more than 6100 brokers. The firm's leadership has remained in the family – current CEO Benjamin Edwards III is a fourth-generation descendant of the founder.

A.G. EXPANSION

While most of the firm's revenues are generated from commissions from selling stocks and bonds to individual investors, Edwards' investment banking division has been expanding rapidly. Its I-banking arm is currently comprised of 100 professionals. The firm apparently invests quite well: Edwards was chosen as the top stock-picker for the first quarter of 1997 by *The Wall Street Journal*, and the second best for the preceding 12-month period. The company also offers asset management and insurance; a subsidiary called A.G. Edwards Trust provides portfolio management and related trust services. A.G. Edwards' customers include a variety of individual, corporate, government, and institutional customers, but it has made its market niche with middle-market companies. This early adopter of high tech, through a Technology Development Committee, continues to upgrade and improve the equipment crucial to its business. With its ability to provide a vast range of services, A.G. Edwards emphasizes building long-term relationships with its clients, rather than profiting from single transactions. Insiders say A.G. Edwards stresses accountability from its management by tying all management bonuses to company profits. The firm is growing so robustly that it had to expand its St. Louis headquarters, where nearly 4000 employees work, in the summer of 1998.

GETTING HIRED

When recruiting, A.G. Edwards looks for team players and leaders, as well as those who have shown a prior interest in the securities industry (e.g., through a summer internship). A.G. Edwards has a somewhat more traditional slant than most other financial firms, and requires its hires to have a very strong code of ethics. New college grads generally start at the analyst level; MBA grads typically begin as associates. New employees in the banking division are slated for generalist slots initially, and can expect a variety of assignments in corporate finance, mergers and acquisitions, and valuations. While new brokers may opt to start at most of the firm's U.S. offices, new hires in Investment Banking all start out of the St. Louis office. Applicants should consult the company's web site, www.agedwards.com, which lists some specific current openings. The company accepts resumes via fax, e-mail, and regular mail.

OUR SURVEY SAYS

NOT THE ARCH TOO?

A.G. Edwards takes employee training seriously, employees report. This commitment is evidenced by the company's training center, which offers employees more than 30 educational programs. One A.G. Edwards broker who has worked in two other brokerage houses calls the firm's culture "more supportive than other major brokerage firms. I wanted to join A.G. Edwards specifically because its policy is to do what's right for the client." Employees also concur that "the firm really cares about a work-life balance." This philosophy pervades all of A.G. Edwards, insiders say. One analyst says "the employees are happy and friendly in every department." Employees at the headquarters in Saint Louis praise the many benefits and perks the firm offers: "free parking, 24-hour security, a subsidized cafeteria and a little gift/convenience store on the premises, discounts to see the St. Louis Arch." All A.G. Edwards

I-Banking Job Seekers: Receive free e-mailed job postings matching your interests & qualifications! Register at www.vaultreports.com

VAULT REPORTS™
www.vaultreports.com

95

can take advantage of a stock purchase plan; senior employees receive stock options. The was rated as one of *Fortune Magazine's* 100 Best Companies to Work For, largely because of the firm's retirement plan, under which 3500 employees have more than $100,000 and close to 200 have more than $1 million.

GOOD TO CLIENTS AND EMPLOYEES

Unlike some brokerage firms, which pressure their brokers to meet sales quotas, A.G. Edwards has a low-key, "client-oriented" atmosphere. One employee sizes up the company as a "Wall Street firm without the Wall Street mentality or egos." In fact the firm's CEO, Ben Edwards, hosts monthly company-wide radio conferences during which he answers employee questions. While some decry "the rather dull and conformist city of Saint Louis," or complain about "the bureaucracy – you have to get approval for transactions from three different groups," most employees relish the opportunities A.G. Edwards offers. "No matter what you do," says one recent hire, "you learn so much here that you end up opening more doors than you knew even existed. If you're willing to learn and work beyond what's expected of you, you'll never dream that so much good could happen to you." Says another: "If you are ready to settle down in a relatively nice Midwestern city with a great, family-oriented company that doesn't work you to death, then you should look very hard at A.G. Edwards."

Allen & Co.

711 Fifth Avenue
New York, NY 10022
(212) 832-8000

LOCATIONS

New York, NY (HQ)

THE STATS

No. of Offices: 1 (U.S.)
A privately-held company
Chairman: Donald R. Keough

KEY COMPETITORS

Goldman Sachs & Co.
Lazard Freres & Co.
Morgan Stanley Dean Witter

UPPERS

- Beautiful, mahogany-paneled offices
- Lucrative profit sharing
- No face time
- Schmooze with the stars

DOWNERS

- Must do own research
- Bad deals can savage salaries
- Extraordinarily competitive and difficult hiring process

EMPLOYMENT CONTACT

Human Resources
Allen & Co.
711 Fifth Avenue
New York, NY 10022

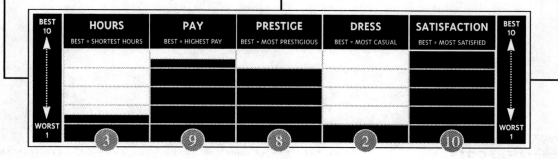

	HOURS	PAY	PRESTIGE	DRESS	SATISFACTION	
BEST 10 ... WORST 1	BEST = SHORTEST HOURS	BEST = HIGHEST PAY	BEST = MOST PRESTIGIOUS	BEST = MOST CASUAL	BEST = MOST SATISFIED	BEST 10 ... WORST 1
	3	9	8	2	10	

THE SCOOP

ALLEN'S HOUSE OF DREAMS

Despite paying its bankers and traders base salaries of $20,000 to $30,000 and expecting them to pay for their travel and secretarial expenses, Allen & Co. remains a dream employer for investment bankers trained at the nation's biggest investment houses. Allen & Co.'s single office on Manhattan's Fifth Avenue houses fewer than two hundred people, compared to Merrill Lynch's 56,600 employees. While larger Wall Street firms often carry billions in debt, Allen & Co. is solidly in the black. The company specializes in the media and entertainment industry, and works only in venture capital, underwriting, private placements and money management, allowing it to follow a unique management philosophy. Allen principals must make a substantial personal investment in all deals they bring in to the firm, ensuring that "if the client pays, Allen pays." Returns on these investments can equal up to 100 percent of a banker's annual pay. Allen's lack of a research department is also unusual; the company's principals perform their own research.

Charles Allen and his brother Herbert founded Allen & Co. as a partnership in 1922, looking for promising companies to invest in. In 1972, Herbert Jr., the founder's son and successor, proved his mettle by putting up $1 million of his own money and $500,000 of the firm's to buy a controlling interest in Columbia Pictures. In 1982, Allen sold Columbia to Coca-Cola. (Coke later sold Columbia.) Allen & Co. has continued to play a key role in the entertainment industry with clients such as Creative Artists, Walt Disney, and Viacom; Allen himself had a hand in hooking up Sony and Columbia. One media mogul has said, "Deals just don't get done in Hollywood unless Allen & Co. has a hand in it."

THE KING OF MEGADEALS

Allen & Co. is a bit different than other investment banks (often functioning more like a venture capital fund). The company does not charge a set fee for putting together its gigantic entertainment deals, because, as Herb Allen told the *Red Herring*, the company feels it cannot "set a fee before adding any value to the transaction. Most of what Wall Street does in mergers and acquisitions is legal protection, not value-added." Allen & Company also deliberately declines to hire security analysts, because Herb Allen dubs them "fairly weak historians and very poor prognosticators. [Analysts] don't buy what they're recommending, so they immediately have a conflict of interest with their customers."

GOING TO PLAY IN SUN VALLEY

Allen & Company is perhaps best known for its famous Sun Valley conference, which gathers together some of the finest minds in business every year for a high-powered schmoozefest. The company brings together 40 "institutional financial buyer" for a conference in the bucolic Idaho setting. In 1998, Allen & Co. featured a panel on management issues, moderated by Allen & Company chair Don Keogh, with panelists like Rupert Murdoch, Barry Diller and Intel chair Andy Grove. A panel on race and business was peopled by panelists like Bob Johnson of Black Entertainment Television and Dick Parsons of Time Warner, and was moderated by mellow-voiced Tom Brokaw. Bill Gates has attended in the past and is allowed to talk about "whatever he wants."

GETTING HIRED

Allen & Co. personnel department does not accept outside calls, does not maintain a job hotline, and does not publicize job openings. The firm does, however, accept resumes mailed to 711 Fifth Avenue, New York, NY 10022. Allen hires only MBAs as bankers and typically

I-Banking Job Seekers: Receive free e-mailed job postings matching your interests & qualifications! Register at www.vaultreports.com

VAULT REPORTS™
99
www.vaultreports.com

requires two to three years of experience. Insiders say getting a job directly out of business school is rare, and getting hired right out of college is "next to impossible."

In an exclusive interview with Vault Reports, Chairman of Allen & Co. Don Keogh had this to say to prospective Allen employees: "My advice to a young person, especially a business school student, interested in Allen & Company is to be sure you become an interesting person. You should develop a full range of interests and not worry about a career... Instead, take courses that interest you – statistics, philosophy and so on... Secondly, any young person who doesn't put the international world into perspective is a damn fool. Any education in today's world must incorporate some part of it outside the United States. We're interested in people who understand other countries and are fluent in other languages... You have to bring something other than a great MBA background to get in the door [at Allen]. You need experience, which means we rarely take undergrads or someone straight out of business school. You need to come in with some credentials from the business world, and we need to be sure that you want to stay here long term. Because we take so few, we have the luxury of taking our time evaluating new people." Adds another insider, "we do a lot in the entertainment and media field, so an interest in that area is helpful."

OUR SURVEY SAYS

"A SPECIAL, SECRET SOCIETY"

Bankers say working at Allen & Co. makes them feel like members of "a very special, secret society." Befitting such a group, working conditions are "optimal." Employees describe their offices as "classy" with "lots of dark mahogany on walls and desks" and "original Norman Rockwell paintings." The office "just oozes success." Dress at Allen is "sharp but conservative," even though employees often work with "flashy media clients." The firm is social, since it is "full of people who schmooze for a living." Senior bankers who have perfected their schmoozing take part in Allen & Co.'s "famed annual retreat for media moguls" in Sun Valley Idaho with "spectacular guests like Bill Gates and Mike Eisner in attendance." This sort of networking means that while Allen "isn't a household name," it "carries almost as much mystique as CAA" in the media business. While some insiders mention there are several women in "senior positions," others report that Allen is "still mostly a male firm."

In addition to "above-average" pay, our sources adore the opportunity to "invest in Allen & Co. deals and share in profits." One banker says: "The culture here is one of risk-taking, both on a personal and corporate level. You must have a significant portion of your net worth at risk if you want to work here, and you must be a fee generator soon after arriving." Confides another contact: "There's salary plus a percentage of the fees from deals that you work on. You get paid when a fee comes in – no waiting for year-end bonus. If you have a bad year, tough luck. On the other hand, there is no theoretical limit on the upside." Because of this payment structure, the firm is "incredibly entrepreneurial" suited for "driven and individualistic" employees: "There is no face time or kissing up to get a big bonus." Workload is "very much dependent on what you are working on" but is generally described as "better than your other Wall Street banks" in part because face time is not a priority. "All that counts is your ability to make abnormally high returns for the firm while maintaining an absolutely clean reputation," explains one insider. "The firm's reputation is paramount. Anyone that does anything unethical or illegal will be removed." As one Allen insider summarizes, "While [Allen & Co.] is a great place, it is unlikely that it would be suited for most people."

I-Banking Job Seekers: Receive free e-mailed job postings matching your interests & qualifications! Register at www.vaultreports.com

VAULT REPORTS™
www.vaultreports.com

101

"There is no face time or kissing up to get a big bonus."

– *Allen & Company insider*

BancBoston Robertson Stephens

555 California St., Suite 2600
San Francisco, CA 94104
(415) 781-9700
Fax: (415) 676-2840
www.rsco.com

LOCATIONS

San Francisco, CA (HQ)
Boston, MA • New York, NY • Palo Alto, CA
• London, England • Tokyo, Japan

THE STATS

No. of Employees: 900 (worldwide)
No. of Offices: 7 (worldwide)
Subsidiary of BankBoston
CEO: Mike McCaffery

KEY COMPETITORS

Goldman Sachs & Co.
Hambrecht & Quist
Merrill Lynch
Morgan Stanley Dean Witter
NationsBanc Montgomery Securities
SG Cowen

UPPERS

- Good support staff
- Entrepreneurial atmosphere
- "Lovely West Coast locale"
- Family-friendly

DOWNERS

- Start days when its dark
- Little training
- Recently became part of more
  bureaucratic giant BankBoston

EMPLOYMENT CONTACT

Human Resources
BancBoston Robertson Stephens
555 California St., Suite 2600
San Francisco, CA 94104

	HOURS	PAY	PRESTIGE	DRESS	SATISFACTION	
BEST 10 / WORST 1	BEST = SHORTEST HOURS	BEST = HIGHEST PAY	BEST = MOST PRESTIGIOUS	BEST = MOST CASUAL	BEST = MOST SATISFIED	BEST 10 / WORST 1
	2	9	8	2	7	

THE SCOOP

A LEADING TEAM PLAYER

BancBoston Robertson Stephens is one of America's leading underwriters of growth companies in the technology, health care, retailing, consumer products, and real estate sectors. The firm is best known for its work in the high-tech industry; Robertson Stephens was the top underwriter of technology IPOs from 1995 to 1997. BancBoston Robertson Stephens is also known as a leader in equity research, with a team of highly-rated analysts. Robertson Stephens is also a notable player in the lucrative mergers and acquisitions business. Since its founding, Robertson Stephens has advised on 300 M&A deals, which together have involved more than $70 billion.

A SUMMER OF MERGERS

The firm isn't just an M&A advisor, but a participant. After toying with the notion of an IPO, the bank decided to seek an acquirer. In 1997, Bank of America the third-largest bank in the United States, agreed to acquire the formerly independent Robertson Stephens in order to take advantage of the smaller firm's expertise in stock underwriting and advising on mergers and acquisitions. The deal was sealed with a friendly handshake after months of negotiation. Clearly captivated by the strong Robertson brand, Bank of America paid $540 million in cash for the bank, approximately five times the book value. Bank of America's deep pockets enabled Robertson Stephens to expand its staff and to venture outside its high tech and health care industry base.

The new merger was thrown into doubt in April 1998 after Bank of America agreed to merge with NationsBank, which already had an investment banking branch – Robertson Stephens rival Montgomery Securities (now Nationsbanc Montgomery Securities). Neither Montgomery nor Robertson Stephens were happy – according to a RS spokesman, the two boutiques have had a "notoriously different approach." In the summer of 1998, BankBoston announced it would pay $800 million for Robertson Stephens' equity and corporate operations (BankAmerica would retain and eventually sell the firm's asset management group, Robertson Stephens Investment Management).

THE AFTERMATH

Shortly after the BankBoston deal was announced, founder and former chairman Sandy Robertson and I-banking head Misha Metkevich announced that they would leave. Despite these departures, the boutique bank retained most of its senior bankers under generous purchase agreement terms, which included a $400 million employee-retention pool. When the deal closed in August 1998, bank officials said they were on track to bring in $480 million in revenue for the 1999 fiscal year. However, weakening world markets in the fall and winter of 1998, hurt investment banking revenue. In November, the firm cut about 5 percent of its workforce. Today, Robbie Stephens is adding e-commerce deals and restaurant banking to its high-tech franchise.

GETTING HIRED

Although the company recruits extensively at top schools around the country, employees still report "it's much easier to be hired if you know someone who works at the firm – many positions are filled through referrals." "Anyone interested in Robertson should definitely hunt out people out any connections through alumni," says one associate who attended a business school at which the firm recruits. "I definitely had to make a lot more of an effort – you didn't see as many people at school as other firms, with all the Goldman and Merrill people walking around."

With the exception of occasional newspaper advertisements, the company does not post specific job openings. Applicants can mail or fax resumes to the company's headquarters, where the resumes will be kept on file for 90 days. The company's interviews are said to be "generally knowledge-based with behavioral questions." Applicants can anticipate an "informal screening interview" and then "an in-house interview with four to six different meetings," although one insider who recently went through recruiting reports a more extensive call-back round. "The final round was meeting with 10 people, all one-on-ones – then a dinner and a cocktail hour, so you spent time with people," reports that contact. Another recently-

I-Banking Job Seekers: Receive free e-mailed job postings matching your interests & qualifications! Register at www.vaultreports.com

VAULT REPORTS™
105
www.vaultreports.com

hired insider suggests that those who expect to be working in equity research should "find out what stocks you might be covering if given the job and research those stocks and their industry." New hires generally work in Robertson Stephens' headquarters in San Francisco headquarters.

OUR SURVEY SAYS

DOWN-TO-EARTH FIRM

Say bankers at BancBoston Robertsen Stephens – fondly known as Robbie Stephens to its employees and others in the industry: "The corporate culture is strong, fun, and best of all, realistic and down to earth." Employees cite "good friendships" with co-workers that "include parties, skiing trips, and jaunts to Las Vegas." Says another insider: "I've really enjoyed the people I work with. I think they're very smart, down-to-earth people. They're not stuffy. They enjoy quality of life. They really have a personal side to them more so than those at most New York firms." A "teamworking environment" warms the hearts of Robertson I-bankers, but on for salespeople, it's a bit different: "In some ways, it can be more competitive, because we are still commission-based, the whole sales force doesn't get a big pool. It's more competitive, but I would say there's less ass-kissing or brown-nosing because of that."

The "lack of structure" at BancBoston Robertson Stephens means "you can learn a lot if you are motivated." The firm offers "little formal training" in favor of "continual on-the-job education." The company's employees also enjoy being on the "cutting-edge" of the banking industry and their frequent contact with the "young, exciting" Silicon Valley companies that play a major role in Robertson Stephens' client base. Employees are able to keep themselves hale and hearty at company expense, as they receive a discount corporate pass to gyms, and full insurance, including medical, dental and vision coverage.

LEAVE WORK AND GO TO SOCCER PRACTICE

Insiders report that the corporate culture at BancBoston Robertson Stephens is "less demanding and more fun" than that of East Coast investment banking firms. Then again, some people might not consider meetings at 5 in the morning fun and undemanding. But, insiders note, early to the office also means early to leave. "The I-bankers get to work at 7:30 or 8, but they don't work all hours of the night. They stay till maybe 8 or 9 at night. The day kind of shifts down." Reports one insider on the sell side: "I get in at 4:30; our first research meeting's at 5. Usually I leave between 2 and 4. Also, there's less entertaining in San Francisco. Most of our clients aren't in San Francisco, so you don't have to go out for drinks after work." That contact continues: "Most of the people I work with are married, and it's great for them. When the day is over, they can go home to the kids, they can go to soccer practice. Some of the guys I work with go to sleep when their little kids go to bed." However, that contact notes that the early-to-bed lifestyle of many Robbie bankers is difficult on those who are still single.

MERGER MANIA

It's a good thing Robertson Stephens bankers are down-to-earth – they've had to be grounded as their employer has changed ownership and names twice recently. "I have to say that morale was certainly seen changes here, although bear in mind, a lot of people I worked with partners and made out pretty well," says one insider, referring to the large rewards that partners in the formerly privately-held firm received from the acquisition by Bank of America and then BankBoston.

Not all of the recent changes have been welcomed, though. Reports one contact about the merger between former Robbie Stephens parent Bank of America and NationsBank: "At first it was scary, because with NationsBank buying Bank of America, obviously there was going to be lots of bloodshed, because Montgomery and Robertson are very similar, and so a lot of people looked around for a lot of jobs and stuff, especially the younger people," says one insider, who notes that "the hard part of being in San Francisco, is, as opposed to New York, where this happens a lot, and there's a lot of places ago, in San Francisco there aren't as many places to go." However, that contact says that after the merged BankAmerica announced that Robertson Stephens would be spun off, "that calmed people down. Basically we were as much

I-Banking Job Seekers: Receive free e-mailed job postings matching your interests & qualifications! Register at www.vaultreports.com

VAULT REPORTS™

107

www.vaultreports.com

as possible going to stay as a group and stay together. At that point we weren't really sure who the end buyer was going to be, but it was more positive."

As for new parent BankBoston, "I should say in general, it's very positive," reports one insider, who notes that culturally, the firm has not been effected greatly. "I think there's been much more of an effort to integrate than we did in BankAmerica, I think there's a lot more synergies. Their client base is a lot more similar, we both target tech and health care middle-market companies. The one concern is that BankBoston will be bought by someone, I mean, they're the 17th- or 18th-largest bank, and everything's consolidating."

SOME NITPICKY COMPLAINTS

Insiders report that Robertson Stephens are irked by the little changes in things because of the acquisitions. For example, previously the firm was automatically billed for travel expenses; now, bankers are billed individually and are reimbursed. "We just got a memo the other day, all business travel has to be pre-approved, and you have to bring receipts, not just your boarding pass, but a copy of the travel plan with itinerary." Another travel gripe: "We changed our travel agency to the travel agency that BankBoston uses, that BankBoston uses American Express, and they get discounts on American Airlines, so they always want to use American. I've heard stories from a couple of people, one guy was going to St. Louis, and he had two stopovers, instead of five-hour flight, it ended up being eight or 10 hours."

To order a 10- to 20-page Vault Reports Employer Profile on BancBoston Robertson Stephens call 1-888-JOB-VAULT or visit www.VaultReports.com

The full Employer Profile includes detailed information on Robertson Stephens' departments, recent developments and transactions, hiring and interview process, plus what employees really think about culture, pay, work hours and more.

Bankers Trust

130 Liberty St., 12th Floor
New York, NY 10006
(212) 250-2500
Fax: (212) 454-1704
www.bankerstrust.com

LOCATIONS

New York, NY (HQ)
14 other major U.S. offices
Additional offices in more than 50 countries
worldwide

THE STATS

Annual Revenues: $12.2 billion (1997)
Net Income: $866 million (1997)
No. of Employees: 18,286 (worldwide)
No. of Offices: 146 (worldwide)
Stock Symbol: BT (NYSE)
CEO: Frank N. Newman

KEY COMPETITORS

BankAmerica
Citicorp
J.P. Morgan
Merrill Lynch
Morgan Stanley Dean Witter

UPPERS

- Good support staff
- Entrepreneurial atmosphere

DOWNERS

- Seemingly constant reorganization
- Recent heavy losses
- Layoffs after acquisition
- Uncertainty from Deutsche Bank acquisition

EMPLOYMENT CONTACT

Human Resources
Bankers Trust
130 Liberty St., 12th Floor
New York, NY 10006

BEST 10 — WORST 1	HOURS BEST = SHORTEST HOURS	PAY BEST = HIGHEST PAY	PRESTIGE BEST = MOST PRESTIGIOUS	DRESS BEST = MOST CASUAL	SATISFACTION BEST = MOST SATISFIED	BEST 10 — WORST 1
	2	9	7	2	6	

THE SCOOP

ONE OF THOSE HYBRIDS

Bankers Trust is not your typical white-shoe investment bank. Unlike Morgan Stanley Dean Witter, Goldman Sachs, and other major investment banks that have established their reputation over decades, Bankers Trust only began to transform itself into an investment bank in the late 1970s. Bankers Trust has gradually evolved into a hybrid bank – half commercial bank and half investment bank, much like its competitor J.P. Morgan, which has undergone a similar transformation.

RECENT TROUBLES

Just a year ago, it seemed as if Bankers Trust had made it back. Lawsuits filed against the firm by clients like Procter & Gamble in the early 1990s for derivatives dealings were behind BT, and the firm had rapidly recovered its reputation – and its revenue. However, all of a sudden (it seemed), in the summer and fall of 1998, Bankers Trust went from a growing firm edging into the upper echelon to a disoriented firm under siege. Although BT reported increased earnings in the second quarter of 1998, analysts noted that the firm was very exposed in Asia for a firm of its size, and speculated that the economic downturn in the area might hurt the bank more than most of its competitors. Bankers Trust hired 650 employees in its third quarter – but when the quarter ended, the bank reported a whopping $488 million loss, which it attributed to losses in emerging markets trading and a decline in investment banking revenue. The loss immediately prompted doubts about BT's viability as an independent firm in an age of consolidation in the financial services industry.

Part of the reason for BT's problems in 1998 was its traditional client base of small companies in fields like high tech, healthcare and telecom. The firm has pursued these smaller clients as the core of its I-banking franchise since its beginnings in investment banking in the 1980s. Banks such as J.P. Morgan and Chase Manhattan, which are also trying to transition from dowdy commercial bank cygnets to glamorous investment banking swans, differ from Bankers

Trust by dint of their client base for commercial lending. Unlike J.P. Morgan, for example, whose pedigree and history have allowed it to provide investment banking services to its blue-chip clients, Bankers Trust's traditional corporate client base has been less-stable companies that are more likely to be hurt by a downturn. On the other hand, BT's client base helps when it comes to businesses like equity or junk bond underwriting, for which larger companies do not have much use.

DEUTSCHLAND, MEIN VATERLAND

The questions of how BT would survive as an independent bank did not last long. In November 1998, just when the world thought that Citigroup had nailed down the title for the "world's largest financial services organization," BT and Deutsche Bank announced that the German giant would acquire the American bank for about $10 billion. The deal will create a financial services behemoth with assets of well over $800 billion. Under the terms of the deal, Deutsche Bank will acquire all outstanding shares of the common stock of Bankers Trust. While the deal has already received a preliminary nod from U.S. regulators, it needs approval from Bankers Trust shareholders and other regulatory bodies worldwide. Insiders expect the deal to close sometime in second quarter 1999.

Anyone who's kept an eye on the post-merger turmoil at Citigroup knows that large scale deals can mean large scale problems within the organization. Deutsche Bank intends to take efforts to smoothly integrate its upper-level management with Bankers Trust counterparts – it has set aside between $400 and $500 million in a retention pool, and insiders told the *The Wall Street Journal* that several Bankers Trust executives, including, Yves de Balmann, Mayo Shattuck (heads of investment banking), Edward Virtue (head of corporate finance), Robert Ferguson (head of BT Australia), and Mary Cirillo (head of global processing), have signed three-year contracts to remain with the company. While execs on both sides are eager to keep BT's top talent, they are just as eager to take advantage of "consolidations" advantages – about 5500 staffers are expected to be cut from the banks because of the deal, with an annual cost savings of $1 billion by 2001. And don't expect all of the employees who remain to be entirely happy campers, either. As opposed to BT's reputation as a sales-and-trading, "wing it" type of culture, Deutsche Bank brings with it a reputation for German conservatism.

I-Banking Job Seekers: Receive free e-mailed job postings matching your interests & qualifications! Register at www.vaultreports.com

VAULT REPORTS™
111
www.vaultreports.com

GETTING HIRED

Applicants should direct their applications to the specific division in which they are interested. The firm's employment web page, located at www.bankerstrust.com, has specific addresses and fax numbers for each division, including separate addresses for offices in Los Angeles and London. MBAs are hired as associates and attend the firm's Financial Services Training Program in New York. BT offers summer internships for MBAs as well; the summer associates are asked to perform the work of a first-year associate. MBAs interested in both financial services and consulting may also apply to the Bankers Trust Management Consulting Group (MCG), a full-service consulting organization within BT. BT interviews are a bit offbeat – reportedly, interviewees have been asked to tell jokes during their first round interviews. Make it good!

OUR SURVEY SAYS

LEAN AND MEAN

Employees consistently praise Bankers Trust's entrepreneurial" corporate culture, with its "very lean and very flat hierarchy," which provides "a lot of upper management contact." "People here are young, they're driven, and they're fair. They're very team-driven, if something needs to be done they won't give it all to you and say, 'Here, get it done.' They'll break it down into little pieces and get it done efficiently," says a trader at BT. Other employees call Bankers Trust a "cosmopolitan place in the sense that the people who work there are varied – BT does not look for a certain personality type." Further, the corporate culture is "very much a meritocracy in which you get paid for performance" – ample incentive for employees to strive for "innovative" thinking. One new analyst remarks that Bankers Trust's corporate culture makes it easier to cope with the "arduous" work requirements: "Often you go to other firms and they're sweatshops. Not that you don't work hard here, but there's a certain collegial atmosphere where everyone gets along and works together. It's like family." However, to thrive in Bankers Trust's corporate work place, employees must be independent and self-driven.

Reports one analyst: "Some companies are very established, have their formula, and will walk you through it. This is not Bankers Trust. Bankers Trust is an entrepreneurial environment, and requires initiative from its people." Those employees who "are aggressive, who are not afraid to be heard, who take initiative and who are willing to work the skin off their butts" are invariably rewarded with better pay and promotions. Sometimes, however, the aggressiveness of fellow employees can get a bit too much. A Bankers Trust veteran remarks: "They give you a huge project and say, 'Run with it,' 'My boss is counting on you,' 'Our client is counting on you.' On occasion, the temperature gets too hot, and people will yell at you, but they later come back and apologize or take you out for a drink. But people do occasionally yell – and it isn't pretty." Summing up the BT experience, an employee observes: "If you want to be coddled or have your hand held, this is not the place for you. But if you're tough, it's a great job."

GET READY TO WORK

Workdays at BT tend to be "typical for the banking industry." New hires in finance should expect to work from "7:30 a.m. to 10 p.m. everyday, plus weekends." Most new hires in the finance unit can "expect to have no life other than work for the first four or five years." One recently hired associate says, "I've done 110-hour weeks. Not every week, of course, but often." One of the advantages of working for Bankers Trust, one employee notes, is that "if you're done with your work, just get out. No one's expecting you to do the 'face time' or be here acting like you're working hard. If you're done at 5 or 6, you can leave." However, the same employee candidly admits: "Leaving at 5 or 6 – that rarely happens. With most people coming just out of school, because it's a heavy learning environment and there's a lot of work to get done, it's fast paced, they definitely do stay longer, and it does bother them." New hires "find that working three out of every four weekends" is "especially hard." Some of them, though, "work like crazy during the week so that they don't have to come in weekends. It all depends on you." The schedules of those working in Capital Markets are much more reasonable; employees usually leave work at "7 or 8 p.m. each night and rarely – if ever – work weekends." Work hours in the non-finance divisions of the bank tend to be "reasonable" for

I-Banking Job Seekers: Receive free e-mailed job postings matching your interests & qualifications! Register at www.vaultreports.com

VAULT REPORTS™
www.vaultreports.com

113

the field, and average at about "45 hours a week." In comparison with the "crazy" hours at the New York office, the Chicago and Los Angeles offices are "much more mellow and laid-back."

To order a 50- to 70-page Vault Reports Employer Profile on Bankers Trust call 1-888-JOB-VAULT or visit www.VaultReports.com

The full Employer Profile includes detailed information on BT's departments, recent developments and transactions, hiring and interview process, plus what employees really think about culture, pay, work hours and more.

Bear Stearns

245 Park Avenue
New York, NY 10167
(212) 272-2000
Fax: (212) 272-8239
www.bearstearns.com

LOCATIONS

New York, NY (HQ)
Atlanta • Boston • Chicago • Dallas • Los
Angeles • San Francisco • Washington, DC •
Beijing • Buenos Aires • Dublin • Geneva •
Hong Kong • London • Lugano, Switzerland
• Paris • Sao Paulo, Brazil • Shanghai, China
• Singapore • Tokyo

THE STATS

Annual Revenues: $6.1 billion (1997)
No. of Employees: 8,309 (worldwide)
No. of Offices: 20 (worldwide)
Stock Symbol: BSC (NYSE)
Chairman: Ace Greenberg

KEY COMPETITORS

Donaldson, Lufkin & Jenrette
Lehamn Brothers
Salomon Smith Barney

UPPERS

- Less bureaucratic than most firms
- Extensive exposure to senior management
- Early responsibility

DOWNERS

- Cramped offices
- Reputation for chintziness
- Rubberbands rare

EMPLOYMENT CONTACT

Investment Banking:
Jennifer Rolnick Rosenthal

Sales, Trading & Research:
Amy Rosen Williams

Bear Stearns
245 Park Avenue
New York, NY 10167

	HOURS	PAY	PRESTIGE	DRESS	SATISFACTION	
BEST 10 ▲ ... WORST 1	BEST = SHORTEST HOURS	BEST = HIGHEST PAY	BEST = MOST PRESTIGIOUS	BEST = MOST CASUAL	BEST = MOST SATISFIED	BEST 10 ▲ ... WORST 1
	2	9	8	1	7	

THE SCOOP

ALWAYS PROFITABLE

Three-quarters of a century is a long time to go without an unprofitable year, but Wall Street luminary Bear Stearns has accomplished just that. Since being founded in 1923, the firm has never operated at a loss. Known as "the Bear" to Wall Street players, the venerable institution is one of the nation's top investment banking, securities trading, and brokerage firms. With about half a million dollars in capital among the three of them, Joseph Bear, Robert Stearns, and Harold Mayer started Bear Stearns at the beginning of the Roaring Twenties. The firm initially operated with a small staff out of a single office at 100 Broadway. Founded as a partnership, Bear Stearns initially focused on brokerage.

TOP OF ITS GAME

Despite consistent returns – the firm has topped 20 percent in return on equity (a common yardstick for a well-performing I-bank) for three straight years – Bear Stearns has not broken into Wall Street's upper I-banking echelon. Apart from some businesses, such as public finance (underwriting and issuing municipal bonds), in which the firm ranks in the middle of the top five consistently, and mortgage-backed securities, in which the firm consistently ranks in the top three, Bear Stearns usually hovers around in the bottom of the top 10 in the league tables.

But the Bear is still a major Wall Street player. In recent years, it has been tapped for some of the world's biggest deals, especially in M&A. The firm advised Starwood Lodging in its high-profile $13.7 billion acquisition of ITT (in 1997), Walt Disney in its $18.8 billion acquisition of Capital Cities/ABC (in 1996), and NYNEX in its $52 billion "merger of equals" with NYNEX (also in 1996). More recently, the firm was tapped to represent American Home Products in its planned $35 billion merger with Monsanto (the merger was called off in the fall of 1998), and Bell Atlantic in its pending $50 billion merger with GTE. In its 1998 fiscal year, the firm also lead managed a $477 million IPO for Young & Rubicam, a $381 million IPO for Avis Rent-a-Car and lead managed the largest municipal bond issue ever – a $3.5 million issue for the Long Island Power Authority.

VAULT REPORTS™
www.vaultreports.com

CLEARING THE WAY

Bear Stearns receives more than a third of its profits from its clearing business. In this business, the firm is hired to execute trades, maintain client records, send out trade confirmations and monthly statements, and settle transactions. (Clearing firms basically do a lot of the paperwork that goes along with brokering, typically for smaller firms.) Close to 2500 clients employ Bear Stearns for clearing, and the department has attracted rivals to the Bear's services. Lehman Brothers is one of a number of top Wall Street firms which take advantage of Bear Stearns clearing services. Such success has become a firm boasting point; ads for Bear Stearns have urged other firms to "Throw Our Weight Around" and claim that "We Clear Everything for Everybody." While Wall Street firms use the Bear for clearing, it is primarily smaller brokerages that use the firm's services, as the firm's prestigious name on paperwork investors receive is often a confidence-selling point. And Bear's clearing services are picking up steam, as are its I-banking businesses. As one analyst told *Crain's* in the summer of 1998: "Clearing is undoubtedly [Bear's] fastest-growing business, but their investment banking has come from nowhere to somewhere."

Unfortunately, Bear Stearns' clearing operations have also generated some unwanted attention. One of the many brokerages that the firm has cleared transactions for, A. R. Baron, collapsed after bilking as many as 8000 investors out of more than $75 million. Currently, the government is still investigating a possible Bear Stearns role in the Baron case, in particular, the ties between former Baron CEO Andrew Bressman and Richard Harriton, Bear Stearns' chief of clearing. The firm has denied any knowledge of Baron's fraudulent activities. Even if, as the firm anticipates, Bear Stearns is cleared of wrongdoing in the Baron case, the recent attention may end up hurting it and other Wall Street firms in the clearing business. Some securities lawyers are pressing for new regulations that would hold clearing firms responsible for the actions of their broker clients. Bear chairman Ace Greenberg has warned that such regulations could lead some clearing houses to "abandon their business outright."

I-Banking Job Seekers: Receive free e-mailed job postings matching your interests & qualifications! Register at www.vaultreports.com

VAULT REPORTS™
www.vaultreports.com

117

GETTING HIRED

For investment banking, the firm has about 10 business schools that it targets heavily. At these schools, either David Solomon, who is a co-head of investment banking, or another high-ranking official makes a presentation. At about five other business schools, the firm interviews, but does not give presentations. These schools are essentially the same every year.

Bear Stearns draws many of its associates through its summer programs. The firm hires about 25 summer I-banking associates (all in New York), and about 40 full-time associates worldwide (NY summer associates can move full-time into one of the firm's regional offices). The summer hiring process is condensed into an about three-week process. The first round is usually on campus, and usually consists of a two-on-one interview. While students at some schools will travel to Bear's New York headquarters for second rounds, the second round for summers is in many cases simply held that evening on-campus. For example, because the University of Chicago business school does not provide for time off from classes to travel for interviews, through three or four two-on-ones. "Depending on what our competitors' schedules are, sometimes it makes sense to just go ahead and give the offer that night," says one recruiter. According to the firm, anywhere from 55 to 75 percent of I-banking summer associates return for full-time positions.

The firm also targets about 25 undergraduate schools each year, which, unlike its target B-schools, can change substantially from year to year, as the firm continually evaluates its success with on-campus undergraduate recruiting. The firm hires about 100 analysts into I-banking worldwide, about 75 of them in New York. For summer analyst positions, although the Bear accepts resumes from all undergraduate schools, and likes to have representation from its core schools, it only recruits on-campus at Wharton.

OUR SURVEY SAYS

YOU'RE NOT GOING TO A FACTORY

One thing that Bear employees love to point out is that the firm offers "so much responsibility that it automatically becomes a rewarding experience." Says one I-banking associate, "You're going to a firm that's large and has its fair share of marquee deals, but you're not going to a factory." Says an associate in sales and trading: "The culture's pretty straightforward as far as giving you important work from day one." That contact notes that his B-school friends at other firms were "given projects that the senior managing director already knew the answer to." Many employees say that they enjoy their "autonomy," which leaves them "free from obnoxious bureaucracy." Reports a sales and trading associate: "The SMD (senior managing director) in my group trades. He's not like just sitting in an office. It's just like the way (Chairman) Ace (Greenberg) sits on the floor." But surely the firm's chairman doesn't roll up his sleeves to do any serious work? Not so, say insiders. "Alan?" says one. "He trades."

MAKE YOUR MARK

Because "there's very little structure, you have to find your own way" at Bear Stearns. The "flat organization," of the firm, meanwhile, enables everyone "to make an impact at any level." Says one insider: ""Every place says they're entrepreneurial – *this* place is entrepreneurial." The firm also allows for "individual stars to shine." Because of Bear Stearns' "thorough commitment to recognizing individual merit, those who perform well can really hold their heads up high." Explains one sales associate: "It's not just that they throw you a big ball and tell you to run with it. They maybe give you a little ball, and you can dribble around with it and if you do well then you get a bigger ball."

SINK OR SWIM?

"You may not get the depth of training that you might get at a J.P. Morgan," says one Bear employee, "but you do have the chance to become a star player for the firm." Some employees

I-Banking Job Seekers: Receive free e-mailed job postings matching your interests & qualifications! Register at www.vaultreports.com

VAULT REPORTS™
www.vaultreports.com

119

say the firm has a "survival of the fittest" mentality which "extends into all ranks." Indeed, the Bear has this reputation outside the firm, which insiders say is overblown. "You hear things, but I quickly found out that it wasn't the case," reports one I-banking associate. "This is not a place where you play duck duck goose, but I think there's as much personal contact as at other firms." Bear employees are quick to point out that the firm is not a sink-or-swim environment, saying that they are provided support from senior employees. I-banking associates are assigned a junior and a senior mentor (a VP as the junior mentor, and an MD as a senior mentor). Says an associate in sales and trading: "The guy who sits behind me is my mentor. The guy who sits in front of me is my mentor. I learn something from them every day." Says one associate: "Bear Stearns is a healthy competitive environment. The bottom line is to make money. If all that they say about backstabbing and sink-or-swim were true, how the hell would we make any money?"

NO PAPER CLIPS FOR YOU

The Bear Stearns support staff has been described by employees as "the best available." Unlike other Wall Street firms, there are plenty of secretaries to go around, though some offices may have a limited number depending upon their needs. Word processing and data entry services are also available. And, of course, interns are plentiful and available for all research needs.

However, several employees confirm that "the firm does emphasize thrift." As one associate laments, "we don't even get paper clips when we start. No paper clips – it's kind of symbolic, a 'you will make due with less' kind of message." Says another insider: "I never got a bag of rubber bands or a box of paper clips. I asked my secretary if I could have some paper clips, and she said I would have to pay for them. No joke, if I see a paper clip on the floor, or a pen on somebody's desk, if somebody's stupid enough to leave a pen on their desk, I take it."

To order a 50- to 70-page Vault Reports Employer Profile on Bear Stearns call 1-888-JOB-VAULT or visit www.VaultReports.com

The full Employer Profile includes detailed information on Bear Stearns' departments, recent developments and transactions, hiring and interview process, plus what employees really think about culture, pay, work hours and more.

I-Banking Job Seekers: Receive free e-mailed job postings matching your interests & qualifications! Register at www.vaultreports.com

VAULT REPORTS™
www.vaultreports.com

121

"No joke, if I see a paper clip on the floor, or a pen on somebody's desk, if somebody's stupid enough to leave a pen on their desk, I take it.

– *Bear Stearns insider*

Bowles Hollowell Connor

101 South Tryon St., 40th Floor
Charlotte, NC 28280
(704) 348-1000
Fax: (704) 348-1099
www.bhc-co.com

LOCATIONS

Charlotte, NC (HQ)

THE STATS

No. of Employees: More than 130
Subsidiary of First Union
Year Founded: 1975

KEY COMPETITORS

Broadview Associates
Raymond James Financial
U.S. Bancorp Piper Jaffray
William Blair & Co.

UPPERS

- Close relationship with senior bankers
- Good launching pad for private
  equity funds

DOWNERS

- Far away from New York
- Some uncertainty because of acquisition
  by First Union

EMPLOYMENT CONTACT

Human Resources
Bowles Hollowell Connor
101 South Tryon St., 40th Floor
Charlotte, NC 28280

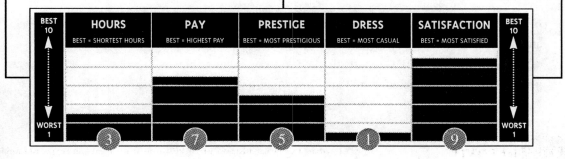

	HOURS	PAY	PRESTIGE	DRESS	SATISFACTION	
BEST 10 → WORST 1	BEST = SHORTEST HOURS	BEST = HIGHEST PAY	BEST = MOST PRESTIGIOUS	BEST = MOST CASUAL	BEST = MOST SATISFIED	BEST 10 → WORST 1
	3	7	5	1	9	

THE SCOOP

A NEW UNION

When North Carolina-based M&A boutique Bowles Hollowell Connor announced it would be acquired by commercial bank First Union in the spring of 1998, much interest focused on one of the firm's name founders, former White House Chief of Staff Erskine Bowles. Was the firm's acquisition only interesting because of the White House connection? Far from it. Bowles Hollowell Connor, or BHC, is a leader in mid-sized M&A advisory – the firm is the national leader in sell side transactions (advising acquisition targets) for deals under $100 million. BHC specializes in M&A advice and financing for companies with annual revenues between $10 million and $150 million. Since 1992, the firm has advised on more than 250 deals worth more than $23 billion; in 1997, the firm participated in 16 M&A transactions worth a total of $2.5 billion. And while BHC was indeed co-founded by Erskine Bowles in 1975, Bowles has sold his stake and is no longer affiliated with the company.

INCREASING AGGRESSION

With its reported $90 million acquisition by First Union, BHC is moving further away from its roots as a closely-held shop. Virginia-based First Union has in recent years aggressively expanded both its commercial and investment banking capabilities. Several months before announcing the BHC deal, First Union acquired Richmond-based boutique Wheat First Butcher Singer, which brought M&A, retail brokerage, and equity underwriting to the growing First Union table. First Union execs believe that the acquisition of BHC is an especially good fit because of First Union's own concentration on middle market business. In announcing the merger, bank officials said that BHC will continue to be headed by CEO Steve Cummings, and will operate under the same name, as a division of First Union Capital Markets.

In large part because of its focus on middle-market companies, BHC has a strong presence among private equity groups – which invest directly in leveraged buyouts and recapitalizations of private companies. BHC reports that it has strong relationships with more than 300 of these groups, and has represented more than 75 of them in the last five years.

GETTING HIRED

BHC hires undergraduates into a two-year analyst program, recruiting primarily from strong Southern schools such as Vanderbilt, University of Virginia and Duke. The firm lists the schools at which it recruits, along with contacts, at its web site, located at www.bhc-co.com. The firm's recruiting of MBAs for associate-level positions is more widespread – BHC journeys to non-Southern institutions Harvard, Kellogg and the University of Chicago.

Reports one insider: "Because Bowles is a strong place culturally, fit is important. [The interview] is certainly not [on the level of] 'How 'bout this weather outside', but as I remember, you're not doing a lot of bond math in the interview."

One insider describes his interview process. "It was two-on-ones first round." During the callback round, candidates "come in for dinner on Friday night, a lot of analysts and associates there, then you go out, but it's not one of these super high-pressure deals where you have go and get hammered." On Saturday, "you start at about 8:30 and have five or six interviews, and close with two-on-two lunch with two recruits, a senior banker and a junior banker."

OUR SURVEY SAYS

BASKETBALL WITH PARTNERS

Insiders agree that one of the best things about working at Bowles is the contact between senior and junior bankers. "[At BHC] there's not a very hierarchical structure – they definitely don't lead you by fear or anything," says one insider. "It's very much a place where you're able to build very good relationships from top to bottom." Says a former analyst: "The senior people cared enough about you as a person to talk to you on a personal basis at work. They knew something about you other than that you showed up with a model for them." While the

I-Banking Job Seekers: Receive free e-mailed job postings matching your interests & qualifications! Register at www.vaultreports.com

VAULT REPORTS™

125

www.vaultreports.com

composition of "the deal team's no different – managing director, VP, associate and analyst – but the managing directors [at BHC] are so cool about your professional development and being friendly – the door's always open," says one insider. "I've spent an inordinate amount of time in partners offices, talking about deals and whatever."

The cozy relationships between senior and junior bankers are not confined to the office, it seems. "We'd have Tuesday night basketball, where the firm would just rent the gym out, and the analysts would come out," one former analyst says. "The partners at the firm would come out and play, not every time, but reasonably regularly."

And the senior bankers apparently are willing to extend the relationship beyond the job. "They have always been pretty supportive, they're great at placing analyst people in positions with private equity firms. They're well known in that circle, and pretty highly thought of. It tends to be a pretty good launching pad for those jobs." Sums up that contact: "The senior guys are very good about giving a damn about what happens to the analysts."

SLIGHTLY LOWER ON HOURS, PAY

"They're pretty good about no face-time, because you do work a lot when you're busy. At the top it can be as busy as Wall Street," reports one insider. Still, that contact says that, on average, the workload at Bowles is shorter than on Wall Street. "The average week is, not 80, maybe 70 hours a week." Notes that contact: "There's an appreciable difference between 70 and 80 – that's two hours every night past midnight that you have to work. Those hours are much more valuable, the last 10."

BHC insiders acknowledge that with shorter hours comes a tradeoff in pay. "I think in absolute terms [pay] is lower. In the past from an analyst perspective, [pay] was a little off-market. For example, Bowles Holowell were not paid as much as NationsBank in the past," says one insider. However, that contact reports that "on the associate level, [salaries are] pretty comparable – they attract some pretty stellar candidates from all over." "The comp is pretty comparable all the way out. The blowout Wall Street numbers are probably not likely to be there, but you're well in the upper half levels," remarks one insider. "And with the cost of living, I mean, multiply it by three." That contact raves about the affordability of North

Carolina. "You can go buy a four-bedroom house in the nicest place of town for $350,000 – you have a mortgage of $18,000 bucks. You've got a house and not a shoebox. You can barely get a nice one bedroom in New York for that."

When Bowles bankers leave home, it's not necessarily to a chi-chi area, either, because of Bowles' focus on middle-market companies. "The travel's OK, sometimes you're at a place where there isn't a decent place to stay, and you just make do," says one insider. "That might be if you were selling the company, and you have to take the buyer to a plant. But typically you're in a town or city where there's a decent place to stay, it's not like you're in mobile home parks."

THE FIRST UNION MERGER

"From a culture point of view, so far, it's had pretty low impact," says one insider about the acquisition of BHC by First Union. "Bowles had already moved into a new offices that are in the NationsBank building, and I think right now, there's no plan to move them in the near future. It's very much operating independently." This independence is symbolized by other factors other than the separate locations: "Bowles hasn't taken its name off the letterhead, and they're still recruiting on their own."

Insiders say that business reasons underly the firm's maintenance of independence. "Bowles brings something that First Union simply didn't have," says one banker. That contact contrasts the Bowles/First Union situation with recent combinations that have resulted in some infighting: "No one's fighting over who's going to do M&A at First Union. They know that Bowles is going to do the M&A." And it's not as if Bowles gets nothing out of the deal, either. "There was just not much chance of doing technology at Bowles Hollowell," explains one insider. "Now they're not going to be a huge player, but they can build some industry groups where First Union is established."

One insider describes the initial reaction to the merger: "I think the junior people kind of looked at it and said, 'Oh shit, what does this mean for me.' But they're all on board. Most of the senior people are pretty rooted there, and the junior people know they wouldn't do something that they didn't think would work." Going from a private partnership to a

I-Banking Job Seekers: Receive free e-mailed job postings matching your interests & qualifications! Register at www.vaultreports.com

VAULT REPORTS™
127
www.vaultreports.com

subsidiary of a public one does have some changes, insiders concede. "At the end of the rainbow there's not partnership as the goal, so you don't have the opportunity to sell out Bowles. But at the same time, with things the way they are, if you were to have joined now, you're rolling the dice that it wasn't going to be sold [before getting a chance to make partner]. And at the same time, comp-wise, there's a lot of incentives First Union can give – stock options, stock discounts – that Bowles couldn't."

Broadview Associates

One Bridge Plaza
Fort Lee, NJ 07024
(201) 346-9000
Fax: (201) 346-9191
www.broadview.com

LOCATIONS

Fort Lee, NJ (HQ)
Boston
Silicon Valley
London
Tokyo

THE STATS

No. of Employees: More 225
A privately-held firm
Chairman & CEO: Paul Deninger

KEY COMPETITORS

BancBoston Robertson Stephens
Hambrecht & Quist
SG Cowen
Wasserstein Perella

UPPERS

- Growing firm
- Social firm
- Close exposure to "cool" partners

DOWNERS

- Commute to New Jersey
- Narrowly defined M&A business

EMPLOYMENT CONTACT

Justin Kulo, Recruiting Manager
Broadview Associates
One Bridge Plaza
Fort Lee, NJ 07024

AnalystRecruiter@Broadview.com
AssociateRecruiter@Broadview.com

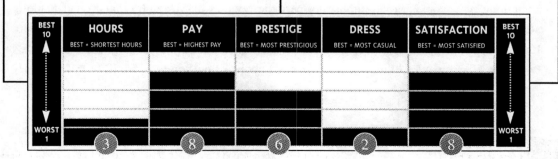

	HOURS	PAY	PRESTIGE	DRESS	SATISFACTION	
BEST 10 / WORST 1	BEST = SHORTEST HOURS	BEST = HIGHEST PAY	BEST = MOST PRESTIGIOUS	BEST = MOST CASUAL	BEST = MOST SATISFIED	BEST 10 / WORST 1
	3	8	6	2	8	

THE SCOOP

TAKING THE LONG VIEW

Broadview Associates has taken the long view when it comes to what industries will be the most important and most active in the coming years – and is enjoying explosive growth and business because of it. The M&A boutique specializes in the information technology, communications and media industries (officially focusing on five "sectors": software products and services, hardware products, telecommunications services, media and information services, and supporting products and services). While the tech banking boom in recent years has enabled the firm to grow rapidly, Broadview forecasts even more rapid growth in the coming years, pointing out that the market capitalization (value according to the stock market) of all the companies in its industries has risen from $200 billion in 1990 to $2.8 trillion in 1997, and that M&A deals in the industries have exploded from about 1200 in 1994 to an estimated 4000 in 1998.

Founded in 1973, the firm has established itself as a leading bank in its industries, handling 81 deals worth more than $4 billion in 1997. The firm was profiled in *Forbes* magazine in 1997 with this teaser: "Who brokered more high-tech mergers last year than Goldman Sachs, Morgan Stanley and Salomon Brothers combined?" (Yes, it was Broadview.) In 1998, the firm was tapped to advise Quarterdeck in its $65 million acquisition by Symantec. Still, although the firm is the leader when it comes to number of deals handled, it hasn't been a player in megadeals like 3Com's acquisition of U.S. Robotics or America Online's bid to purchase Netscape.

ENTER VENTURE

Along with its advisory role in deals within its target industries, Broadview also functions in something of a wonkish role, publishing periodic reviews of M&A, IPO, and other banking activity in the industries. The firm has also entered into a venture capital joint venture with Electra Fleming, a private equity group. The VC fund, Kennet Capital, invests in mid-sized European IT companies (with revenues between about $2 million to $15 million). In January

1998, the firm's chairman, Charles Federman, stepped down, and Paul Deninger, already the firm's CEO, took on the additional post.

GETTING HIRED

Broadview recruits analysts and associates at leading schools in the U.S. and Europe. Calenders for presentations and on-campus interviews can be found at www.broadview.com. Unlike some other investment banks, Broadview prefers one-on-one interviews to two-on-ones. The process for analysts involves an on-campus interview (or one at the firm's headquarters) and then a "Superday," usually a Saturday, with four to six interviews.

Despite the firm's focus on the IT industry, insiders say that "they don't specifically look for a tech background." Explains one contact: "I would say you need to have a passion for tech, there's just as much talk about acronyms like ISDN [ed note: that's Integrated Services Digital Network] as there is about P/E ratios," says one insider. "They'll ask, say, to 'Tell me something about technology that interests you.' If you say the Internet is the coolest thing in the world, they'll ask you to qualify that."

The firm hires undergrads into a two-year analyst program. Analysts begin with a three-week training program in the New Jersey office, which brings analysts from all of the firm's offices together. "It's all taught by internal people," reports one contact. "It's a lot of finance, some [tech] industry stuff." If an analyst does a third year, which the firm reportedly encourages, he or she can switch offices. The firm will pay business school tuition for outstanding analysts who pledge to return, insiders say. The firm also promotes a few analysts to the associate level without requiring that they receive an MBA.

In the past, associate classes at Broadview were comprised of "engineers that went back for MBAs," but as the firm grows, insiders say, it is looking at more business school students with straight finance backgrounds. Reports one insider: "When you come on as an associate at Broadview, they expect you to become a partner." This insider outlines the career path to

I-Banking Job Seekers: Receive free e-mailed job postings matching your interests & qualifications! Register at www.vaultreports.com

VAULT REPORTS™
www.vaultreports.com
131

partnership: one and a half year until making senior associate, at which time an associate begins to specialize in a sector like hardware or software; two years to "phase I" principal, three or four years to "phase II" principal, and then a year or so to partnership.

OUR SURVEY SAYS

LUCKY NICHE

Broadview is a rapidly growing firm. Explains one insider: "Basically Broadview turned a corner from concentrating on a niche that nobody gave a shit about to a niche that everybody gave a shit about. They got kind of lucky in that tech went nuts." Still, the firm is far from a machine, and insiders note that its lifestyle maintains the characteristics of a small firm. Says one contact about the firm's growth in the past several years: "If you take a look at Wall Street and say, at the typical Wall Street bank the people are sort of nasty, and the hours are grueling, if that's a 10, Broadview went from being a 1 to a 4 or a 5." Says that contact: "The hours are maybe 60 to 65 a week – that's a week at Club Med compared to Wall Street." Another contact pegs the hours a little higher. "You have the occasional all-nighter, it's all about a deal cycle. It's minimum 60 or 70." Still, says that contact, "it's not expected that you'll be there on the weekends. Though most people do put some time in the weekends, on Fridays, it's not like, 'I'll see you tomorrow.'"

NO CEO FEAR

The firm's small size also effects issues like career path and responsibility, insiders report. "Because you're in a small environment, if you're talented, everyone will know that," explains one insider. "The people who are moving quickly, everyone knows about." One former analyst recounts leading a six-hour meeting with the CEO of a client. "I'm not saying that's typical, but if you know your shit, you'll get to do some cool stuff," says one insider. "One of the great things about working at Broadview is that after, you have no fear. You get on the phone with CEOs, and you have no fear, because you're doing this all the time at Broadview."

FORT LEE: SUCKS?

Broadview is headquartered in Fort Lee, New Jersey, just across the George Washington Bridge from Manhattan. "Fort Lee itself sucks, no doubt about it, but I don't think it really matters when you're in the office all day," says one insider. There are other reasons that the location may be less than desirable, contacts note. Because most young bankers, "and even some of the marrieds" live in Manhattan, "you have to file estimated taxes in New York once a quarter. It's such a pain, the CFO sat us down and told us how to do it." But the actual travelling is not a headache. "It's a nice reverse commute. It's, like, 15 minutes to the Upper West Side," reports one contact. Also, the firm pays for "a car home after 8 p.m. Most people would catch rides in with people in the morning, and take the car at night." Says one insider about the cab rides home: "It's a New Jersey taxi cab. The people who don't have cars know all the drivers and their life stories." For drivers and those not inclined to lending sympathetic ears, Broadview offers "free parking in the building."

I LOVE NEW YORK

Although the firm's headquarters may be located in suburban New Jersey, insiders say Broadview bankers maintain social lives more representative of their Manhattan homes. "You meet up with each other in the city on Friday or Saturday night," says one insider, "and there are a lot of firm events. They have a welcome picnic, and a Halloween party and a holiday party." Reports another insider: "There's a partner there who shoots hoops with all the analysts, of course, we suck because we're all investment bankers, but he can practically dunk – and he goes out with you to the bar after." And, according to insiders, the firm's CEO, Paul Denninger, likes to mix it up too. At the firm's functions, "he's the last person to leave the dance floor, he outlasts me," says one analyst. "He's just very cool. In some ways, you say, 'Wait a minute, I don't want to see the CEO on the dance floor.' But on the other hand, it's cool."

I-Banking Job Seekers: Receive free e-mailed job postings matching your interests & qualifications! Register at www.vaultreports.com

VAULT REPORTS™
www.vaultreports.com

133

ABROAD BILL OF FARE

Aside from firm functions, other perks Broadview bankers can take advantage of are the dinners when staying late. "There's no real rule" on how late a banker must stay in order to qualify for the dinner. There are also no strict policies on how much a banker can bill for dinner. As one insider points out, "it's New Jersey. It's not like New York, where you could actually bill a very expensive meal. And you know, people are reasonable." Another perk at the firm's headquarters are weekly analyst lunches on Fridays, educational and training lunch. "The firm buys lunch for everyone," explains one insider. "It's usually good – it's not Burger King. We've had sandwiches or Italian or sushi. They've gotten very creative."

Brown Brothers Harriman & Co.

59 Wall Street
New York, NY 10005
(212) 483-1818
Fax: (212) 493-8003
www.bbh.com

LOCATIONS

New York, NY (HQ)
Boston, MA • Charlotte, NC • Chicago, IL •
Dallas, TX • Jersey City, NJ • Los Angeles,
CA • Palm Beach • Philadelphia, PA • Hong
Kong • London • Naples • Tokyo • Zurich

THE STATS

No. of Offices: 16 (worldwide)
A privately-held company
CEO: Anthony T. Enders

KEY COMPETITORS

Bear Stearns
Goldman Sachs
J.P. Morgan
Morgan Stanley Dean Witter

UPPERS

- Broad-minded analysis welcome
- No face time
- Somewhat shorter hours
- Hallowed tradition

DOWNERS

- Few women in top positions
- No casual dress
- Conservative culture

EMPLOYMENT CONTACT

Human Resources
59 Wall Street
New York, NY 10005

Fax: (212) 493-7287
jobs@bbh.com

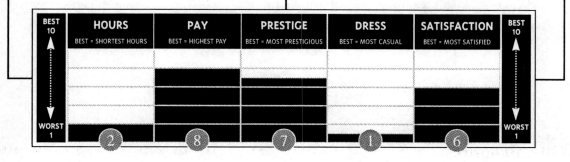

	HOURS	PAY	PRESTIGE	DRESS	SATISFACTION	
BEST 10	BEST = SHORTEST HOURS	BEST = HIGHEST PAY	BEST = MOST PRESTIGIOUS	BEST = MOST CASUAL	BEST = MOST SATISFIED	BEST 10
WORST 1	2	8	7	1	6	WORST 1

THE SCOOP

THE OLDEST NAME

The Brown name, while not as dominant in American investment banking as the Morgan name, has the longest history. Alexander Brown, an auctioneer from Northern Ireland, emigrated to the United States and in Baltimore, established an eponymous firm that is now America's oldest investment bank – BT Alex. Brown. His sons, the Brown Brothers of England – William, George, John, and James – founded a merchant bank in England (called Brown Shipley), and branched out to Philadelphia in 1818 as Brown Brothers & Co. Today, Brown Brothers Harriman is America's oldest owner-managed private bank.

After its founding in America, and in partnership with the Brown Shipley, the firm established offices in New York (1825) and Boston (1845), making its money by financing the textile and other forms of trade and transportation, and capturing a sizable portion of the East India trade. The transatlantic partnership ended in 1917. In 1931, Brown Brothers combined its business and client base with two other family-owned firms with serious pedigrees – they had been founded by members of the famed Harriman family (one was founded by W. Averell Harriman, who became Governor of New York).

STILL OLD SCHOOL

Brown Brothers Harriman & Co. provides commercial and private banking, global custody of securities, and investment advisory services from nine domestic and seven international offices. The firm is perhaps the epitome of the old-school, private banking stereotype, (think the old guys in the Eddie Murphy flick *Trading Places*), in both its practice and its reputation. The firm's client base focuses more than other I-banks on private companies and wealthy individuals. And it wasn't until 1998 that the firm named its first two women partners (who now have ownership stakes) – Susan C. Livingston and Kristen Fitzwilliam Giarrusso.

TURNING JAPANESE

Reflecting its European origins, BBH & Co. retains a heavy international flavor. Its custodial businesses (which entails actually keeping the documentation that shows that a customer, say a mutual fund, owns securities) is highly regarded – in 1997 the firm ranked most highly in a survey of mutual funds in all categories of global custody. (Chase Manhattan, the Bank of New York and State Street Bank ranked highly in domestic services.) Mutual fund assets, run out of Brown Brothers' large Boston office, represent more than 50 percent of the firm's $500 billion assets under custody. In 1998, the firm formed a partnership with Japanese banking giant Daiwa Bank, which will involve the training of Daiwa bankers at Brown Brothers Harriman. Brown Brothers Harriman also runs several private equity funds, which invest the firm's and partners' (including the California Public Employees' Retirement System and the pension fund of the World Bank) funds in non-controlling equity investments of private companies.

GETTING HIRED

Brown Brothers Harriman maintains helpful employment web pages at its web site, located at www.bbh.com. The pages include an opportunity to fill out a resume on-line, to contact the firm's HR department, and to check out info on the firm's training programs and job openings.

Brown Brothers recruits MBAs for a variety of positions, including investment management (both as portfolio managers and equity research), and I-banking advisory, including M&A. For the few (usually around three) analysts BBH & Co hires each year, the firm recruits at the "usual Ivy League schools, but also a few schools like Bowdoin and Colgate." The hiring process for analysts usually consists of two rounds. In the first round, one insider tells us, "you'll meet two or three analysts who will spend 30 or so minutes each asking you a range of questions – no brainteasers but definitely stuff about why you want to work in finance." For the second round, for which the firm foots the bill: "You'll meet just about everyone else in the

I-Banking Job Seekers: Receive free e-mailed job postings matching your interests & qualifications! Register at www.vaultreports.com

VAULT REPORTS™
137
www.vaultreports.com

department on the second trip and they'll take you out to lunch." BBH employees report that the firm's hiring process is relatively casual for the finance industry: "I think [the BBHers] try to really get to know what you're like to work with."

BBH & Co. looks for intelligent people who are balanced socially and academically. According to one insider, "The firm prefers students who are not single-minded in their career focus and have a broad perspective on what they might like to do." Applicants should have a true interest in investment banking, as one contact warns, "several current members of the department are very wary of students who choose investment banking without giving it much thought – you should have a genuine interest."

OUR SURVEY SAYS

NO BRAVADO

Can you say… conservative? Aiming to maintain the "oldest bank on the Street" atmosphere, partners at BBH reportedly keep the firm's culture strictly conservative. Employees wheel and deal in formal dress five days a week, year round. Reports one insider: "there are no dress-down days, not even in the summer." Says another insider: "Regarding the culture of Brown Brothers, I would categorize it as being quite conservative." Although the firm may be conservative, says one source, it is somewhat more laid back than other firms, "there is no face time – if you don't have work, you go home, there is no one to impress by staying late." Says that insider: "There is no 'trading floor' bravado at BBH."

COOPERATIVE AND FRIENDLY

Though the firm's executives reportedly work shorter hours than the norm for the Street, analysts at BBH can expect the same 70- to 80-hour workweeks Wall Street is infamous for. Employees describe co-workers as cooperative and friendly, with partners often inviting analysts to important meetings. As for perks? "You get $25 for dinner if you work late and you get private cars home at night and on the weekends." Other benefits, detailed at the firm's web site, include pre-tax medical spending accounts (up to $500 a month), tuition reimbursement for six classes a year, and two retirement plans: a pension plan that requires no employee contribution, and a 401(k) program with a company match.

I-Banking Job Seekers: Receive free e-mailed job postings matching your interests & qualifications! Register at www.vaultreports.com

VAULT
REPORTS™
139
www.vaultreports.com

"There are no dress down days, not even in the summer."

*– **Brown Brothers insider***

BT Alex. Brown

One South Street
Baltimore, MD 21202
(800) 638-2596
Fax: (410) 783-3356
www.alexbrown.com

LOCATIONS

Baltimore, MD (HQ)
New York, NY • San Francisco, CA •
Geneva, Switzerland • London, England •
Tokyo, Japan • Additional U.S. locations in
CA • DC • GA • IL • MA • PA • TX

THE STATS

No. of Employees: 5,000 (worldwide)
Subsidiary of Bankers Trust
Co-Chairmen and Co-CEOs:
Yves C. De Balmann and
Mayo A. Shattuck III

KEY COMPETITORS

BancBoston Robertson Stephens
Hambrecht & Quist
Nationsbanc Montgomery Securities
SG Cowen

UPPERS

- Better quality of life than most firms
- Loose structure
- Ample crab crackers

DOWNERS

- Poor diversity
- Less prestige than Wall Street
- No love of Baltimore
- Soon to be owned by Deutsche

EMPLOYMENT CONTACT

Human Resources
BT Alex. Brown
One South Street
Baltimore, MD 21202

(410) 895-5350
recruit_office@alexbrown.com

	HOURS	PAY	PRESTIGE	DRESS	SATISFACTION	
BEST 10 / WORST 1	BEST = SHORTEST HOURS	BEST = HIGHEST PAY	BEST = MOST PRESTIGIOUS	BEST = MOST CASUAL	BEST = MOST SATISFIED	BEST 10 / WORST 1
	2	9	8	2	7	

THE SCOOP

WE GO WAY BACK

Few investment bank have more history than Alex. Brown. Prior to its acquisition by Bankers Trust in June 1997 (it is now called "BT Alex. Brown"), the firm was the oldest independent investment bank in the country. Founded by Alexander Brown in 1800, Alex. Brown has had an important financial hand in our nation's history. (Alexander Brown's sons founded what is now called Brown Brothers Harriman & Co., the nation's oldest and largest privately-held bank.) In 1827, Alexander Brown and family were instrumental in forming and financing the pioneering Baltimore and Ohio Railroad. After the Civil War ended, conveniently situated Alex. Brown spearheaded the rebuilding of devastated Southern cities, by shipping goods and financing construction. Alex. Brown built an impressive brick-and-Tiffany glass headquarters in 1900, a solid edifice which survived a 1904 fire that destroyed most of Baltimore's downtown. After the fire, Alex. Brown then helped refinance the rebuilding of its hometown. Alex. Brown's innate caution and sense have helped the firm weather all market corrections and slumps. The firm went public in 1986, ending 186 years of partnership at Alex. Brown.

In 1997, the bank moved into new skyscraper digs in downtown Baltimore. In June 1997, New York-based Bankers Trust acquired Alex. Brown, effectively ending the bank's long independent history. The eight-largest bank in the United States, Bankers Trust splits its operations between commercial banking and I-banking. In November 1998, Bankers Trust itself was acquired, by German monolith Deutsche Bank.

YOU'VE GROWN SO FAST

Alex. Brown didn't simply gain a large parent, it grew substantially as a result of the merger. Bankers Trust consolidated its investment banking group under its BT Alex. Brown subsidiary. Before the merger, Alex. Brown had about 2700 employees. After assimilating Bankers Trust bankers, BT Alex. Brown had 5000 employees around the world. In December 1997, Bankers Trust announced its acquisition of the equities business of the U.K.-based NatWest Markets' for $220 million. (NatWest Markets is the investment banking unit of the venerable National Westminster Bank.) NatWest's businesses were merged with BT Alex. Brown. And now it seems that BT Alex. Brown is about to be subsumed into an even larger financial services unit – in fact, the largest in the world. In November 1998, Deutsche Bank announced that it would acquire Bankers Trust for about $10 billion. That would bring BT Alex. Brown together with Deutsche Bank Securities, the investment banking arm of Deutsche.

HELPING OTHERS GROW

Alex. Brown is known for plugging capital into hot growth companies through equity (stock) offerings. The bank has taken public now-booming businesses such as America Online, Oracle, and Outback Steakhouse. Aside from its growth company financing, the firm is also known for its strong equities research team.

Like other banking boutiques, Alex. Brown focuses on a limited number of industries, most notably health care and high tech. Explains one insider: "The firm focuses on mid-sized to smaller growth companies in a couple of core industries. High tech, health care, media, real estate, transportation – those are really the prime groups."

The combination of Bankers Trust and Alex. Brown has, as expected, brought an enhanced ability to attract new clients, especially in the fields of equity underwriting, trading and sales, high-yield debt, risk management, and M&A (mergers & acquisitions). Alex. Brown, which posted just over $1 billion in revenue in the year before it was acquired by BT, was, prior to the merger, strong in businesses related to equities (stocks), such as equity research and underwriting, while BT was strong in fixed income (bonds and currency) businesses, especially high-yield debt (junk bonds). Bankers Trust reported that in the first quarter after the merger, which closed in September 1997, one-third of the firm's domestic equity and bond financing came from cross-selling to BT and Alex's Browns clients – the firm's work in fixed income with pre-merger Alex. Brown clients and in stocks with pre-merger BT clients. As an example, the firm cited to a March 1998 $1.3 billion stock offering for radio giant Chancellor Media Corp., for which it served as co-lead manager, as evidence of a growing equity business.

I-Banking Job Seekers: Receive free e-mailed job postings matching your interests & qualifications! Register at www.vaultreports.com

VAULT REPORTS™

143

www.vaultreports.com

GETTING HIRED

BT Alex. Brown's recruiting process usually begins with an on-campus interview. A pared-down group of candidates is then invited to visit the firm's offices, where candidates typically interview with several of the firm's employees. The firm says that it looks for candidates who demonstrate "initiative" and "excellence" and who will work well in a team environment. Current bankers suggest applicants "talk to people with experience in the industry" before interviewing at BT Alex. Brown. Consult either the firm's job hotline or its web site located at www.alexbrown.com for a list of current job openings.

New college grads or hires without previous work experience begin their careers as analysts. New employees with several years of banking experience or an MBA enter BT Alex. Brown at the associate level. Both analysts and associates are recruited by, and hired directly into, specific departments. One financial analyst reports that "Alex. Brown looks for smart people, and thinks that grades are very important in determining mental horsepower. Also, the company looks for a strong work ethic, and an outgoing and engaging personality, because you have to get along with clients when away from the office, and with peers when working 100 hours a week."

The firm reportedly cares about that elusive "fit" a great deal. "They want an outgoing, engaging personality," says one analyst. "BT Alex. Brown wants people who can get along with the clients on a two-week 'roadshow' and be able to work with their peers during a couple of 100-hour week projects." A recent hire says that "athletes are definitely favored strongly at BT Alex. Brown. We look for people who are not only smart and hardworking, but cool guys who get along with others." Alcohol is a social lubricant, and the firm apparently doesn't mind a little imbibing. One associate relates the tale of a recent Super Saturday. "After everyone was through with their interviews, we take [the prospective applicants] out to dinner and have some drinks. Well, some of the guys had a bit too much, and decided to go swimming in Baltimore harbor. They got a little wet, but it didn't affect them jobwise – a bunch of them got offers."

OUR SURVEY SAYS

CHARM CITY; BALTIMORE BLUES

BT Alex. Brown's Baltimore headquarters plays a crucial role in shaping its corporate culture. Insiders describe the firm as being both "less intense" and "less structured" than its Wall Street competitors. A "loose" organizational structure gives junior employees opportunities to develop "long-term relationships" with senior management and with clients. Some employees think that "the fact that the firm is not in New York makes for a more livable experience." As another analyst explains: "We are still an incredibly intense and successful firm, but at the same time, the analysts here are not beaten into the ground."

As for pay, says one associate: "It's comparable with the Street, otherwise they couldn't attract the people." The cost of living in Baltimore, of course, is significantly less than in New York. Reports one associate: "I live in a really superb condominium complex. I have maybe a 1300-square foot apartment, it's two-bedroom, with an indoor garage and fitness center, for $1350. I could have gotten a really nice one bedroom for about $1000." Another insider agrees that "the rents are incredibly cheap. Three analysts can live in a three-story house, with each getting his own bedroom, for $400 each. With those kind of expenses, you can afford to drive a nice car."

The perks make Alex. Brown employees happy too. "All the facilities are topnotch," says one analyst, "especially in the San Francisco branch, where the offices are on the top floor of a building that overlooks the city and the bay." The computer systems "have improved a lot over the last three years, all the better for faster-running Excel programs." The gabby and stressed should know they can make "unlimited long distance phone calls" at Alex. Brown. Other lovely perks: overtime meals, taxis, and bonuses paid twice a year. "Bonuses can be 80 percent of base compensation," says one employee. "When you travel you stay in the top hotels," says another. However, bemoans one Brown insider, "there is no company gym."

Baltimore itself has its good points and bad points, according to employees. One analyst says that "Baltimore sucks. There is nothing to do here. There are bars and things like that, but no

I-Banking Job Seekers: Receive free e-mailed job postings matching your interests & qualifications! Register at www.vaultreports.com

VAULT REPORTS™
www.vaultreports.com

145

clubs or other interesting places to go." A former employee points out that "Baltimore is really limited in the number of places you can live, because it's basically a crumbling city. You can live in a few neighborhoods, like Federal Hill or Phelps Point." Be wary of where you park it, however – we hear that "in January 1998, the garage attendant at Alex. Brown's new parking garage was shot and killed." (Baltimore also has one of the highest homicide rates in the nation.)

WHAT ABOUT THE 'RENTS?

How Bankers Trust has affected Alex. Brown depends largely on the group, insiders report. "High tech is so strong at Alex. Brown, they kind of run their own show," reports one associate. "It's the same with health care." However, in other groups, "we have substantial contact with New York, a lot of our deals come from New York, and we actually work on deals with [Bankers Trust]." As for the upcoming acquisition by Deutsche Bank, "the mood's not bleak, but the mood's not euphoria either," says one insider at BT Alex. Brown. "Everybody's very anxious. It could be very good thing, it could be very bad. It's a period of uncertainty."

That contact talks about a visit by Deutsche Bank chairman Rolf Breuer shortly after the Deutsche/BT deal was announced. Reports one BT Alex. Brown insider: "He said Deutsche Bank is not interested in being a bulge-bracket U.S. player, that they're more interested in being what the American firms are in Europe. He wants to be a full-service firm, with all the capabilities, but is not seeking to compete with the Goldmans or Merrills." Continues that insider: "I got the feeling that he was very candid, very forceful. He said that Bankers Trust will not be set free on a long leash. He brought up [Deutsche Morgan Grenfell, Deutsche's I-banking arm now folded into the bank], and said 'We learned from DMG, we just let those guys run wild.'"

NOT THE BEST FINANCIAL TRAINING

While BT Alex. Brown may be a good place to work, it's not necessarily the best for financial training, insiders say. "With Alex Brown, it's equities, it's bringing companies to the market, IPOs, secondary offerings," explains one insider. "Equities is really not an analytically challenging type of work. It's highly profitable – if you do well, you'll make a lot of money, but it's not the type of thing where you're doing a lot of analytic work. If you do M&A, you're going to do be doing a lot of the financial modeling, financial analysis, you learn a good deal, and you develop a set of tools. When you do equities, it's much more process-oriented work – you have to be in tune with the market and have to know the market, you have to understand what it's doing. It's 'Can this company with this type of rating place a preferred offering?' It's more of a feel type thing."

To order a 10- to 20-page Vault Reports Employer Profile on BT Alex BRown call 1-888-JOB-VAULT or visit www.VaultReports.com

The full Employer Profile includes detailed information on BT Alex Brown's departments, recent developments and transactions, hiring and interview process, plus what employees really think about culture, pay, work hours and more.

I-Banking Job Seekers: Receive free e-mailed job postings matching your interests & qualifications! Register at www.vaultreports.com

VAULT REPORTS™

147

www.vaultreports.com

"We are still an incredibly intense and successful firm, but at the same time, the analysts here are not beaten into the ground."

– *BT Alex. Brown insider*

CIBC Oppenheimer

Oppenheimer Tower
World Financial Center
New York, NY 10281
(800) 999-OPCO
Fax: (212) 667-4444

LOCATIONS

New York, NY (HQ)
Atlanta • Boston • Chicago • Ft. Lauderdale •
Houston • Los Angeles • Miami • San
Francisco • Seattle • London • Tel Aviv, Israel
Lima, Peru • Milan, Italy • Sao Paulo, Brazil

THE STATS

No. of Offices: 16 (worldwide)
Subsidiary of Canadian Imperial Bank
of Commerce
Chairman and CEO: Rulle Michael

KEY COMPETITORS

Bankers Trust
Deutsche Bank
Donaldson, Lufkin & Jenrette
TD Securities

UPPERS

- ◆ Laid-back Canadian culture
- ◆ Excellent vacation time and hours

DOWNERS

- ◆ Recent problems in wake of mergers
- ◆ Cutbacks and layoffs
- ◆ Conservative leadership

EMPLOYMENT CONTACT

Human Resources
CIBC Oppenheimer & Co.
Oppenheimer Tower
World Financial Center
New York, NY 10281

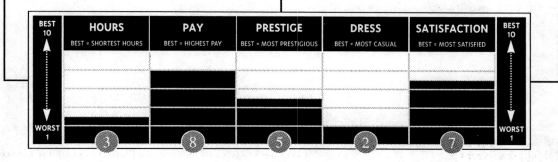

	HOURS	PAY	PRESTIGE	DRESS	SATISFACTION	
BEST 10 ... WORST 1	BEST = SHORTEST HOURS	BEST = HIGHEST PAY	BEST = MOST PRESTIGIOUS	BEST = MOST CASUAL	BEST = MOST SATISFIED	BEST 10 ... WORST 1
	3	8	5	2	7	

THE SCOOP

CANADA DRAMA

Founded in 1950, CIBC Oppenheimer is the U.S. investment bank and brokerage arm of Canada's second-largest bank, the Canadian Imperial Bank of Commerce (CIBC). CIBC purchased Oppenheimer in November 1997 for $525 million to boost its North American I-banking presence. Oppenheimer, which was acquired in 1982 by a British merchant banking firm, but whose senior management took the bank private again in 1986, had been shopping itself around for a couple of years. Oppenheimer's parent was set to get larger. In 1998, CIBC announced a $14.3 billion merger with Toronto-Dominion (TD), which would have created North America's ninth-largest bank. However, in December 1998, the Canadian government blocked the proposed deal.

GROWING BANKING

CIBC Oppenheimer operates under CIBC World Markets, the bank's global investment banking division. Also under this umbrella is CIBC   was viewed as a high point in the growth of a firm; Oppenheimer brought to CIBC about 650 retail brokers who concentrate on high net-worth (rich) clients. After the announcement of the merger with TD, CIBC Oppenheimer officials announced plans to move forward with hiring and expansion.

However, both CIBC and Oppenheimer have stumbled a bit since the merger, largely because Oppenheimer's client base of mid-size corporations was hurt by slumps in global market conditions. In September 1998, CIBC Oppenheimer cut 27 people from its mortgage-backed securities and emerging markets trading desks, stating an intention to abandon those risky businesses. In October 1998, CIBC announced that it would lay off about 5 percent of its staff from its investment banking division.

GETTING HIRED

Hiring at CIBC Oppenheimer is somewhat decentralized – for example, the high-yield group handles its own hiring. However, insiders agree that because the firm doesn't have the same cachet as those in the bulge bracket, interviewers are impressed by candidates who can express a specific interest in the firm. "I think they're looking for people who have a strong interest in the firm," says one insider. "[CIBC is] a relative unknown, so they're looking for someone who, if they can extend an offer, is going to take it. It matters how strong your interest is."

As for quant questions, "interviews will just try to check out quantitative ability. At MBA schools, we don't come out and ask direct financial questions. The overall number one question is 'Do you know what you're getting into?'"

OUR SURVEY SAYS

LESS INTENSE

"In general there is just more of a laid-back culture among the bankers," reports one insider at CIBC Oppenheimer. "It could be because it's a Canadian institution and its world headquarters are in Toronto. It's not like people could rush around and put themselves on the line, because they had to get approval from Toronto to do things like make crazy loans." This laid-back atmosphere, isn't always to the liking of CIBC bankers. Reports one insider about life among the Canadians, "The only impediment that it creates is that any amount of capital over $100 million has to be approved by Toronto, and Toronto is notoriously conservative and slow." Says that insider: "It takes an extra two to four days. In banking that's a long time for approval, especially if you are competing with people."

I-Banking Job Seekers: Receive free e-mailed job postings matching your interests & qualifications! Register at www.vaultreports.com

VAULT REPORTS™ 151

www.vaultreports.com

What the firm may lose in competitiveness, however, it makes up for in lifestyle issues, as far as insiders are concerned. "The firm very generous about benefits. There's good sick time, vacation – basically good HR policies." Says one insider who has worked at bulge-bracket Wall Street firms: "[At other firms], the attitude is win win win, get your deals, where the attitude at Oppenheimer is a lot more team oriented, more "win on our principles." It's a friendlier place," says one contact. That insider continues: "[CIBC Oppenheimer is] a pretty hard-working place, but they're not up there in any of the league tables. They're not up they're managing their league table status, whereas at larger banks, I know they're managing their status. They don't pursue the large Fortune 500 companies. They stick with, not the middle market, but middle-sized larger companies."

CIBC Oppenheimer's more relaxed attitude doesn't extend to every department. For example, the firm's high-yield group, formerly called the Argosy Group before CIBC acquired it in 1995, isn't so casual. The group is "led by three Drexel guys," reports one insider, referring to Mike Milken's famed junk bond shop, Drexel Burnham Lambert. "They're pretty aggressive."

THE FIRST MERGER

Although CIBC and Oppenheimer have merged, operations in New York are still "split between [CIBC's] 425 Lexington, and the Oppenheimer space in the World Financial Tower." Says one insider, "There has been talk of slamming the two groups together, so that investment banking will be all together, but they haven't figured out how yet." Another source points out that "CIBC got their headquarters at the top of the market, so if they sublet right now, they take a huge negative cashflow," reports one insider.

Bankers haven't much had to move offices between the two locations, either. "Oppenheimer and CIBC had pretty distinct groups. Oppenheimer mostly covered equity and M&A, CIBC was mostly debt-oriented, so there wasn't a lot of overlap. Where there was overlap was in client executives, or origination. The ones that remained were mostly Oppenheimer, a lot of CIBC was pushed they really wanted to have bankers and not lenders."

THE NEW CULTURE

This small overlap in origination, however, is indicative of a culture shift in the firm. "Oppenheimer is pretty much the new culture," says one insider. "If I were to categorize CIBC, it was a bunch of lenders as opposed to a bunch of bankers. Lenders are very conservative, they're really into looking into credits and risk characteristics, as opposed to bankers, who want to make their money off of leading deals. Lenders tended to focus on getting credit deals, getting your foot in the door by participating in another deal. Bankers like to lead deals." Despite this shift, insiders seem happy with the merger. "It was a lot more dynamic, I thought it was a better place than before," says one insider from the CIBC side. "Oppenheimer people were definitely excited about it. What was constraining to them was the capital. They didn't have the capital to grow, and CIBC has a ton of capital, which helped underwriting capability."

I-Banking Job Seekers: Receive free e-mailed job postings matching
your interests & qualifications! Register at www.vaultreports.com

VAULT
REPORTS™
153
www.vaultreports.com

"In general there is just more of a laid-back culture among the bankers."

– *CIBC Oppenheimer insider*

D.E. Shaw

120 W. 45th Street
New York, NY 10036
(212) 478-0000
Fax: (212) 478-0100
www.deshaw.com

LOCATIONS

New York (HQ)
Boston
London
Tokyo
Hyderabad, India

THE STATS

No. of Offices: 5 (worldwide)
A privately-held company
No. of Employees: 750 (worldwide)
CEO: David E. Shaw

KEY COMPETITORS

Long-Term Capital Management
Soros Fund
Tiger Fund

UPPERS

- Potentially huge bonus
- Way casual dress for Wall Street
- Hang out with super-smart people
- Tradition of firm-wide retreats and happy hours
- Short hours for finance
- Diverting brainteasers

DOWNERS

- Intellectual, somewhat nerdy culture
- 401(k) does not vest until three years
- Firm took severe hit by markets in 1998

EMPLOYMENT CONTACT

Strategic Growth Department
D.E. Shaw
120 W. 45th Street
New York, NY 10036

career@deshaw.com

	HOURS	PAY	PRESTIGE	DRESS	SATISFACTION	
BEST 10 ▲ ... WORST 1	BEST = SHORTEST HOURS	BEST = HIGHEST PAY	BEST = MOST PRESTIGIOUS	BEST = MOST CASUAL	BEST = MOST SATISFIED	BEST 10 ▲ ... WORST 1
	4	8	7	8	8	

THE SCOOP

ATYPICAL WALL STREET

D.E. Shaw is not your average Wall Street hedge fund and securities operation. The firm owns Juno Online Services, a free e-mail service with close to six million subscribers, and DESoft, an on-line brokerage system. Its alums include Amazon.com founder Jeff Bezos. Sound like a particularly technology-oriented financial firm? You bet. D.E. Shaw is the most prominent "quant" firm on Wall Street. These firms use computer programs and complex math to take advantage of tiny "inefficiencies" (discrepancies) in market prices, through a method called statistical arbitrage. It's similar to a situation where Dell stock is trading for $100 in New York and $101 in Tokyo – only muchmuchmuch more complex. These inefficiencies involve relationships between currency rates, interest rates, and all sorts of other factors that affect the prices of financial securities.

Founder David Shaw wasn't the first to come up with the idea to use rocket-science math and apply it to the market, he's just been the most successful. Compounded annual returns for the first 10 years of D.E. Shaw's hedge fund have averaged about 19 percent – after fees. Shaw, a former Columbia University computer science professor, started the firm in 1988 with $28 million in capital to play with. Initially, the firm was only a hedge fund – using its quantitative techniques to invest the money in its own account. Now with a worldwide staff of about 750 and offices in New York, Cambridge, London, Tokyo and India, the notoriously secretive firm uses its smarts in other financial arenas, such as market making. In U.S. equities, for example, the firm provides liquidity for clients (buys and sells so clients can move their stock) in more than 3000 stocks. In recent years, D.E. Shaw had also made a big push into online banking and brokerage: in 1994, it launched a service to provide online personal financial services, including home banking. In 1997, the firm announced a partnership with what was then the nation's third-largest bank, Bank of America. Under the partnership, the bank provided the firm with financing, while D.E. Shaw has provided the bank and its clients with access to some of its equity-related products.

THE FAILURE OF BRAIN POWER

However, that deal hit an extremely rough patch in the fall of 1998, when BankAmerica Corp. (the result of the merger between Bank of America and NationsBank, and now the second-largest bank in the country) announced that it would take a $372 million write-down on a $1.4 billion loan it made to D.E. Shaw as part of a trading joint venture. The firm explained that it had taken huge hits in the bond market because of turmoil in foreign markets. Its hedge fund in mid-October was down 13 percent for the year. After a decade of astounding growth, the most technology-savvy firm on Wall Street was forced to announce layoffs of 264 employees, or 25 percent of its workforce at the time, in December 1998. The firm also announced that it was seeking to sell subsidiaries FarSight Financial Services (its online brokerage) and D.E. Shaw Financial Technology (which develops Internet technology for financial services firms).

GETTING HIRED

"They have these really elitist-sounding recruiting philosophies, like, 'If you're brilliant we'll hire you,'" says one insider about D.E. Shaw's hiring process. Indeed, the firm founded by a Computer Science professor boasts that it includes a disproportionate amount of computer scientists and systems architects, and that it extends an offer to only one out of about 150 of the candidates it considers.

Unlike most financial firms, D.E. Shaw does not salivate when it sees an MBA next to one's name. Reports one insider: "They hire almost no MBAs, they're not really interested in MBAs. They do interview them, but they don't really recruit them heavily. The people they recruit very heavily are graduate students in computer science, math, and physics, but also any graduate students." These graduate students need not be successfully receiving their PhDs. Reports one insider: "The philosophy is if you can get them before the doctorate, that's even better, because it means they're smart enough, but they don't yet have the complete drive to be theoretical. Other things drive them – like money."

I-Banking Job Seekers: Receive free e-mailed job postings matching your interests & qualifications! Register at www.vaultreports.com

VAULT REPORTS™

157

www.vaultreports.com

For undergraduate recruiting, the firm generally has a screening round on campus, followed by a visit to the firm's New York headquarters. "When you come back [for interviews] it's usually a range of people, not real senior people, but usually a lot of vice presidents, senior vice presidents who are very young," reports one contact. Perhaps surprisingly, recruits won't necessarily be grilled with intense math questions. "Recruiting is sort of free form, so each interviewer has their own style. They don't coach you how to interview you before you do it," says one insider who has helped with the recruiting effort. "Some people will ask you quant questions, some people won't, some will depending on your background." Undergrads with humanities backgrounds are not necessarily out of the running. "They had a psychology major make partner six years after graduating from Brown," notes one insider. "But you can't be any English major, you've got to have a really logical, mathematical head."

OUR SURVEY SAYS

WELCOME NERDS

Almost as well known on the Street as D.E. Shaw's strong performance (previous to its 1998 collapse) are the firm's idiosyncrasies: a super-lax dress code ("jeans, shorts, people walk around without shoes on"), a secretive and somewhat paranoid partnership ("they're very hyper about confidentiality") and super-smart finance whizzes who are often more like your stereotypical graduate student than your stereotypical back-slapping, steak-eating, cigar-smoking banker. Says one insider diplomatically: "There are definitely some folks who would not really be socially well-adjusted in a normal company, and yet could function fine at D.E. Shaw." The banter at the firm is also apparently a bit more cerebral than the fare served up at most banks. Reports one former employee: "If it was quiet or we were bored, somebody would throw out a brainteaser and we'd all try to sit around and try to figure it out."

AMAZINGLY SHORT HOURS AND EXTENSIVE BONUSES

D.E. Shaw employees also work "way way less" than their Wall Street counterparts. "Some groups tend to work longer than others, but on average it's maybe 50 hours a week," says one insider. "There were no weekends. I never worked a weekend. There was one tight-knit group who were workaholics – and they'd work 70 to 80 hours, they were definitely an exception." As for pay: "They claim to pay a little better than standard, but I would say it's about even," says one insider, "but it can go up really really fast." As an example of the "really really fast" increases, that contact cites one trader who received a $1 million bonus in his fourth year out of undergraduate college. "That's the exception," that source says, "but that's also the possibility."

But perhaps a more important mark of the culture at the firm is a conscious attempt to level hierarchy. For example, the firm has quarterly firm-wide meetings at which any employee can pose questions to firm leaders. Reports one insider: "You're on a first-name basis with everyone." That contact continues: "Basically there's associate, vice president, senior vice president and partner. Those are the only four titles – they have very young people in the senior vice president level. They have no problems having young people take over."

FREESTYLE

This flat organization structure has drawbacks – it means that "everybody does their own crap. There are no secretaries until you get to the very top level (senior VP)." The career path at D.E. Shaw is about as chaotic as it gets. Most undergrads start in what is called the general associates program. The firm places them in positions, and from there, it's up to the associate. Unlike most other financial services firm, new hires are not initiated through a group training program. "They don't have any training program. It's totally free form – everybody's experience is totally different at D.E. Shaw," says one insider. "Ideally, as you work there for a while, you also figure out what people are doing, and they keep it pretty mobile." Says that contact: "It's sort of up to you, to say 'Oh wait, I'm really interested in that and blah blah blah." This free-market system is still more structured than D.E. Shaw's past practice. "They used to throw all general associates into the mailroom," says one insider about the firm's training

I-Banking Job Seekers: Receive free e-mailed job postings matching your interests & qualifications! Register at www.vaultreports.com

VAULT REPORTS™
159
www.vaultreports.com

program about five years ago. "You would deliver people's mail and figure out what they did, and talk to them – and based on your motivation, you'd figure out what you'd want to do."

The firm also has made traditions of firm-wide bonding events, like Friday happy hours featuring "some kind of food – wings, quesadillas – and then beer, wine and soda." In past years, the firm also indulged annual retreats. For example, says one insider, "they sent us all to Florida for a weekend. They used to try to do a trip every year. They had gone to Jamaica before, once it was upstate at Sagamore." Says that insider: "They paid for airfare, gave us meals, rented out a dance club place at a resort one night, and they gave us free tickets to Disney World." Unlike at some I-banking or law firms, where retreats are reserved for just bankers or lawyers, the D.E. Shaw retreats were for "every single person in the company."

SHOCKING LAYOFFS

Of course, those happy days at D.E. Shaw should be over for a while, because of the firm's major losses and layoffs in 1998. Insiders say that while in the summer there was a "vague sense" that the firm was losing money, the losses were officially addressed at one of the firm's quarterly meetings. "From the time of that meeting to the time of the layoffs, there was no word from management about what was going to happen." However, among colleagues, "there were constant discussions." "It was always a discussion of how many they would lay off," says one contact, "but it's really hard to think that there will be layoffs without anyone saying it directly. So people were talking but no one was looking (for other jobs)." Layoffs occurred the week after Thanksgiving; they were announced and occurred on the same day. Reportedly, the cuts were "larger then most people anticipated." And while the firm officially reported laying off only 25 percent of its staff, insiders say the cuts were more severe – some employees were told that they would be kept on for several months but eventually laid off.

The firm is reportedly settling down after the layoffs. "There are always cases of people whose lives have gotten better because of this sort of thing," notes one insider, alluding to promotions. "I know of one case where that happened." And although D.E. Shaw has consciously worked to fend off the stilted hierarchy that marks many Wall Street firms, its size and success had birthed a hierarchy nonetheless. No more. One contact describes a formerly removed executive: "Suddenly that person is now talking to lower-downs. They've gone back to the earlier company – it's less of a hierarchy because there are fewer people." Says another contact: "[D.E. Shaw is] basically going back to their hedge fund days, going back to what they were. They were branching out into all these customer-related businesses. They're going to go back to just proprietary trading."

I-Banking Job Seekers: Receive free e-mailed job postings matching your interests & qualifications! Register at www.vaultreports.com

VAULT REPORTS™
www.vaultreports.com

161

"There are definitely some folks who would not really be socially well-adjusted in a normal company, and yet could function fine at D.E. Shaw."

– *D.E. Shaw insider*

Deutsche Bank

31 West 52nd Street
New York, NY 10019
(212) 469-8000
www.db.com

LOCATIONS

New York, NY (U.S. HQ)
San Francisco, CA
Frankfurt, Germany (worldwide HQ)
Tokyo, Japan • Other offices in 30 countries

THE STATS

Annual Revenues: $36.7 billion (1997)
Net Income: $566 million (1997)
No. of Employees: 76,000 (1997)
No. of Offices: 67 (worldwide)
Stock Symbol: DTBKY (ADR)
Chairman: Rolf Breuer

KEY COMPETITORS

ABN Amro
Citicorp
Credit Suisse First Boston
Dresdner Bank
Warburg Dillon Read

UPPERS

- Huge signing bonuses in past
- Lots of get-to-know-each-other events

DOWNERS

- Stalled firm
- No unified corporate culture
- Larger presence in Europe and Asia than in the U.S.

EMPLOYMENT CONTACT

Human Resources
Deutsche Bank
31 West 52nd Street
New York, NY 10019

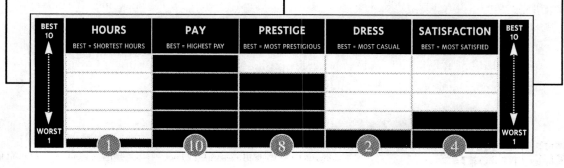

	HOURS	PAY	PRESTIGE	DRESS	SATISFACTION	
BEST 10 ↑ WORST 1	BEST = SHORTEST HOURS	BEST = HIGHEST PAY	BEST = MOST PRESTIGIOUS	BEST = MOST CASUAL	BEST = MOST SATISFIED	BEST 10 ↑ WORST 1
	1	10	8	2	4	

THE SCOOP

DEUTSCHE'S PRIDE

The young investment banking division of Deutsche Bank represents a lot of ambition. The enterprise, known as Deutsche Bank Securities in the United States, traces its roots to Deutsche Bank's acquisition of the English merchant bank Morgan Grenfell in 1989. The firm's parents had between them 383 years of experience – Morgan Grenfell with 158, Deutsche with 125. In 1994, Deutsche Bank announced its intentions to transform the firm, then known as Deutsche Morgan Grenfell (DMG), into a global investment banking player, especially in the U.S.

REWORKING THE I-BANK

In its brief existence, London-based DMG quickly achieved high rankings in industry publications such as *Risk* and *Institutional Investor.* The firm's assiduous raiding of talented personnel from rivals such as Morgan Stanley and SBC Warburg helped its rise to prominence, as did support from the deep pockets of Deutsche Bank. Having apparently conquered cultural differences between Deutsche and Morgan Grenfell, DMG was poised to take advantage of what it viewed as an opening for a European entry in the top echelon of investment banking.

IT'S NOT THAT EASY

However, in 1997 and 1998, the firm's fortunes fell. American and German bankers clashed over the parent Deutsche Bank's commitment to U.S. investment banking (funding the U.S. operations) and the lavish expenses accrued by partying U.S. bankers (funding the U.S. operations). In early 1998, Deutsche Bank decided to fold DMG back into its universal banking operations, and lost some of DMG's key talent (including bankers it had lured away from rivals a couple of years earlier). To rebound, Deutsche began sniffing around U.S. banks for acquisitions it believed could enhance its position. The bank was rumored to be courting J.P. Morgan, Hambrecht & Quist, and PaineWebber.

TAKING OVER THE TRUST

Those deals, however, were not to be. Deutsche Bank announced at the end of November 1998 that it would acquire Bankers Trust, thereby creating a financial services behemoth with assets of well over $800 billion. While the deal has already received a preliminary nod from U.S. regulators, it needs approval from Bankers Trust shareholders and other regulatory bodies worldwide. Insiders expect the deal to close sometime in the second quarter of 1999. The deal is the largest acquisition of a U.S. financial group by a European bank, uniting Germany's largest bank, $675 billion in assets, with the United States' eighth-largest bank, counting $156 billion in assets. The combined group will be the undisputed leader in asset management.

GETTING HIRED

When hiring new employees, Deutsche Bank looks for candidates who demonstrate strong leadership, communication, and "problem solving" skills. Given Deutsche's international focus, applicants who speak a foreign language have an edge, although this proficiency is not required. For its associate positions, Deutsche prefers previous work experience in finance. New hires should expect to go through an extensive orientation and training program, covering topics such as corporate tax, accounting, valuation, and financial modeling. DBS's target business schools are Wharton, MIT, Stanford, Chicago, Kellogg, Tuck, Harvard, NYU and Columbia. New MBA hires in Global Markets undergo a 12-month rotation program.

I-Banking Job Seekers: Receive free e-mailed job postings matching your interests & qualifications! Register at www.vaultreports.com

VAULT REPORTS™

165

www.vaultreports.com

OUR SURVEY SAYS

AAA AND STAYING THAT WAY

Insiders say working for Deutsche entails a lot of hard work, and some cultural uncertainty. The firm, for example, wants you to know that "MBAs joining the Investment Banking Division of Deutsche can be expected to be pretty well thrown in at the deep end on arrival. That is not because we want to see whether they can sink or swim. After completing the MBA from a good school, we already know the answer to that. The reason is that the MBAs we recruit tend to be people who pick things up quickly and apply themselves to the task with little supervision." As might be expected at a European bank, Deutsche's global culture "revolves around conservatism. The Directors (the Vorstand, the Germany-based committee) will do whatever is necessary to maintain the bank's AAA rating," say insiders. A former employee says: "In my opinion, the bank is highly bureaucratic and has many inefficiencies that hamper deal execution. The problem stems from cultural differences between the U.S. branch and overseas management, compounded by a strong German-based controlling presence."

MANY MINI GROUPS

So what is the culture like at Deutsche? The short answer: prognosis inconsistent. "The first thing you're asked when you arrive is 'Where are you from?' That is, at which bank did you formerly work?" says one investment banker. Insiders tell Vault Reports that "at present, no one seems to know what the corporate culture is. There are many mini-cultures. Much depends on the firm from which the managing director of a particular group was recruited." Another employee agrees: "There are little groups and subgroups – a Goldman group, a Lehman group, etc." Insiders say the firm does seem to host alumni from the best firms on Wall Street. One associate reports that "if you go around the table in New York and ask people where they're from, you'll hear Merrill, Goldman, Lehman, Salomon, Morgan Stanley, J.P. Morgan – all the other top banks."

MAKING IT IN NEW YORK?

Deutsche's reputation gained strength with the early strong performance of Deutsche Morgan Grenfell, but industry insiders say the firm's name still doesn't carry the aura of its Wall Street rivals. A Deutsche associate informs us that "Deutsche's reputation varies widely from region to region and among business areas." One employee expounds on Deutsche's reputation. "Across the different business areas, Deutsche's rep is heavily slanted toward the fixed-income and FX [foreign exchange] business. We are not yet a top player in the equities markets or core investment banking areas." Another employee breaks down Deutsche's reputation by region: "In Europe, Deutsche Bank is one of the top names, and certainly one of the main players in the London markets. Only the big Swiss-owned firms (Warburg Dillon Read and Credit Suisse First Boston) and a few of the top U.S. names (Merrill, Goldman, and Salomon Smith Barney) have the same presence and prestige in Europe. In Asia, same story, different competitors – here main rivals include J.P. Morgan. The above names are also strong here – except for Salomon, who are nobody in Asia." What's missing from the analysis? "New York is the only major market where I'd say we're not in the same league as the top names," says a Deutsche vice president.

To order a 50- to 70-page Vault Reports Employer Profile on Deutsche Bank call 1-888-JOB-VAULT or visit www.VaultReports.com

The full Employer Profile includes detailed information on Deutsche Bank's departments, recent developments and transactions, hiring and interview process, plus what employees really think about culture, pay, work hours and more.

I-Banking Job Seekers: Receive free e-mailed job postings matching your interests & qualifications! Register at www.vaultreports.com

VAULT REPORTS™   167

www.vaultreports.com

"The first thing you're asked when you arrive is 'Where are you from?' That is, at which bank did you formerly work?"

– *Deutsche Bank insider*

Jefferies & Co.

11100 Santa Monica Blvd, 11th Fl.
Los Angeles, CA 90025
(310) 445-1199
Fax: (310) 914-1014
www.jefco.com

LOCATIONS

Los Angeles, CA (HQ)
Atlanta, GA • Boston, MA • Chicago, IL •
Culver City, CA • Dallas, TX • Houston, TX
• Jersey City, NJ • New Orleans, LA • New
York, NY • San Francisco, CA • Short Hills,
NY • Stamford, CT • London • Hong Kong •
Tokyo • Zurich

THE STATS

Annual Revenues: $764.5 million (1997)
Operating Income: $116 million (1997)
Chairman & CEO: Frank E. Baxter

KEY COMPETITORS

Charles Schwab
Donaldson, Lufkin & Jenrette
E*Trade
Salomon Smith Barney

UPPERS

- ◆ Above-market pay
- ◆ Great 401(k) when firm performs well
- ◆ Early responsibility

DOWNERS

- ◆ No extensive training
- ◆ Can be very aggressive
- ◆ Poor diversity for women

EMPLOYMENT CONTACT

Human Resources
Jefferies Group
11100 Santa Monica Blvd, 11th Fl.
Los Angeles, CA 90025

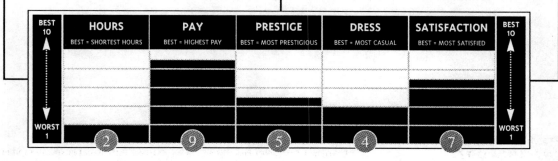

	HOURS	PAY	PRESTIGE	DRESS	SATISFACTION	
BEST 10 ... WORST 1	BEST = SHORTEST HOURS	BEST = HIGHEST PAY	BEST = MOST PRESTIGIOUS	BEST = MOST CASUAL	BEST = MOST SATISFIED	BEST 10 ... WORST 1
	2	9	5	4	7	

THE SCOOP

AN OTC PAST

Founded in the 1962 in the West (Los Angeles, actually) by former cowboy Boyd Jefferies, fast-growing investment bank Jefferies & Co. has always had something of a wild reputation. The firm made its mark in the 1960s and 70s as a trader of over-the-counter (also called "third market" stocks) – managing trades outside the normal exchanges (like the NYSE). The firm became popular among corporate raiders like T. Boone Pickens and Ivan Boesky, who could accumulate large piles of stock for hostile takeovers, without the scrutiny from the SEC would have faced had they bought the stock on an exchange. However, after the stock market crash of 1987, some of Jefferies' dealings were found to have violated SEC regulations; Jefferies was banned from trading and resigned.

ON EDGE

Led by current CEO Frank Baxter, the firm continues to thrive on cutting-edge financial businesses. In recent years, the firm's junk bond underwriting business has exploded. In 1990, Baxter hired 60 bankers from Mike Milken's collapsed junk bond shop, Drexel Burnham Lambert; from 1992 to 1997 the firm underwrote $17.1 billion in junk bond offerings, including the largest high-yield offering managed by a single firm in the 1990s (a $1.6 billion financing of TransAmerican Corp in 1997). Although the firm's equity trading business is still its major moneymaker, the firm's junk bond business grew 60 percent in 1997; junk bond offerings underwritten by Jefferies also have among the lowest default rates in the industry. Overall, Jefferies' corporate finance revenues jumped 134 percent in 1997 to $229 million. The firm's investment banking businesses, which aside from underwriting, also includes M&A and restructuring work, targets small to midsize companies.

VAULT REPORTS™
www.vaultreports.com

GYRATING FORTUNES

Jefferies & Co. is actually a part of a holding company called Jefferies Group, which also controls a computer-automated stock trading company Investment Technology Group. In the spring of 1998, as its profits soared, the company announced that it would spin-off both Jefferies & Co. and Investment Technology Group (in separate offerings) in a move designed to allow Jefferies & Co. develop as a firm focused solely on investment banking. However, largely to weakening market conditions worldwide, the firm's corporate finance revenues have plummeted, down to a meager $13.5 million in the third quarter of 1998. Although the Jefferies Group's overall earnings remain healthy, thanks to trading commissions for the Investment Technology Group, some observers have expressed concern over the falling I-banking revenues. The firm has reported staff reductions, but has not provided specifics.

GETTING HIRED

Jefferies & Co. recruits at select college and business school campuses, especially on the West Coast, owing to the firm's L.A. headquarters. Says one insider about the firm's interviews: "I would classify it as typical banking, you get some technical questions, it depends on the interviewer. Some are real lax, others are real intense." Unlike some firms which like to employ two-on-one interviews, however, "all we do pretty much is one-on-ones," reports an insider.

Although in the past, Jefferies has recruited primarily for full-time, rather than summer positions, the firm is developing a more structured summer associate hiring process. "They're definitely moving that way, because they've grown so much," reports one insider.

Those who have a banking or finance background have perhaps more of an edge over other applicants than at other firms, insiders say. "By and large, Jefferies likes to hire people who've been in banking before, because they don't have a large training program that the bulge-bracket firms have," reports one contact. That source describes the firm's analyst training program:

I-Banking Job Seekers: Receive free e-mailed job postings matching
your interests & qualifications! Register at www.vaultreports.com

VAULT
REPORTS™

171

www.vaultreports.com

"It's helpful, but it's only a week. It's modeling, Excel, just kind of walking you through the basics."

OUR SURVEY SAYS

THOSE DREXEL GUYS ARE EVERYWHERE

One insider at Jefferies explains the firm's recent history: "It's traditionally a high-yield firm. When Drexel blew up, basically half of them went to DLJ, half went to start Jefferies Corporate Finance. Over the last four years, we've moved into basically every product group." That contact says the notorious aggression of Mike Milken's bankers at Drexel has been preserved at Jefferies. "I would say it's very aggressive, very hard-working. There's some competition amongst bankers."

FLYING FREE

What does this "aggressive" atmosphere mean for bankers looking at Jefferies? "It's one of the few places where you can have a completely general experience. You're not pushed into a product group right away. Although they have those groups, you're free to move on your own," reports one insider. "Maybe there's a lack of controls, but that's just the tradeoff. You've got to be aggressive. If you're looking for structure, you're not going to be happy."

"Because there's the lack of controls, it's a real relaxed expense policy. You can travel business class everywhere, pretty much stay at whatever hotel you want," adds that insider. Another points out that these travel perks aren't to be sneezed at. Because Jefferies is a small firm, "analysts and associates are going to drafting meetings, not just doing spreadsheets."

One insider discusses the responsibility afforded at a smaller firm: "You definitely have much more responsibility. As a second-year analyst, you're pretty much playing associate roles. It's not as structured. There's a lot of deal teams without an associate or VP, just an analyst going to work with a managing director."

ABOVE-MARKET PAY

"I think they pay above market," says one insider. "Definitely in the bonus, the base is on par with Wall Street, the analyst base might be a little above Wall Street. When you're a smaller firm... sometimes that's the only way you can differentiate yourself." Also, the firm reportedly has an outstanding 401(k) program. "The matching's pretty attractive," reports one insider. "It's based on Jefferies profitability, so it can be over 100 percent."

How hard do the bankers work for the money? "It's right on par with most Wall Street firms, analysts are at about 80 to 85 per week, associates maybe 70." Work may be less painful, though, our contacts say. "It's a more casual atmosphere, more of a West Coast feel, without a doubt," says one insider. "There's more personality." As an example of the firm's laid-back 'tude, consider that Jefferies & Co. bankers – firmwide – have recently been able to dress casually all summer.

I-Banking Job Seekers: Receive free e-mailed job postings matching your interests & qualifications! Register at www.vaultreports.com

VAULT REPORTS™
www.vaultreports.com

173

"You've got to be aggressive. If you're looking for structure, you're not going to be happy."

– *Jefferies insider*

Legg Mason

111 South Calvert Street
P.O. Box 1476
Baltimore, MD 21203
(410) 539-0000
www.leggmason.com

LOCATIONS

Baltimore, MD (HQ)
Over 100 locations throughout the U.S.
and worldwide

THE STATS

Annual Revenues: $889 million (1998)
Net Income: $76.1 million (1998)
No. of Employees: 3950 (worldwide)
No. of Offices: 115 (worldwide)
Stock Symbol: LM (NYSE)
CEO: Raymond A. Mason

KEY COMPETITORS

A.G. Edwards
BT Alex. Brown
First Union
Raymond James Financial

UPPERS

- Expanding company
- Supportive environment
- Ambitious growth in I-banking

DOWNERS

- Regional firm
- Skimpy vacation

EMPLOYMENT CONTACT

Personnel
Legg Mason
111 South Calvert Street
P.O. Box 1476

Fax: (410) 528-3101

	HOURS	PAY	PRESTIGE	DRESS	SATISFACTION	
BEST 10 / WORST 1	BEST = SHORTEST HOURS	BEST = HIGHEST PAY	BEST = MOST PRESTIGIOUS	BEST = MOST CASUAL	BEST = MOST SATISFIED	BEST 10 / WORST 1
	2	8	5	2	8	

THE SCOOP

A Legg up in Washington

Founded in Baltimore in 1899, Legg & Company merged with the eight-year-old Mason & Company in 1970, resulting in great changes for the regional brokerage firm – by one measure, cited at the "top ranked regional investment bank in the United States." Mason & Company founder Raymond A. Mason became president of the combined firm, adopting a new strategy in the early 1980s for expansion in the rapidly changing financial services market. Legg Mason's strategy included increasing capital, expanding its traditional brokerage business, investing in technology, and entering the investment advisory business. Recently, Legg Mason served as financial advisor to the Washington Bullets, the Washington Capitals (NHL) and Ticketmaster. Legg Mason also has securities brokerage, commercial mortgage and asset management subsidiaries. The firm's investment banking businesses operate under a subsidiary called Legg Mason Wood Walker.

Double down

By 1990, Legg Mason had increased revenues nearly ten-fold since 1980, with a significant percentage of revenues and profits coming from non-brokerage sources. Today, Legg Mason is a publicly-owned, diversified financial services firm with a major presence in securities brokerage, investment management, investment banking and commercial mortgage banking. Legg Mason has grown its investment banking practice especially aggressively. From late 1996 to early 1998, the firm doubled its professional staff in both research and sales and trading, and nearly doubled its corporate finance personnel.

The firm has built some impressive niche practices, such as its business in lease-backed securities; the firm was expected to do $1 billion in deals involving such securities in 1998. In 1998, the firm reported revenues of $889 million, up from $665 million in 1997. Investment banking revenues increased 35 percent to a record $97 million. "About 30 percent of Legg Mason's revenues come from fees, not buy or sell transactions, which makes Legg Mason less cyclical compared to most other firms in the business," says one insider.

GETTING HIRED

Legg Mason looks for team players with integrity and a strong drive and commitment to excellence. Desired experience levels vary depending on the job. To find out about job opportunities, visit the "Employment Opportunities" section of Legg Mason's web site (www.leggmason.com). Applicants can send or fax resumes to the personnel department at Legg Mason's headquarters in Baltimore. Interested interviewees will first be interviewed at a local branch of Legg Mason. Promising candidates will then be flown to headquarters in Baltimore for a second round of interviews. For financial advisors and trainees, Legg Mason says a Series 6 or 7 registration is preferred; financial analysts are hired at the college graduate level without previous experience for a two-year generalist program which involves exposure to mergers and acquisitions, public offerings, and private placements of debt and equity.

OUR SURVEY SAYS

Legg Mason is described as "a great place to work." One employee at the firm's Baltimore headquarters describes the culture as "very warm and friendly," and "much more of a pleasant and helpful atmosphere than in New York." Though hours and pay vary by division, most employees can expect to work long hours for top pay, with formal dress. "The company doesn't have any casual days," says one contact, "though I think women get away with more." The environment is described as fast-paced and supportive. Employees are "incredibly diverse" – the Boston office reportedly has a 90-year-old employee, and "women, blacks, Asians, all the traditional indicators of diversity, we've got them. All full-time employees are eligible for benefits from the day of hire; these benefits include "a decent health care PPO that charges 10 dollars for any drug prescription or basic office visit," though employees are "unhappy with the skimpy vacation time. Basically you get a day of vacation for every month you work, and you don't even accumulate vacation in June and July."

I-Banking Job Seekers: Receive free e-mailed job postings matching your interests & qualifications! Register at www.vaultreports.com

VAULT REPORTS™
www.vaultreports.com

177

Employees call the company "prestigious" and "with a good name" – "Chip Mason [the CEO], Jim Brinkley [President] and the other powers that be protect Legg Mason protect that reputation carefully." In general, say employees," Legg Mason is a great company with a bright future." One analyst says: "Anyone interested in investment banking should look at Legg Mason. While money management and brokerage are huge, and research is getting better, investment banking is relatively small – but Legg Mason wants to grow that business."

Morgan Keegan

Morgan Keegan Tower
50 North Front Street
Memphis, TN 38103
(901) 524-4100
Fax: (901) 579-4406
www.morgankeegan.com

LOCATIONS

Memphis, TN (HQ)
44 offices in 12 states: AL • AR • FL • GA •
KY • LA • MA • MS • NY • NC • TN • TX.

THE STATS

Annual Revenues: $407 million (1998)
Net Income: $48.2 million (1998)
No. of Employees: 1,683 (U.S.)
No. of Offices: 44 (U.S.)
Stock Symbol: MOR (NYSE)
CEO: Allen B. Morgan, Jr.

KEY COMPETITORS

A.G. Edwards
Raymond James Financial
Robinson-Humphrey
Wheat First Union

UPPERS

- Tuition reimbursement
- Choice of generous health benefits
- Friendly, team-oriented work environment

DOWNERS

- Lack of workplace diversity
- Memphis not financial center of U.S.

EMPLOYMENT CONTACT

Human Resources
Morgan Keegan
Morgan Keegan Tower
50 North Front Street
Memphis, TN 38103

jobs@morgankeegan.com

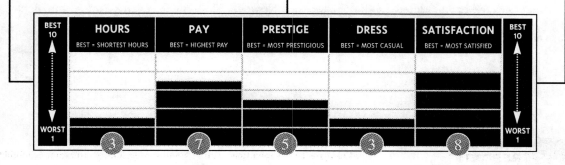

	HOURS	PAY	PRESTIGE	DRESS	SATISFACTION	
BEST 10 → WORST 1	BEST = SHORTEST HOURS	BEST = HIGHEST PAY	BEST = MOST PRESTIGIOUS	BEST = MOST CASUAL	BEST = MOST SATISFIED	BEST 10 → WORST 1
	3	7	5	3	8	

THE SCOOP

LITTLE, AMBITIOUS MORGAN KEEGAN

Small is beautiful – and profitable – at Morgan Keegan. Four friends founded the firm in Memphis, Tennessee in 1969. They pooled half a million dollars to start the business, making it the largest securities firm in the city the day it opened. One year later, the company secured a seat on the New York Stock Exchange. Morgan Keegan was one of the first companies in the industry to go public (in 1983), a move that brought in enough cash for the company to expand into the retail business and strengthen its corporate finance division. It began acquiring other companies in 1988, allowing most of them to operate independently of the original investment firm. This has allowed the parent company hold move into a variety of new areas. For example, in 1995, Morgan Keegan acquired Athletic Resource Management, a sports agency representing professional football, baseball and basketball players.

ON AN ACQUISITION TEAR

More recently, the company scooped up two other Southern investment firms, Memphis-based Weibel, Huffman Keegan Inc. and Atlanta's Knox, Wall & Co. Managing director C. David Ramsey believes that these new elements will help make Morgan Keegan the "leading investment firm" in the South. The acquisition of Weibel Huffman boosted the firm's asset management business (the firm managed $2.2 billion at the end of its 1998 fiscal year). Morgan Keegan is also one of the few firms outside Wall Street with an independent fixed-income research unit. The investment firm now includes 44 offices in 12 states.

The firm has a healthy I-banking business. In 1998, Morgan Keegan had a hand in 37 equity offerings totaling $3.4 billion. Since January 1994, the firm ranked as the leading IPO underwriter headquartered in the Southeast. However, Morgan Keegan's M&A and debt underwriting businesses are fledgling.

A SON OF THE SOUTH

Over the years, Morgan Keegan has proven its commitment to the region by consistently promoting Southern businesses. In 1986, it established the Southern Capital Fund, a mutual fund invested in Southern companies. Morgan Keegan & Co. also provides extensive equity research on more than 200 Southern-based stocks, and prides itself on the fact that it focuses on "the undiscovered, growing concerns striving to be tomorrow's blue chip stocks." In the near future, the company plans to develop a proprietary database that will provide information on southern companies. The company has been consistently ranked as the leading manager of municipal bonds in the Southeast, and in 1996 it was tapped by *Forbes* as one of the top 200 small companies in America. The company was also ranked 13th among the world's 20 fastest-growing companies by The Conference Board in 1997. Some may think Morgan Keegan foolish to concentrate so heavily below the Mason-Dixon Line (well, the firm does have an office in NY), but Morgan Keegan proves that there's an abundance of opportunity in the region.

GETTING HIRED

Applicants should direct their resumes to Morgan Keegan's headquarters. Positions are offered in investment banking or stock and bond research, and both undergraduates and MBAs are considered. Those interested in banking should contact the managing director, and research enthusiasts may write the director of research. The firm's web site does not list job openings. Inquiries can be addressed to jobs@morgankeegan.com

I-Banking Job Seekers: Receive free e-mailed job postings matching your interests & qualifications! Register at www.vaultreports.com

VAULT
REPORTS™
www.vaultreports.com

181

OUR SURVEY SAYS

NOT JUST JULEPS

Morgan Keegan prides itself on being "a Southern company with southern manners." Employees say co-workers are "warm and friendly," and everyone is "eager to help." At the same time, insiders report that "if you don't like someone hovering over you while you work, this is the place." They report Morgan Keegan is a "great place to learn the ropes," and "opportunities for advancement are great." Still, life at the firm is not all mint juleps and Southern hospitality. Insiders in the firm's I-banking department say "this is still a man's business," so "if you have difficulty taking criticism, or standing up for yourself, this is not the place." "Signs of discrimination," however are not evident, and women are reportedly "treated fairly." Insiders do admit "there are not an overabundance of minorities" employed by firm. Workers have different experiences with the hours. While some remark happily that "overtime is not encouraged," others bemoan "tough" hours for investment bankers. But benefits are universally praised – they're "really good," with "several different options" for health plans, a tuition reimbursement program and a "terrific" 401(k) program that allows employees to decide how their money is invested. The company also sponsors an outstanding stock purchase plan – 54 percent of the firm's stock is owned by its employees and directors. And the stock's performance has been outstanding; Morgan Keegan was named one of the "Top 50 Stocks of the 1990s" in August 1998.

NationsBanc Montgomery Securities

600 Montgomery Street
San Francisco, CA 94111
(415) 627-2000
Fax: (415) 249-5058
www.montgomery.com

LOCATIONS

San Francisco, CA (HQ)
Boston, MA • Charlotte, NC • Dallas, TX •
Los Angeles, CA • New York, NY • Seattle,
WA • London

THE STATS

No. of Offices: 8 (U.S.)
Subsidiary of BankAmerica Corp.
CEO: Lewis Coleman

KEY COMPETITORS

BT Alex. Brown
BancBoston Robertson Stephens
Donaldson, Lufkin & Jenrette
Hambrecht & Quist
SG Cowen

UPPERS

- Company gym
- Generous paid vacation policy
- Lots of parties
- Get to live in San Francisco

DOWNERS

- Parent merged again
- Awake at 4:30 a.m. if you're on the sell side

EMPLOYMENT CONTACT

Human Resources/
Corporate Employment
NationsBanc Montgomery Securities
600 Montgomery Street, 13th floor
San Francisco, CA 94111

Fax: (415) 627-2028
jobs@montgomery.com

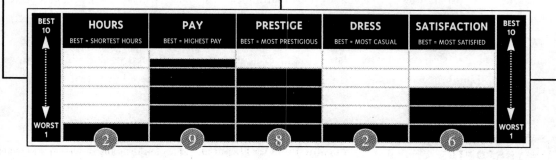

BEST 10 / WORST 1	HOURS BEST = SHORTEST HOURS	PAY BEST = HIGHEST PAY	PRESTIGE BEST = MOST PRESTIGIOUS	DRESS BEST = MOST CASUAL	SATISFACTION BEST = MOST SATISFIED	BEST 10 / WORST 1
	2	9	8	2	6	

THE SCOOP

THE HEART OF SAN FRANCISCO

Historically, the San Francisco-based investment banking firm of Montgomery Securities has enjoyed success that rivals that of its New York peers. Montgomery Securities' strategy has been to focus on companies in nine industries: financial services, consumer (products, retail and hospitality), media and communications, business services, energy, industrial growth, real estate, and health care. In addition, the company relies upon its ability to integrate its large research department with its trading department, one of the largest outside New York City. Montgomery Security's Private Client Department utilizes the resources of the firm to provide investment services to wealthy individuals and families.

A BEAR HUG FROM NATIONSBANK

In 1997, the firm was acquired by the much larger NationsBank Corporation, then the fourth-largest bank in the United States. NationsBank paid a pretty penny for its new subsidiary – the pact cost NationsBank an estimated $1.2 billion in cash and stock. While Montgomery was said to have been searching for a partner to take a minority stake, the overwhelming embrace of NationsBank may have taken the firm by surprise.

MUCH MERGING

More changes are in the works. In early 1998, NationsBank announced a merger with BankAmerica in a deal that created the second-largest commercial bank in the U.S. (trailing only Citibank in size). In September 1998, then-Montgomery Chairman/CEO Thomas Weisel resigned his post after close to a year of power struggles with NationsBank. The bank had been extremely aggressive in its efforts to tame the "highly entrepreneurial" securities firm. His exit was not a complete surprise – firm insiders report that Weisel had voiced objections to a number of decisions made by NationsBank concerning its new securities division. For example, though it was understood that the Montgomery Securities would control the firms' combined (extremely lucrative) high yield business, NationsBank eventually took control of it – reportedly in preparation for the bank's merger with BankAmerica Corp. The situation was further aggravated when NationsBank announced that the private equity investing business would be turned over to BankAmerica instead of staying with Montgomery. Industry observers expect that bankers loyal to Weisel may follow his lead. However NationsBank execs say most will find it hard to leave a bank with such a wide variety of products and broad customer base. Lewis Coleman, the firm's COO, will fill Weisel's position. Industry observers say Weisel's departure is probably just the first of many such defections from similar firms acquired by commercial banks in 1997. (BankAmerica's own investment bank subsidiary, Robertson Stephens, was sold to BankBoston in September 1998.)

GETTING HIRED

NMS conducts on-campus recruiting at select universities. Applicants from schools not visited by Montgomery can send an e-mail to jobopps@montgomery.com for graduate hiring information. Consult the company's Web page www.nationsbancmontgomery.com – for a list of contact names and addresses.

The firm hires MBAs into I-banking as generalists who work across product and industry groups before specializing in either one of the firm's nine industry groups (technology, health care, etc.) or one of its product groups (private equity, etc.). NMS also hires MBAs as as associates into its sales and trading, research, and private client departments. MBAs are hired into all of NMS' offices except Seattle: Boston, Charlotte, Dallas, Los Angeles, London, New York and San Francisco. In addition, business school students can join the firm as a summer associate in San Francisco, but only in I-banking.

I-Banking Job Seekers: Receive free e-mailed job postings matching your interests & qualifications! Register at www.vaultreports.com

VAULT REPORTS™
www.vaultreports.com

185

OUR SURVEY SAYS

WEARYING HOURS

Nationsbanc Montgomery is an "aggressive company" that offers "constant challenges" in a "high-pressure" environment." Employees travel "frequently" and often work "consecutive long days." Those days start early. In the San Francisco office, "traders have to come in around 5 a.m. to be there before the market opens on the East Coast. The rest of us have more reasonable hours." These hours often wear on NMS employees. One banker "was so miserable after working five consecutive days of 15+ hours a day that I almost walked in front of a car so I wouldn't have to go to work." Another insider says "I lost a lot of friends from working so much." Still, it all comes with the territory, say NMSers. "As an analyst, you have to be prepared to dedicate two years out of your life to the job. There were plenty of times when I had weekend plans that I had to cancel," says a philosophical former employee.

All this toil is not for naught, however. We hear that NMS is "a first class company," where employees " have the most up-to-date computers" and "love working in the Pyramid, the most famous building in San Francisco." And the "golden salaries" provide "superb" compensation for the "rigorous" schedule, and middle management is "eager" to "share their experience" with recently hired employees. In general "the pay is 10 to 20 percent above average."

AGGRESSIVE CULTURE

Employees report that "quite honestly, the place is very male dominated, like the entire industry," and that "the culture is pretty aggressive – there are many former athletes working here." One insider describes the difference between Nationsbanc Montgomery and its archrival BancBoston Robertson Stephens: "Robertson was founded with sort of a philosophy of research, Montgomery was founded more on the trading side. Montgomery is much more feisty and aggressive; Robertson is more laid-back." Despite this aggressive culture, employees "don't see much of a difference in the way men and women are treated. If you work hard and do a good job, you will be rewarded." One associate offers some straightforward advice to prospective employees: "An investment bank is very hierarchical. It's kind of like the army. In order to succeed, you must respect the hierarchy. This sucks as an analyst, because you're at the bottom of the pile. Being responsive to one's superiors, though, definitely gets you noticed." Ambitious employees are pleased that "Montgomery likes to promote from within." As for the merger with NationsBank, insiders are excited: "We have access to a lot more financial products and capital, and can advise our clients on many more ways to raise capital."

To order a 10- to 20-page Vault Reports Employer Profile on NationsBanc Montgomery Securities call 1-888-JOB-VAULT or visit www.VaultReports.com

The full Employer Profile includes detailed information on NMS' departments, recent developments and transactions, hiring and interview process, plus what employees really think about culture, pay, work hours and more.

I-Banking Job Seekers: Receive free e-mailed job postings matching your interests & qualifications! Register at www.vaultreports.com

VAULT REPORTS™   187
www.vaultreports.com

"It's kind of like the army. In order to succeed, you must respect the hierarchy."

– *NMS insider*

PaineWebber

1285 Avenue of the Americas
New York, NY 10019-6028
(212) 713-2000
Fax: (212) 713-4889
www.painewebber.com

LOCATIONS

New York, NY (HQ)
Weekhawken, NJ • Offices across the U.S.
and in France • Hong Kong • Japan • Puerto
Rico • Singapore • United Kingdom

THE STATS

Annual Revenues: $6.7 billion (1997)
Net Income: $415 million (1997)
No. of Employees: 16,600 (worldwide)
No. of Offices: 310 (worldwide)
Stock Symbol: PWJ (NYSE)
CEO: Donald B. Marron

KEY COMPETITORS

E*Trade
Merrill Lynch
Morgan Stanley Dean Witter
Salomon Smith Barney
Prudential Securities

UPPERS

- Job training
- Year-end bonuses
- Company fitness centers
- Free ferry in NYC

DOWNERS

- Constant acquisition rumors
- Long workdays
- Less prestige than rival securities firms

EMPLOYMENT CONTACT

PaineWebber Incorporated
Corporate Staffing
1000 Harbor Boulevard, 10th Floor
Weehawken, New Jersey 07087

Fax: (201) 902-4281
hrresumes@painewebber.com

	HOURS	PAY	PRESTIGE	DRESS	SATISFACTION	
BEST 10 / WORST 1	BEST = SHORTEST HOURS	BEST = HIGHEST PAY	BEST = MOST PRESTIGIOUS	BEST = MOST CASUAL	BEST = MOST SATISFIED	BEST 10 / WORST 1
	3	8	7	2	7	

THE SCOOP

THE BROKER ARMY

The PaineWebber Group is currently the fourth-largest retail broker in the country. The firm employs over 16,000 people in 300 offices in all 50 states and around the world, including an army of 6700 brokers. PaineWebber provides a range of products and services in private client brokerage, investment banking, real estate, institutional equity, fixed income, and asset management (with $54.7 billion under its management). The company has more than 2 million customers, including a variety of state and local governments.

A RECENT REVIVAL

William Paine and Wallace Webber opened their brokerage house in Boston in 1879. Before the end of the century, the company had joined the New York Stock Exchange and opened its first branch office. In the 1960s, the company began to move onto the national stage by moving its offices to New York, acquiring other houses throughout the U.S., and opening offices overseas. After the stock market crash of 1987, PaineWebber consolidated, shedding some of the more exotic businesses that it had acquired over its years of growth, including a venture capital arm in 1988, and its commercial paper operation in 1987. Though PaineWebber's ill-advised loan to bankrupt Federated Department Stores in 1988 dogged the firm for years, a capital infusion from the insurance company Yasuda (which at one point held a 20 percent equity stake in PaineWebber) provided a much-needed jolt, as did the revival of the stock market in the early 1990s. In late 1998, the firm announced that it would begin testing online trading.

A LIGHT FROM GE

In 1994, in an effort to bolster its own I-banking unit, PaineWebber purchased Kidder Peabody, General Electric's investment banking concern (GE now owns 23 percent of PaineWebber). However, establishing a major presence on Wall Street has proved to be more difficult than

PaineWebber had expected. Although the firm is perennially among the leaders in municipal bond underwriting, it usually finishes just outside the top 10 in stock underwriting. The firm is an attractive choice as a co-manager because its strong retail force can be used to sell offerings to individual investors, but has had difficulty winning lead manager spots.

MERGER NEGOTIATIONS

The firm's difficulties in building a top-tier investment banking franchise has spawned talk of mergers and acquisitions. In the summer of 1998, PaineWebber was reportedly negotiating with Prudential Securities about a merger that would have propelled both groups into the top ranks of several I-banking categories, namely municipal bond underwriting, mortgage- and asset-backed securities, and real estate investment trusts (REITs). Later that summer, PaineWebber was reportedly approached by German giant Dresdner Bank, which was considering buying the firm for as much as $10 billion.

GETTING HIRED

Entry-level employees at PaineWebber are hired into one of three groups: Investment Executives, Information Systems, and General Employment. Investment Executives (brokers) come from a wide variety of backgrounds; communication and problem-solving skills are crucial to these positions. The company offers new employees in this area a challenging education program designed to give them the skills they will need to succeed. Information Systems careers include positions at the company's data center as well as in the development of its technical system. The remainder of the positions at PaineWebber fall under General Employment. Each of these three groups has its own mailing, fax, and e-mail addresses, which are all available on the company's web site, www.painewebber.com. While PaineWebber has opportunities throughout the U.S., the majority of its employees begin in either its New York headquarters or its Weehawken, NJ, office facilities. MBAs have the option to join as

I-Banking Job Seekers: Receive free e-mailed job postings matching your interests & qualifications! Register at www.vaultreports.com

VAULT REPORTS™
www.vaultreports.com

191

associates in investment banking, public finance, or real estate. Initial hires spend time as generalists, which gives new employees exposure to different product groups and practice areas within PaineWebber.

OUR SURVEY SAYS

EVERYTHING TO EVERYONE

While "PaineWebber would like to be all things to all people, potential employees are cautioned that "PaineWebber is a brokerage firm first and an investment bank second." Still, we hear that the firm is committed to the company's goal of "growing and establishing a presence as a premier bank on Wall Street." According to one veteran banker: "PaineWebber definitely offers a better [banking] lifestyle than at other firms. The atmosphere is collegial and the hours, while long at times, were much better than at other firms." While life at PaineWebber is "challenging," "demanding," and "rewarding" as any in the industry, the corporate culture is said to be much less "stuffy" and "overbearing" than that at many of its competitors. Employees in real estate praise the firm's top executives for "being so approachable," and employees generally say that "PaineWebber, despite its size, has a small business feel." Says one insider who served a stint as a summer associate with PaineWebber in New York while in business school: "It was a very good experience. I had exposure to VPs constantly. Exposure to [managing directors] was limited to special meetings, three to five during the summer."

At this Wall Street firm, "dress is businesslike, no particular guidelines for women, but men are expected to wear suits. Friday is a casual day." However, an insider informs us that "the firm will soon go to business casual every day." Employees in New York and New Jersey say "there are fitness centers here, and if you live in New York City, you can take the ferry free to PaineWebber at Lincoln Harbor (in Weehawken, NJ) if you work there. Otherwise in car-clogged New Jersey "the commute is a nightmare." At PaineWebber, "women and minorities are treated very well, and women constitute a good portion of management. Complaints regarding harassment and discrimination are handled very seriously." While employees think the firm is "relatively liberal – I see some long-haired and multi-earringed employees," and "sensitive, for a place on the Street," "the culture is fragmented and people tend to keep to their own divisions."

As for the experience thousands of PaineWebber employees have with the firm's retail side, brokers tend to "work 50-hour weeks including Saturdays, though usually by choice." Brokers "can make over six figures in as little as five years, thought the first few years are usually quite lean, since you're putting together your client list."

I-Banking Job Seekers: Receive free e-mailed job postings matching your interests & qualifications! Register at www.vaultreports.com

VAULT REPORTS™
www.vaultreports.com

193

"PaineWebber is a brokerage firm first and an investment bank second."

– *PaineWebber insider*

Peter J. Solomon Company

767 Fifth Avenue
New York, NY 10153
(212) 508-1600
www.pjsolomon.com

LOCATIONS

New York, NY (HQ)

THE STATS

Year Founded: 1989
No. of Employees: 37
No. of Bankers: 22

KEY COMPETITORS

Goldman Sachs
Greenhill & Co.
Lazard Freres & Co.
Merrill Lynch
Morgan Stanley Dean Witter
Wasserstein Perella

UPPERS

- Great contact with senior bankers
- Excellent training in M&A
- Prime Midtown offices

DOWNERS

- Small firm; lonely at night
- Small firm; tighter expense policy

EMPLOYMENT CONTACT

Diane M.Coffey, Director
Peter J. Solomon
767 5th Avenue,
New York, New York 10153

careers@pjsolomon.com

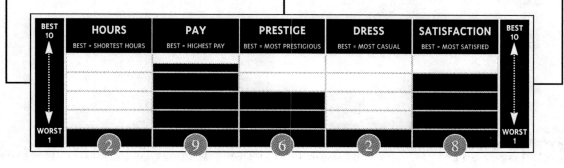

BEST 10 ⬆ WORST 1	HOURS BEST = SHORTEST HOURS	PAY BEST = HIGHEST PAY	PRESTIGE BEST = MOST PRESTIGIOUS	DRESS BEST = MOST CASUAL	SATISFACTION BEST = MOST SATISFIED	BEST 10 ⬆ WORST 1
	2	9	6	2	8	

THE SCOOP

ON HIS OWN

After co-chairing Lehman Brother's investment banking division, Peter J. Solomon left to form his own firm in 1989. Solomon, who also served a stint as deputy mayor for economic policy under New York mayor Ed Koch, developed a reputation as a leading banker in the retail and distribution industries. His eponymous firm, an M&A boutique, has followed suit, first building its rep in the retail and consumer goods industries, and now branching out into other sectors, such as healthcare and media.

A PROFICIENT BOUTIQUE

PJSC is one of Wall Street's most successful M&A specialty firms. Since its founding, the firm has advised on more than 100 deals. Recent deals have included pharmaceutical wholesaler McKesson Corp's $14.46 billion acquisition of medical software supplier, announced in October 1998, and McKesson's proposed purchase of Ameri-Source Health Corp in 1997, which was dropped because of opposition from the Federal Trade Commission. The McKesson/HBO deal, if approved, will create the world's largest healthcare services company.

Another of PJSC's big deals, the merger between office supply giants Staples and Office Depot proposed in 1997, was also blocked by the FTC. The firm was representing Office Depot in the deal. Office Depot again turned to Peter Solomon for its $2.71 billion acquisition of Viking Office Products, announced in May 1998. Other recent deals that the firm has advised on include Montgomery Ward's

The firm has also been busy with restructuring and other non-merger advisory work, including assignments with Bradlees, Filene's Basement, Guess?, and Ralph's Grocery Company.

VAULT REPORTS™
www.vaultreports.com

GETTING HIRED

With only about two dozen bankers and less than 40 total staff, positions at PJSC are extremely competitive. The firm hires both analyst and associate-level bankers for M&A, restructuring and corporate finance work. The firm provides contact information at its web site, located at www.pjsolomon.com

"[PJSC] recruits at Harvard, Wharton, Stanford, Berkeley, maybe Yale. But I don't think they've had too much luck. They also get a lot of resumes off the fax, so sending your resume by the fax is probably a good idea," says one contact. "They've just started hiring associates in the past year or two – on-campus – Harvard and Wharton.

"I think it's better there to have a quantitative or finance background. You do go through training – it's about a month – and they do bring in accountants, but they really want you on the job really quickly," explains one insider. "If you have some experience, you're going to be happier. That's not to say that you can't get there without it." Says that contact: "The Wharton candidate is almost the ideal candidate for [PJSC]. They come in understanding discounted cash flows." As for those discounted cash flows and other yummy quantitative finance questions, "if you have it on your resume, you better be sure you can talk about it. If you have zero experience, you better be focused on the fact that you're smart. Bring up examples where you've been quantitative."

Applicants can expect to travel to PJSC's headquarters twice andm "definitely meet all the senior people at the firm." What about the big man himself? "Peter, if he's around, he'll pop his head in and say why Peter Solomon is great, but he won't ask you questions."

I-Banking Job Seekers: Receive free e-mailed job postings matching your interests & qualifications! Register at www.vaultreports.com

VAULT REPORTS™

197

www.vaultreports.com

OUR SURVEY SAYS

DEEP M&A KNOW-HOW

"If you really want to learn how an M&A deal works," says a firm insider, "you'll get depth at Peter Solomon. You'll get depth, though you won't get the breadth." That contact elaborates: "They don't underwrite, so you don't get financing experiencing. You're not going to do an IPO or a debt deal. You'll get to see it, but you won't actually work on it." On the upside, "you definitely work on smaller teams. At Peter Solomon, the working group is one page of people. If you look at DLJ or Goldman, the working group list is 100 people." "You see a much smaller piece of a bigger deal at a bigger bank," says one insider. "At Peter Solomon, you're much more likely to see something from start to finish. You won't necessarily get to see as many things, but you'll know a lot more about what you've seen."

PART OF THE TEAM

Getting to see more of deals also means working more closely with senior bankers, insiders say. "The senior banker contact is great. You just walk into the partners' offices, there's no appointment making," says one insider. "Even if there's a conference call, you can just walk into the office and listen to it if you want to, even if it's not something you're working on." Working at a small firm also provides for an extra type of learning experience for the business-minded. "At a lot of banks, you think of yourself as an investment banker and not part of a business," explains one insider. "At Peter Solomon, you get both. It's small enough so you understand what its like to run a business – which computer to buy, how best to market the firm. And if you're entrepreneurial and interested in what its like to run a professional services firm, that's really interesting."

THE ASTOUNDING PETER SOLOMON

Working with senior bankers, of course, can mean working with Peter Solomon, of whom, one insider notes: "You would hear the secretary say who was on the phone. It's incredible. If you think about the mid- to late-1980s or early 90s, and who were the hitters. It's those names, all the time." As far as working with Solomon is concerned, "he's extremely demanding, and he doesn't really believe in the concept of titles, so he just expects you to know everything," says one insider. "He'll cut you some slack because you're a junior person, but if he wants something done, if you happen to be in his line of sight, you'll be the person to do it, whether it's VP work or not."

Peter J. Solomon bankers work in "offices with a beautiful view overlooking Central Park in Manhattan." Says one insider: "There's lots of places to go shop nearby, though you have no time to do that. You will be there for dinner all the time, it's just a better place than downtown." The firm pays for its bankers' dinners, and "you get taxis home, and they reimburse you for those." Peter Solomon bankers take taxis "because to take a car from Midtown to Downtown it's $15, for a cab its $8. Those little things count. They'll take care of you, but you have to recognize that they're a small firm and they have to take into account those things."

Although small benefits like cabs versus limos may differ between PJSC and larger firms, "your hours won't be any different than at a big firm. [Workweeks are] definitely sometimes over 100 [hours], sometimes less than 70." Those late night hours might look a bit different at a smaller firm, though. "At a big firm if you're there at 10 or 11 o'clock at night, it looks like 4 o'clock in the afternoon. At a smaller firm, late at night, it gets a little lonely, but it's not that bad, you're getting work done." And, the firm helps make up for solitary nights with pretty decent social contact. "In the summer there's outings. We went on a fishing trip one time in the Hamptons. There was some other boat cruise thing that they did. We go bowling, do things at Chelsea Piers," says one former Peter J. Solomon banker. "There are times when, because you have that senior banker contact, the senior guy will say, 'OK, who wants to leave and can go to dinner. Before you know it, you and two other analysts will be out at a nice place and talking to a managing director about whatever."

I-Banking Job Seekers: Receive free e-mailed job postings matching your interests & qualifications! Register at www.vaultreports.com

VAULT REPORTS™

199

www.vaultreports.com

"At a smaller firm, late at night, it gets a little lonely, but it's not that bad – you're getting work done."

– *Peter Solomon insider*

VAULT REPORTS™

www.vaultreports.com

Prudential Securities

One New York Plaza
New York, NY 10292
(212) 778-1000
Fax: (212) 778-6880
www.prusec.com

LOCATIONS

New York (HQ)
Atlanta
Houston
Los Angeles
San Francisco

THE STATS

No. of Brokers: 600
A division of the Prudential Insurance
Company of America
President and CEO: Hardwick Simmons
Year Founded: 1879

KEY COMPETITORS

Charles Schwab
Merrill Lynch
Morgan Stanley Dean Witter
PaineWebber
Salomon Smith Barney

UPPERS

- Kind hours for I-banking
- Good exposure to deals

DOWNERS

- Less prestigious than bulge-bracket firms
- Short on women

EMPLOYMENT CONTACT

Prudential Securities
Attention: Corporate Staffing
One New York Plaza
New York, New York 10292
Fax: (212) 778-3298

	HOURS	PAY	PRESTIGE	DRESS	SATISFACTION	
BEST 10 — WORST 1	BEST = SHORTEST HOURS	BEST = HIGHEST PAY	BEST = MOST PRESTIGIOUS	BEST = MOST CASUAL	BEST = MOST SATISFIED	BEST 10 — WORST 1
	3	8	7	3	7	

THE SCOOP

HUGE INSURANCE, GROWING BANKING

The financial services arm of Prudential Insurance, Prudential Securities is one of the largest insurance companies in the U.S. Along with the fifth-largest retail brokerage force in the U.S. with 6000 brokers, and a large mutual fund that oversees $76 billion, Prudential Securities includes a growing investment banking arm. Headquartered in New York, the company's I-banking practice targets seven industry groups: consumer, energy, financial services, health care, real estate, technology, and telecommunications and media. The firm touts this industry specialization as an advantage when it comes to competing against I-banking heavies.

WE GO WAY BACK

Prudential Securities traces its roots back to 1879 and a concern called Leopold Cahn & Co. Brokers and Investment Bankers. Shortly after its establishment the firm brought Jules Bache on board, who in 1892 reorganized the company as J.S. Bache & Co. In 1981, the company was acquired by Prudential and called Prudential-Bache Securities. The firm shortened its name to Prudential Securities in 1991.

The firm's parent, Prudential Insurance, traces its long history back to the Prudential Friendly Society, founded in 1875. The next year, Prudential issued its first death claim – for $10 – and adopted the Rock of Gibraltar as its corporate symbol. The company began to diversify outside the insurance business in 1981 through the acquisition of the securities brokerage firm Bache Halsey Stuart Shields. Currently Prudential's business operations are organized into four business lines: individual and group insurance, investments and other financial services, health care, and real estate. Insurance is still Prudential's mainstay, however; more than 50 million people around the world have their own "piece of the rock." The company's image was tarnished in the early 1990s when it received a multi-million dollar fine for fraudulent sales practices, but its reputation has bounced back, thanks in part to its new CEO, Arthur Ryan, and a successful public relations campaign.

GETTING HIRED

Prudential Securities visits college and B-school campuses for on-campus presentations and interviews. The firm's recruiting schedule for both analysts and associates can be found at its web site, located at www.prusec.com. Says one I-banking associate: "It's very competitive. They hire only the top graduates from half a dozen top schools and B-schools in the country." There are fewer I-banking analysts than associates, insiders say, reflecting the firm's emphasis on lean staffing.

The firm also offers summer positions for both undergraduates and business school students, although the number of summer analyst positions is reportedly small. Says one former summer associate: "I was involved in several live transactions and had extensive client and senior management contact. I was impressed by the amount of responsibility I was given for the summer." Another summer associate complains about the "long hours" but lauds the "great opportunity to work with senior bankers." The summer associate program is quite structured; summer hires are assigned to a particular industry or product group. Says one insider: "Everybody puts down a couple of groups, and they try to match you up."

The summer associate program is also reportedly diverting. Says one alum: "They did a lot of stuff, compared to other places. There were a couple of big dinners, a couple of baseball games, a couple drink events. It seemed to me from talking to my [I-banking] friends we did a lot more than they did."

I-Banking Job Seekers: Receive free e-mailed job postings matching your interests & qualifications! Register at www.vaultreports.com

VAULT REPORTS™
203
www.vaultreports.com

OUR SURVEY SAYS

MODEST GOALS

Working at Prudential, not usually thought of as a securities firm, has its ups and downs, insiders say. "The drawback is that Prudential is not a 'bulge bracket' firm and in many cases, when pitching a deal, you can't win against the likes of a Morgan Stanley, Goldman, or Merrill," explains one insider. "However, at Prudential, you will get much more exposure to clients, and senior management, and they will allow you to take responsibility up to the level of your capabilities." Another insider agrees, saying that "the deal teams are much leaner than at other firms. It's an associate, maybe an analyst, maybe an MD. Of course, at other firms, those deals might be a lot bigger."

Where are the firm's strengths? "Certainly their real estate group is the strongest. [Prudential] competes with Merrill for the most revenue generated in real estate," says one insider. "They do a lot of asset-backed stuff, sort of in the financial services stuff. They're also doing some of those music bonds, like those David Bowie revenue bonds."

COLLEGIAL, LOW ASSHOLE QUOTIENT

The firm's modest ambitions and I-banking businesses are reflected in its culture, Pru insiders say. "Certainly, in a general way, the people are a little bit more laid-back," says one insider. "They love to say this – and their big credo is – they have a low asshole coefficient. From my experience there's a strong correlation between your arrogance level and where you are on the league tables. Goldman and Morgan – they do a lot of business and they are definitely not humble people." Reports another contact: "I think the way they're trying to sell the firm is, 'We're a middle-market firm, we're not trying to compete with the bulge bracket by buying bankers. We're going to stick to this and we're doing a good job and making a lot of money.' They want to sell that it's a collegial, cultivating atmosphere." To help promote this groovy feeling of togetherness, Prudential Securities CEO Hardwick "Wick" Simmons "speaks regularly over the firm's broadcast system to keep employees abreast of developments within the firm, and welcomes questions at these times."

Despite the emphasis on quality of life issues, Prudential has had trouble attracting and retaining women in I-banking, insiders report. "Pru is getting killed on women, they've got virtually none. They're looking to boost up women, which they should, because it's pretty bad," one contact reports. "The Street's notoriously bad, but Pru is especially bad. It's because the good women can go to Goldman, Morgan, and Merrill."

STILL HARD WORKING

Prudential Securities bankers aren't slackers. Says one source: "Pru has changed from a laid-back I-bank to a pretty hard-driving, determined organization." Hard-driving, of course, means long hours. One I-banking associate reports reports working "up to 110 hours per week." However, Prudential insiders on the whole are pleased with their hours. "Hours are low-end to middle for investment banking, meaning 70 hours a week or so, worse on occasion," reports one contact. The tradeoff for the somewhat kinder hours is that "pay is decent but not as good as Prudential thinks it is paying for the junior people." Another insider agrees: "Just as much not having the arrogance and the money, you're going to have a little more of a life at Pru than at a Merrill or a Morgan. You still get paid a good bit of money, and you don't work as much." And, shock of all shocks – "people definitely take some weekends off."

Perks I-bankers with Prudential Securities enjoy include "lunch at the Downtown Club," "dinner at the 21 Club" and of course, "car rides and free dinners when working late." The niceties aren't confined to food and travel, either. Reports one insider: "I was given a window office as an associate. The working space was very good." The firm also provides a 401(k) plan with a 25 percent match of the first 3 percent of an employee's gross pay. Prudential employees also anjoy a retirement fund for which they are 100 percent vested after five years.

I-Banking Job Seekers: Receive free e-mailed job postings matching your interests & qualifications! Register at www.vaultreports.com

VAULT REPORTS™
www.vaultreports.com
205

"Just as much as not having the arrogance and the money, you're going to have a little more of a life at Pru than at a Merrill or a Morgan."

– *Prudential insider*

Raymond James Financial

The Raymond James Financial Center
880 Carillon Pkwy
St. Petersburg, FL 33716
(813) 573-3800
Fax: (813) 573-8244
www.rjf.com

LOCATIONS

St. Petersburg, FL (HQ)
Offices in DE • FL • GA • IL • NC • SC • TN • TX • Belgium • France • Germany • India • Luxembourg • South Africa • Switzerland • United Kingdom

THE STATS

Annual Revenues: $928 million (1997)
Net Income: $98.9 million (1997)
No. of Employees: 3244 (U.S.)
No. of Offices: 1100 (worldwide)
Stock Symbol: RJF (NYSE)
CEO: Thomas A. James

KEY COMPETITORS

A.G. Edwards
First Union
Legg Mason

UPPERS

- Shorter hours than most I-banks
- Extensive art collection in the company HQ
- Lots of company activities

DOWNERS

- Low pay for the industry
- Few minorities
- Not a party firm
- Stressful hiring process

EMPLOYMENT CONTACT

Undergraduates:
Kathryn McCann
(813) 573-3800 ext. 5102
Fax: (813) 573-8058
kmccann@ecm.rjf.com

MBAs:
Flinn L. Flexer
(800) 248-8863
Fax: (727) 573-8365
fflexer@exec.rjf.com

	HOURS	PAY	PRESTIGE	DRESS	SATISFACTION	
BEST 10 ↑ ⋮ ↓ WORST 1	BEST = SHORTEST HOURS	BEST = HIGHEST PAY	BEST = MOST PRESTIGIOUS	BEST = MOST CASUAL	BEST = MOST SATISFIED	BEST 10 ↑ ⋮ ↓ WORST 1
	4	8	6	4	9	

THE SCOOP

THE GROWING SOUTHEASTERN FIRM

The largest investment banking and brokerage firm headquartered in the Southeastern U.S., Raymond James Financial began in 1962 as Raymond and Associates. Two years later, the firm was sold to associate Bob James, whose son Thomas is now the CEO. Raymond James went public in 1983. In recent years, the company has branched into a wide variety of financial services. In 1994, it bought three branches of a failed thrift, Security Federal, and created Raymond James Bank. In 1996, the firm began offering retail banking services; in 1997, Raymond James established a merchant banking subsidiary. The firm's stockbrokers, who are independent contracters, make up the 10th-largest retail force in the U.S. The firm is rapidly growing its affiliated brokerages.

GREAT PICKS

Backing up its army of stockbrokers is an equity research department with an astounding record. (The firm's 1997 "best picks" portfolio went up 53 percent versus the S&P 500's 31 percent gain. The previous year, the portfolio gained 35.8 percent versus 19 percent for the S&P 500.) At the beginning of 1998, the firm introduced a mutual fund research division, and will offer information and advice to individual investors. As opposed to services that simply track past performance, Raymond James' reports offer opinions on the prospects of a fund. It's the first time in more than 50 years (since the Depression) that a securities firm has offered predictions on fund performance.

Although the firm's stockpicking prowess generates much of its press, it is the firm's investment banking (a subsidiary called Raymond James & Associates) and asset management (called Eagle Asset Management) businesses that have enjoyed the most impressive recent growth. The firm's I-banking business, like its research, focuses on stocks rather than fixed income, and targets several industries. Insiders describe the firm's information technology group as particularly robust.

In its 1998 fiscal year, Raymond James' revenues topped $1 billion for the first time. The firm's rapid growth spurred a recent $35 million expansion of its headquarters. Although the firm has not had great luck overseas, it continues to look for openings in the global securities market. In September 1998, the firm announced the launch of a Latin American I-banking and brokerage joint venture in Argentina, in a long-anticipated step. Earlier that summer, the firm had been in talks concerning the purchase of U.K.-based Caspian Securities' Latin American businesses, but decided not to make an acquisition.

GETTING HIRED

Raymond James' web site, located at www.rjf.com, provides information on applying for jobs at the St. Petersburg, FL headquarters, at other U.S. offices and at overseas offices. The site includes job descriptions, contact information, and recruiting schedules at both undergraduate and business schools. The firm hires one business school graduate each year to serve as an assistant to Thomas A. James, chairman of Raymond James Financial, for a two-year period. One insider describes that position as largely focused on special projects like geographic or new business expansion. That contact describes the position as ideal "if you wanted to see how investment banking works from 30,000 feet – how the whole thing works."

Raymond James' recruiting effort for MBA investment bankers, (for both summer and full-time positions), is rather unique. To start with, "the recruiting is done by a fairly high individual, the No. 2 guy with the firm," reports one insider. "He does the interviewing for investment banking on campus. He usually brings in another banker, typically a junior banker, but he asks most of the questions." The questions asked in the screening interview are somewhat atypical as well; candidates are reportedly often asked about high school and other areas of life not normally covered in on campus interviews. "Not many people ask you questions like that," says one insider. "They'll ask you about things on your resume or throw out some finance questions. Raymond James asked about high school: What were you doing in high school? Were you doing well in class? Were you playing any sports? He may ask you

I-Banking Job Seekers: Receive free e-mailed job postings matching your interests & qualifications! Register at www.vaultreports.com

VAULT REPORTS™

209

www.vaultreports.com

'Did you just bum through high school?' What he wants to know is: Did you take on all you can handle and still do more?"

The same day as the screening interview, several candidates at the school are called and invited for a "dinnerview." Explains one contact: "They'll go to dinner, and see how you act in a dinner environment. It's usually at one of the best restaurants around – and you'll just talk about whatever." The firm waits until it completes its on-campus interviews before deciding on call-backs to the firm's headquarters. While thorough, "the interview process is also a little nerve-wracking. If you're at one of the first schools they visit, it could be months before you get the call, you get a little acid indigestion."

The visit to Raymond James' headquarters isn't much stress relief, though the firm makes sure to provide amusement. Candidates are usually flown to Florida on a Thursday evening and go through a "full slate of interviews in the morning." These interviews are usually two-on-one or three-on-one . "They're all just peppering you with questions, just to get a sense of who you are," recounts one recent candidate. After lunch, candidates take a set of five 10-minute tests. "All of it's just fundamental math, it's not one of those 'Here's this shape and do something funky with it.' It's: You've got 10 minutes to solve these fraction multiplication problems. You've got to do a bunch of these and do them in a hurry." After these tests, the firm administers a standardized personality test on a Scantron form. It's like one of those where you have two choices: 'I'm standing in a line, and someone cuts in front of me. I would fly into a rage, or approach them calmly.' It's something like 300 questions." All of the candidates take the test in the same room: "Everybody's just sitting around and plugging away."

After the interviews and tests, the firm finally lets the candidates relax. On the Saturday after interviews, Raymond James' hopefuls have been treated to deep-sea fishing and golf in recent years. Some lucky candidates have been treated to Tampa Bay Bucaneers football games (the firm owns the naming rights to the team's stadium).

OUR SURVEY SAYS

A VERY INTENSE FAMILY

Raymond James bankers enjoy a working environment that is "not as stuffy as some of the workplaces in New York City." Reports one source: "RJ's culture is still like that of a small firm. Almost like family." Although some describe the firm as laid-back, one I-banking insider disagrees. "I personally find that the laid-back term is not an accurate term – everybody there is extremely competitive, I was actually kind of surprised. They're all extremely intense." Continues that banker: "What they want to do is fit work into their life. They get to work in the morning and they work real hard until 8 o'clock and then they quit. There's not a whole lot of sitting around staring at the ceiling, you're pretty much on task from the moment you get there. Not a whole lot of gabbing in the hallway."

SMOOTHLY RUN

Insiders say RJ is "very well run," and "a great company to work for." "There is a strong sense of teamwork and respect," bankers say. Insiders are especially pleased with the company's policy of promoting from within. One longtime employee describes ascending from a back-office position to an I-banking VP spot. Says one trader: "I have gained more experience at RJ than I could have with a larger firm. There's an excellent training program, and it's easier to get on the trading floor than at a bigger firm." One I-banker agrees about the opportunities the firm affords. "You get exposure there pretty quickly to just about everybody," says that associate. "I could go knock on virtually everybody's door." That contact reports that this emphasis creates a selective hiring process. "They like to look at it as if they're hiring a partner, someone who will be with them for a long time.

I-Banking Job Seekers: Receive free e-mailed job postings matching
your interests & qualifications! Register at www.vaultreports.com

VAULT REPORTS™
211
www.vaultreports.com

FUN IN FLORIDA

"The pay is not good by industry standards," admit insiders, but it's decent for the areas where the offices are located. (One insider notes approvingly that Florida does not have a state income tax.) Another insider says he came to Raymond James "not for the money, but rather the working environment." Benefits include insurance ("good if you are single, a bit expensive for families"), a 401(k) plan ("not up to NY standards"), profit sharing, and a "good" employee stock purchase plan. Employees also observe with pride that "RJ supports a lot of local arts programs." Sources say "the company does lots of neat things," including "Breakfast with the Boss" each quarter, and "yearly employee days at Busch Gardens or Sea World." The firm also sponsors an annual cultural awareness week, "that showcases different cultures," complete with "exhibits, food, and information from different countries." RJ employees also enjoy "going all out with the decorations" at Halloween, and fundraising for each department's favorite charity during the winter holidays. These firm-sponsored social events notwithstanding, don't expect to be partying hard with colleagues at Raymond James, insiders say. "A lot of the bankers are married," says one. "They make really no bones about spending time with family."

Raymond James' offices are located in two "brand spanking new" towers in St. Petersburg, about 20 minutes from downtown Tampa. "St. Pete's a little more of a retirement area, but it's right across from the water from Tampa. Most of the bankers live in Tampa, and they seem to really like it, there's a nice trendy area in South Tampa," reports one insider. In one of the two towers, the firm houses most of its institutional finance groups (investment banking, research, trading, but not asset management). "There's two cafeterias [one in each tower], they have a barber shop, a guy who shines your shoes. You can drop your laundry off there." The company even boasts a "superb" art collection at its headquarters.

"As with most male-dominated industries," relates one female insider, "the climb for women is much harder, but it is possible." She goes on to add, "there are minorities here, but not many." Most insiders report that opportunities for women and minorities, however, are wide open. Says one woman: "I think that everyone is treated equally by most of the company." Comments another insider: "There's many cultures at all levels. Your success is based on your merit and determination."

SG Cowen

Financial Square, 8th Floor
New York, NY 10005
(212) 495-6000
Fax: (212) 495-7477
www.cowen.com

LOCATIONS

New York, NY (HQ)
Albany, NY • Atlanta, GA • Boston, MA •
Chicago, IL • Cleveland, OH • Dayton, OH •
Houston, TX • Phoenix, AZ • San Francisco,
CA • Geneva, Switzerland • London, England •
Paris, France • Tokyo, Japan • Toronto, Canada

THE STATS

No. of Employees: 1,650
No. of Offices: 15 (worldwide)
A subsidiary of Societe Generale
Chairman: Joseph Cohen

KEY COMPETITORS

BancBoston Robertson Stephens
BT Alex. Brown
Hambrecht & Quist
Nationsbanc Montgomery Securities
Volpe Brown Whelan

UPPERS

- Great offices
- Good client contact

DOWNERS

- Taken over by Societe Generale

EMPLOYMENT CONTACT

Undergraduates:
Debbie Chang
SG Cowen
1221 Avenue of the Americas
New York, NY 10020

MBAs:
Jodi Fasula
SG Cowen
Financial Square
New York, NY 10005

	HOURS	PAY	PRESTIGE	DRESS	SATISFACTION	
BEST 10 / WORST 1	BEST = SHORTEST HOURS	BEST = HIGHEST PAY	BEST = MOST PRESTIGIOUS	BEST = MOST CASUAL	BEST = MOST SATISFIED	BEST 10 / WORST 1
	2	9	7	2	6	

213

THE SCOOP

A FOCUSED APPROVAL

Founded in 1918 in Wall Street as a bond broker, SG Cowen has pursued a strategy of focusing on a limited number industries. A leading full-service securities firm, SG Cowen perennially receives top rankings in certain markets, most notably health care, and high tech. In 1997, the tied for the lead in health care offerings and ranked No. 3 in technology offerings. The firm has the Street's largest health care research team with 25 analysts covering more than 100 companies. Recently the firm was tapped to help underwrite the IPO of high-profile software company pcOrder.com. Like rivals BT Alex. Brown, NationsBanc Montgomery Securities, and BancBoston Roberston Stephens, SG Cowen has been acquired by a large commercial bank. In 1998, Cowen & Company (as it was formerly called) was acquired by French commercial giant Societe Generale for $615 million. The deal included a $75 million bonus pool designed to keep key bankers and analysts from leaving.

With the purchase by Societe Generale, Cowen is focusing almost entirely on investment banking businesses. Previous to its acquisition, Cowen had close to $6 billion under management by its subsidiary, SG Cowen Asset Management, and managed six mutual funds with about $1.8 billion in assets. Despite this apparent success, in October 1998, the firm laid off the CEO of the asset management arm and the firm's director of marketing (who also had a key role in the asset management business), explaining that their roles were redundant. While cutting back its asset management business, the firm is looking to expand its industry expertise. Observers speculate the firm hopes to conquer the media and entertainment industry, after poaching all-star analyst Edward Hatch from Warburg Dillon Read in October 1998.

GETTING HIRED

SG Cowen looks for accomplished and motivated individuals with strong academic backgrounds, and analytical, computer, and communication skills. Visit the investment banking section of Cowen's web site for job descriptions and contact information. Send or fax resumes to offices in New York or California. For analyst positions (entry-level finance positions, the firm recruits on-campus at select schools in January and February. For associates (MBA-level positions), responsibilities include financial and strategic analyses such as structuring and executing equity and debt financing and identifying, evaluating and implementing mergers and acquisitions in Cowen specialty areas. Contact information is on Cowen's web site at www.cowen.com.

One recent associate hire explains her interview process: "I did a two-on-one for the first round. The second round was a round robin of one-on-ones. I interviewed with four people, each interview was 30 to 45 minutes." That contact reports that Cowen lobs finance questions at associate candidates if they do not have a particularly strong banking background. "Because it's small, you need to hit the ground running, because they don't have the resources to train people – they will give you the time, but they would rather not."

Because of its focus on industries, bankers at Cowen are generally hired into specific groups. While a deep knowledge of an industry isn't necessary, "what's important to them is that you have a thirst to learn. In underwriting you have to write documents describing the company, and its products and strategy, so you have to exhibit that interest." Analysts in the past have been asked their industry preference, which is generally accommodated, insiders say. While in past the firm has promoted analysts to associates without requiring an MBA, it is reportedly moving away from such promotions.

I-Banking Job Seekers: Receive free e-mailed job postings matching your interests & qualifications! Register at www.vaultreports.com

VAULT REPORTS™
215
www.vaultreports.com

OUR SURVEY SAYS

FRIENDLY CULTURE

With a small- to medium-size company atmosphere, insiders note that each department and office at SG Cowen has its own distinct culture. The firm's technology group, for example, has reportedly been more fractious than its healthcare group in the past. However, insiders agree that bankers are in general closer to each other at Cowen than at bulge-bracket firms. One source praises relationships with upper management, saying upper management is interested in developing the abilities of their staff, and are "even willing to make themselves available to anyone who needs them." Others "manage to get together outside the office, which is nice." Says one associate in the firm's San Francisco office: "It's a friendly, family-like environment. I think the lines between professional and personal relationships get crossed. People know when someone's been on a date, and people celebrate birthdays a lot." Reports a former analyst in New York: "The MDs take people out once a month to have a big event, whether it's bowling, or out for drinks, or whatever, just to keep morale high, they did a good job bringing people to travel."

Because of its size, entry-level bankers at Cowen are given high levels of responsibility from the start. "In your first year here," say analysts, "you will get to work with CEO clients, something that would not happen in a larger firm."

But even though employees are proud that "Cowen is a company with a history of success," they acknowledge that "there are drawbacks. You will also perform the mundane tasks that would not be required of you in a larger company. You will do copying, filing, take out the garbage – whatever needs to be done."

THE SG ACQUISITION

Reports one insider about the acquisition of Cowen & Company by Societe Generale: "There were the cosmetic changes – new business cards, new stationary, new logos and everything. Templates for producing pitchbooks changed." That contact continues: "The policies changed a bit, there were more people were added to committees. One of the things that SG did was actually reduce the number of steps that had to be taken before deciding to take on a deal."

More important than cosmetic or policy changes, however, is a generally change in name recognition and identity. "From a marketing standpoint, it changes somewhat," explains one insider. "You now have a parent company that's a French bank, and you try to offer more products for clients, you're able to do debt and equity. But some people don't understand what SG means, whereas NationsBank or Bank of America is more recognizable."

And more important than prestige and name recognition has been cultural change and turnover, most notably at the firm's NY headquarters. Reports one associate: "Some of the SG people are coming in and taking over more, the head of I-banking is an SG person, where it used to be all Cowen." Another insider reports: "Basically the tech group got decimated, a lot of them didn't stick around to see how it would work out. Also, a lot of the dead wood got fired."

RESEARCH-ORIENTED

SG Cowen has grown rapidly into a full-service bank from a research firm. For one, the firm is moving into industries outside of its traditional focus. "It was health care and technology, now it's everything from retail, media – they're trying to be cross all industries," says one insider, who notes that Cowen has been unsuccessful thus far in duplicating the success that it has enjoyed in its original industries.

Still, the emphasis on research distinguishes the firm from others where research analysts may be pressured to work in ways that will promote banking work, insiders say. "The research people don't take any shit from the bankers," explains one insider. "Those guys have built enough power, since they were there first. They never felt any pressure from the bankers to do anything more than they wanted to do."

THE HIGH LIFE

In the past, Cowen has paid its bankers pretty much the industry average. "They always do a real good job finding out what the median was in Wall Street – from my point of view, always

I-Banking Job Seekers: Receive free e-mailed job postings matching your interests & qualifications! Register at www.vaultreports.com

VAULT REPORTS™
www.vaultreports.com

217

disappointing. When you're Goldman you can see not paying as much, because you've got the name," says one insider. "It just wasn't near the top." However, the firm offered other niceties. Cowen's New York offices are "as nice as you'll see on Wall Street." Unlike most Wall Street bankers who sometimes feel a bit like veal, "analysts get windowless offices rather than cubes. Nine times out of 10, associates get windowed offices." Also, Cowen bankers have taken advantage of a "gourmet kitchen on the 30th floor, that's like a five-star restaurant" and "barber on the 28th."

TD Securities

31 West 52nd Street
New York, NY 10019
(212) 468-0633
Fax: (212) 262-1922
www.tdbank.ca

LOCATIONS

New York (HQ)
Calgary • Hong Kong • London • Montreal
Toronto

THE STATS

No. of Offices: 6 (worldwide)
A division of Toronto-Dominion
Chairman and CEO: G.F. Kym Anthony

KEY COMPETITORS

Charles Schwab
CIBC Oppenheimer
E*Trade
Merrill Lynch
Morgan Stanley
Royal Bank of Canada

UPPERS

◆ High marks for diversity
◆ Good advancement opportunities
◆ Good quality of life for I-banking

DOWNERS

◆ Recent instability because of planned
   merger with CIBC

EMPLOYMENT CONTACT

Human Resources
Toronto-Dominion Securities
31 West 52nd Street
New York, NY 10019

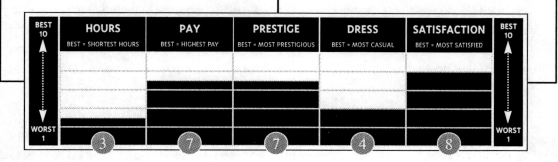

	HOURS	PAY	PRESTIGE	DRESS	SATISFACTION	
BEST 10 → WORST 1	BEST = SHORTEST HOURS	BEST = HIGHEST PAY	BEST = MOST PRESTIGIOUS	BEST = MOST CASUAL	BEST = MOST SATISFIED	BEST 10 → WORST 1
	3	7	7	4	8	

THE SCOOP

TD SCORES NEW BUSINESSES

TD Securities is the investment banking arm of the Toronto-Dominion Bank (TD), Canada's fifth-largest commercial bank. TD has grown its I-banking capabilities in recent years, successfully moving into new geographic markets. The firm opened its New York office in 1996. In April 1998, the bank received a license from Japan's Ministry of Finance to operate a securities business in the country. TD Securities' corporate finance and advisory activities are organized into several industry groups: media and communications (in which the firm is especially strong); paper and forest products; mining, oil and gas; financial institutions; real estate; health care; utilities and power; technology and biotechnology; governments and infrastructure; and diversified industries. The firm also has a product group dedicated to M&A work.

The firm has also started new business groups, receiving clearance to underwrite debt in 1995. In June 1997, the firm's fixed income group celebrated its first global bond offering, a five-year issue by the The Federal National Mortgage Association (Fannie Mae) in New Zealand Dollar-denominated financing that it jointly lead managed. The new debt underwriting capability has also paved the way for the establishment of a high-yield debt group. In 1997, the firm began making markets in U.S., Canadian, and NASDAQ stocks out of its New York office, and changed its name from Toronto-Dominion Securities to TD Securities. The firm has also established a merchant bank, TD Capital Group, which today has a portfolio of more than $800 million.

CIBC MERGER DENIED

Formed by the 1955 merger of two large Canadian banks, TD has been expanding in the U.S. since the U.S. division was established in 1980. In 1998, Toronto-Dominion agreed to merge with the Canadian Imperial Bank of Commerce (CIBC). That deal would have created a bank with more than $320 billion in assets and 2300 branches across Canada. (Canadian Imperial owns U.S. investment bank CIBC Oppenheimer Corp.) Both Oppenheimer and TD Securities, however, took punches after the announcement of the merger. TD Securities took a $36 million loss in its last quarter of 1998. At the beginning of December 1998, TD Securities laid off 65 employees because of the poor performance, according to the *National Post of Canada*. In mid-December, the Canadian government blocked the proposed merger. (At the same time, it nixed a planned merger between the Royal Bank of Canada and the Bank of Montreal.)

TD's corporate I-banking services are bolstered by strong retail support. The bank's discount brokerage business, Greenline Investor Services, moved into the top brokerage ranks in the U.S. with its 1996 acquisition of New York-based Waterhouse Investor Services. The purchase of Australian-based Pont Securities in 1997 helped establish the bank as a leading global discount broker. But it is in cyberspace that TD's brokering is making the most waves. Its subsidiary, Waterhouse Securities is battling E*Trade and Ameritrade for Web trading market leadership.

GETTING HIRED

TD Securities has opportunities in Toronto, Montreal, Calgary, Vancouver, New York and London. The firm allows candidates to register online at www.tdbank.ca, and check out I-banking analyst and associate, and sales and trading job descriptions. The hiring process is reportedly relaxed. Reports one insider: "The most technical questions I got were from the head of HR."

The firm also offers summer internships for both analysts and associates. Reports an insider about the summer program: "It's not an MBA-heavy program. In terms of the summer program, they didn't really make a distinction in terms of what we did, for training and social things." What are the social things that the firm provides for summer interns? "We went out one night and played laser tag [in Times Square]. One night, they had a dinner with pretty much every managing director in the New York office, and they forced us to do the skits and do the entertainment for them." Summer hires also get other non firm-bonding perks" including "$250 to take out whoever we wanted for drinks or whatever."

I-Banking Job Seekers: Receive free e-mailed job postings matching your interests & qualifications! Register at www.vaultreports.com

VAULT REPORTS™
221
www.vaultreports.com

OUR SURVEY SAYS

RESPECTFUL, KIND

Insiders at TD Securities remark that their employer is a bit different than your average American Wall Street firm. Says one associate at the firm's New York office: "The corporate culture here is very positive – friendly, probably a bit more laid-back internally than other firms, team-oriented and fun." For example, the dress code in the summer at the firm's offices in New York is business casual. For the rest of the year, employees at TD Securities can get loose(r) on Fridays, enjoying casual days.

A former analyst praises his experience with supervisors. "Opinions are respected," he says. "Comments and questions are encouraged." "It's a great place to work," reports one associate. "A lot of people came from other big banks because of the lifestyle and opportunities." Why might the opportunities at TD be better than at the big-name firms? "The associates who are there joined because they thought there was a lot of opportunity without five or 10 people in front of you," explains one insider. "That was a lot of the reason they joined – that the upside would be a lot greater than somewhere else." Another contact agrees, saying that TD Securities is "relatively young in the I-banking industry, but building it and its reputation rapidly." Because it is a "growing firm," one insider suggests there is "lots of opportunity to take responsibility and learn."

GOOD MARKS FOR DIVERSITY

Insiders also praise the opportunities and treatment for women and ethnic minorities at TD Securities. Says one insider: "Everyone attends a diversity awareness program that the firm designed based upon extensive research and feedback from employees. In my opinion, the awareness program, combined with the corporate culture, makes it a great place for minorities and women." Another insider agrees: "Women are in senior positions and command respect." To illustrate this point, one summer associate explains that twice a week, the heads of groups make presentations to interns: "As many women as men came in."

However, like all I-bankers, those at TD Securities can look forward to killer hours. Reports one former analyst: "I often worked in excess of 80 hours a week. It's really like having two jobs." Thankfully, those hard-working bankers receive dinner if they "work past 8 p.m.," free car rides home, and can "keep airmiles from travel." However, some insiders maintain that "there's less punching the clock than other firms, where you're expected to stay late and go out every night. It isn't really that type of atmosphere. The quality of life there is very high."

MERGE FEAR

With the expected merger with CIBC Oppenheimer, however, TD Securities employees haven't been too happy lately. "I think a lot of people's morale is really low," reports one insider. "I would say that people just expect that there will be significant layoffs because of overlap." For example, an insider notes that TD Securities essentially shut down its U.S. equities operations over the summer of 1998, perhaps in preparation for the merger (although, that insider admits, possibly for other strategic reasons). One summer associate recalls peers sneaking out to sniff out other positions: "I saw a lot of analysts go out shopping during the day." Those fears were allayed at the end of 1998, however, because of the Canadian government's decision – in part because of feared layoffs – to block the merger.

I-Banking Job Seekers: Receive free e-mailed job postings matching
your interests & qualifications! Register at www.vaultreports.com

VAULT
REPORTS™   223
www.vaultreports.com

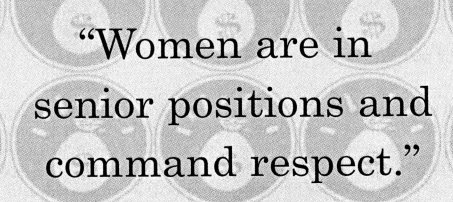

"Women are in
senior positions and
command respect."

– *TD Securities insider*

U.S. Bancorp Piper Jaffray

Piper Jaffray Tower
222 South Ninth Street
Minneapolis, MN 55402
(612) 342-6000
Fax: (612-342-6996
www.piperjaffray.com

LOCATIONS

Minneapolis, MN (HQ)
Denver, CO • Des Moines, IA • Great Falls, MT • Kansas City, MO • Los Angeles, CA • Menlo Park, CA • Milwaukee, WI • Phoenix, AZ • Portland OR • San Francisco, CA • Seattle, WA • Spokane, WA • St. Louis, MO London, United Kingdom

THE STATS

Annual Revenues: $602 million (1997)
Net Income: $1.0 million (1997)
No. of Employees: 3,180 (U.S.)
Subsidiary of U.S. Bancorp
CEO: Addison L. Piper

KEY COMPETITORS

A.G. Edwards
Dain Rauscher
William Blair & Co.

UPPERS

- Spiffy new HQ
- Rising profits
- Friendly for an I-bank

DOWNERS

- Not strong diversity
- Headquarters not in finance hot spot
- Tough for single folk

EMPLOYMENT CONTACT

Employment Coordinator – BR
U.S. Bancorp Piper Jaffray
Piper Jaffray Tower
222 South Ninth Street
Minneapolis, MN 55402

(612) 342-6918
applicant@piperjaffray.com

	HOURS	PAY	PRESTIGE	DRESS	SATISFACTION	
BEST 10 / WORST 1	BEST = SHORTEST HOURS	BEST = HIGHEST PAY	BEST = MOST PRESTIGIOUS	BEST = MOST CASUAL	BEST = MOST SATISFIED	BEST 10 / WORST 1
	3	8	6	2	8	

THE SCOOP

THE TRUE NORTH BANK

Founded in 1895, Piper Jaffray views itself as a different sort of investment bank. The firm's most obvious distinction is the location of its Minneapolis, MN, headquarters, a location that contributes to Piper Jaffray's strength in investment banking activities outside of New York. Founded in 1895, Piper Jaffray Companies has several subsidiaries: Piper Jaffray Ventures, a private equity VC firm which focuses on emerging-growth companies; Piper Capital Management Incorporated, an institutional money fund manager with about $12 billion under management; and Piper Trust Company, a Minnesota state chartered trust company. The main subsidiary, Piper Jaffray Inc., offers a full range of securities brokerage and investment banking services through its 90 branch offices located in 17 states. The firm's I-banking practice focuses on select industries: consumer, financial institutions, health care, industrial growth, and technology. Piper Jaffray is also the top municipal bond underwriter in the Midwest.

A NEW OWNER

In December 1997, Piper Jaffray Companies agreed to be acquired by U.S. Bancorp (also based in Minneapolis), in a cash deal valued at $730 million. Piper Jaffray added brokerage offices and 1500 brokers to U.S. Bancorp's significant private financial services capability, creating the 11th-largest brokerage in the United States. U.S. Bancorp, the 15th-largest bank holding company in the U.S., is the largest provider of Visa corporate and purchasing cards in the world.

MORE ROOM

Since the acquisition, Piper Jaffray's investment banking business has grown dramatically. In October 1998, the firm reported that its I-banking revenue had risen by 70 percent in the previous 12 months, driven largely by a 155 percent rise in advisory fees (mostly M&A

advisory). In the 18 months previous to October 1998, the firm had doubled its number of I-bankers to 90. The firm is building a new Piper Jaffray Center in Minneapolis to accommodate its growth. Piper will house 2000 employees in the $150 million development; fewer than 800 worked at Piper's current headquarters, called the Piper Tower, when it opened in 1985. Piper Jaffray predicts that its annual revenue, which was more than $600 million in 1997, will hit $900 million in the year 2000.

Despite its rapid growth, Piper Jaffray continues to focus on emerging-growth companies. In its 1998 fiscal year, the firm represented private companies in 64 percent of the 60 M&A deals it advised on. Piper's had some large clients also – the firm served as an underwriter in a $709 million stock offering by health care giant Medtronic in September 1998. A list of recent deals and offerings the firm has handled is available at Piper's web site, located at www.piperjaffray.com.

GETTING HIRED

Piper Jaffray's web site, located at www.piperjaffray.com, provides a listing of current job opportunities and contact addresses. Applicants can submit their resumes to the Employment Department at the company's corporate headquarters. Most new employees in the corporate finance department start as generalists with the latitude to pursue the specialty of their choice.

"They typically don't recruit for analysts, but for associates they definitely recruit from the top five schools – they draw a lot from Chicago and Northwestern because they're in the Midwest, but they have a lot of Harvard Business School people. Also, they opened an office in Menlo Park, and are hiring a lot in Stanford too," says one recent hire.

Unlike other I-banks, Piper Jaffray doesn't do most its hiring through summer programs. As one insider explains: "People who want to do I-banking don't necessarily want to do a summer in Minnesota." "They want to get the best candidates they can, but they don't want them to leave six months later, either. I think they try to hire people who have Piper Jaffray as their first or second choice.

I-Banking Job Seekers: Receive free e-mailed job postings matching your interests & qualifications! Register at www.vaultreports.com

VAULT
REPORTS™   227
www.vaultreports.com

Piper, according to contacts, "doesn't come on campus and take you to dinner and stuff – other firms will come down to dinners and other things, so you get to express your interest there." At Piper, "it's sort of up to the person to express an interest. Maybe you can call them up before the interviews and express your interest." Potential applicants, take note.

The sneaky may do well to try to get hired by the equity research firm Dain Rauscher. "Dain has a prestigious reputation in the Midwest, but not nationally," reports one insider. "However, Dain and Piper raid each other all the time, so if you work at Dain, you can easily be lured to Piper in two years with big money."

OUR SURVEY SAYS

HIGH-LEVEL

Piper Jaffray employees call their firm's work environment a "superb" place to begin a career, thanks to an "interactive" atmosphere and "genial" colleagues who help new hires "learn the subtleties of the business." Explains one insider: "Traditionally they've been a very top-heavy firm. They don't win deals based on their name recognition. They win based on research, and because the companies that work with them know they're going to get senior-level attention. So they don't leverage analysts as much as other firms do – senior people need to be more involved." This means, in part, that moving up the ladder at the firm is somewhat easier than at larger firms. In fact, promotions can happen rapidly: one insider reports that associates can move up to the VP level in two years.

The firm is also different when it comes to job responsibilities for junior bankers. "Associates don't do any modeling, analysts do all the modeling. You could literally never do a model there if you're an associate," reports one insider. "It's great for an analyst because you do all the models, including the complex ones. The associates get a lot of client time, they're always included in the meetings." I-banking analysts can stay on for a third year, and, in rare instances, can be promoted to associate without getting an MBA. "It was a dramatic mind change," reports one insider about this possible career path. "Four years ago they wouldn't let anyone."

GOOD PAY (ESPECIALLY FOR MN)

The firm offers "healthy salaries" that tend to vary with the performance of the stock market and "some of the best employee benefits" in the industry, including an "unbeatable" employee stock ownership program. When it comes to starting pay, the firm isn't all that different from the big boys back East. Reports one insider: "First-year associates can get paid close to what they get paid in New York. Where it gets skewed is in the four or five years and up. Here, people make a million dollars but it's not the rule. But here, people can buy a huge house for $250,000 10 minutes out of town." Piper Jaffray's largesse also includes "a free turkey for Thanksgiving, up to 22 pounds." Says an I-banking insider: "You get to expense meals if you work past 7. I turned in my cell phone bills, and no one checks receipts. You're given a lot of leeway."

STUFFY DRESS AND MANAGEMENT

At Piper, you'll be wearing "formal business attire, long sleeves, dark blue or gray – plus a huge down parka during the winters!" However, "Fridays are casual days, and one sees a lot of L.L. Bean." Some employees also complain about bureaucracy at the company: "The corporate culture is a bit stuffy and prone to micro-management," says one employee. "There is a lot of red tape," concurs another contact.

MORE WOMEN PLEASE

Insiders comment that "Piper, like Minnesota itself, is homogenous, with few minorities," though "it is an open environment and the only criteria for advancement is hard work." Says another insider: "I think Minnesota in general, doesn't have a strong mix of ethnicity. If you wanted strong cultural diversity, you'd be somewhere else." However, says that I-banking contact: "I think they're very good with the male/female ratio. They're not 50/50 at the top, but they definitely have some strong women there."

I-Banking Job Seekers: Receive free e-mailed job postings matching your interests & qualifications! Register at www.vaultreports.com

VAULT REPORTS™
www.vaultreports.com

229

NOT FOR THE SINGLE

Minneapolis has some advantages aside from the cost of living, however. Reports one insider: "There's a lot of young people. They've got Pillsbury and General Mills and the banks. The downtown area's not that big, and you run into a lot of people – they've also got the Timberwolves, the Vikings and the Twins, so there's a lot of entertainment to do at night." You might want to qualify entertainment as "family entertainment" though, because while "it's a phenomenal place to be if you're married and want to have kids. If you're single, it's not the best place. Most people are married."

MORALE STILL STRONG

How has Piper Jaffray's recent acquisition affected life at the bank? "It is affecting morale, though not as much in the investment banking division." Says one I-banking insider: "It's still run the same as a wholly-owned subsidiary – and they haven't affected compensation."

LIFE OK

Because of Piper Jaffray's Midwestern location, employees usually start the day early, in order to be open during East Coast market hours. For I-bankers, "the hours are extreme, 12 to 14 hours a day, plus weekends for bankers, thought it's still not quite as bad as New York." Says one former analyst: "You work hard, but they allow you to have a life. Workweeks are in the range of 70 to 80. You do work on weekends but it's not all weekend. You work hard, but it's not like New York. If you had a birthday party, or concert tickets – you can get away. A lot of times you have to cancel, but it's not like other places. Here they're more lenient – it's the Midwestern values."

Warburg Dillon Read

677 Washington Boulevard
Stamford, CT 06912-0305
(203) 719-1000
Fax: (203) 719-1410
www.wdr.com

LOCATIONS

Stamford, CT (HQ)
U.S. offices in Boston, MA • Chicago,IL •
Dallas, TX • Edina, MN • Houston, TX • New
York, NY • Philadelphia, PA • San Francisco,
CA • Offices in more than 40 countries

THE STATS

No. of Employees: 15,000 (worldwide)
A subsidiary of UBS Group
CEO: Hans de Gier
CEO, The Americas: Dick Capone

KEY COMPETITORS

ABN Amro
Credit Suisse First Boston
Deutsche Bank
Merrill Lynch

UPPERS

- Ambitious firm
- Great for analysts

DOWNERS

- Messy merger
- Lumpy culture
- MBAs devalued

EMPLOYMENT CONTACT

Recruitment Officer
Warburg Dillon Read
Human Resources
UBS Center
677 Washington Boulevard
Stamford, CT 06912

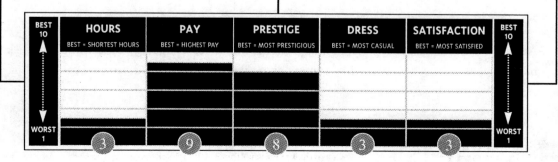

	HOURS	PAY	PRESTIGE	DRESS	SATISFACTION	
BEST 10 / WORST 1	BEST = SHORTEST HOURS	BEST = HIGHEST PAY	BEST = MOST PRESTIGIOUS	BEST = MOST CASUAL	BEST = MOST SATISFIED	BEST 10 / WORST 1
	3	9	8	3	3	

THE SCOOP

NOT A GREAT BEGINNING

There's been a whole lot of name-changing going on to create Warburg Dillon Read, a U.S.-based investment bank whose parent, Swiss banking giant UBS, hopes will soon be challenging the Goldmans and Merrills of the world for I-banking primacy. Established in 1832, Wall Street investment bank Dillon Read was thrown into the churning mix of global financial services merging in September 1997, when it was acquired by SBC Warburg, and was renamed SBC Warburg Dillon Read. SBC Warburg had been created by the 1995 purchase of London investment bank S.G. Warburg Group by Swiss Bank Corporation, one of Switzerland's largest banks. When Swiss Bank merged with rival giant Union Bank of Switzerland in 1998 to form UBS, the two firms merged their I-banking businesses under the name Warburg Dillon Read.

Since the merger, however, little has gone right for the combined investment bank. As with virtually any merger, what was pitched as a merger-of-equals has not turned out that way. The firm's head, Hans Grier, came from SBC Warburg Dillon Read, as did the heads of equities, foreign exchange and corporate finance. (Corporate finance is headed by former Dillon Read chief Fritz Hobbs.) Between the time the merger was announced in January and completed in June, many of UBS' top bankers left, mostly to competitor Donaldson, Lufkin & Jenrette. Also, UBS had to confront the highly-publicized suit brought against it and other Swiss Banks by relatives of Holocaust victims, agreeing to pay out two-thirds of the $1.25 billion settlement (Credit Suisse Group is paying the other third). And in September, UBS announced that it had lost $780 million in the blow-up of hedge fund Long-Term Capital. UBS' chairman, Mathis Cabiallavetta, abruptly resigned.

HOPE SPRINGS ETERNAL

Amid UBS' problems, as top bank officials met to mull over its strategy concerning high-risk businesses like investment banking, rumors about the possible divestiture of Warburg Dillon

Read began hitting the Street. The I-banking firm laid off 80 employees in Russia in August 1990 and 40 in Asia a month later. Still, most analysts do not believe that UBS will abandon investment banking altogether. One of Warburg Dillon Read's joint-COOs, David Solo, has, in fact, been promoted to oversee UBS' risk management. Despite its recent problems, Warburg Dillon Read hopes to become one of the world's premiere I-banks. It is already the leader in Europe, and is among the top three in Asia and Latin America. The firm hopes that it's only a matter of time until it seriously challenges the big Wall Street boys on their home turf.

GETTING HIRED

One's experience at Warburg Dillon Read may depend a lot on whether one is hired out of college or business school. Insiders warn that a business degree doesn't carry the same weight at WDR as it does at most American banks. Says one contact at WDR's Stamford U.S.: headquarters: "The biggest thing is that they don't hire huge MBA classes, so there's not a huge MBA culture." For example, this sales and trading contact notes, MBAs and analysts are lumped into the same training program once they join the firm. The same system is used in corporate finance. Says one insider who went through corporate finance training in the U.S." "They threw us in with college graduates. It was totally ridiculous – it was eight weeks of being treated like a kid. I think that was pretty much a consensus feeling."

On the other side of the coin, those associates note, the firm provides greater opportunity for undergrads. Says one contact: "For undergrads in the analyst position, it's a fantastic place. If you're a Wharton undergrad, it's really ideal. They really love that profile, the really hungry young person."

Insiders explain the lack of value of the business degree to WDR as a difference in American and European traditions regarding the business degree. Says one associate about the prevailing culture of Swiss Bank, and eventually WDR: "I mean, it was nice to have an MBA. But you had to prove yourself. You were not considered automatically higher than the guy next to you who didn't have an MBA." One insider argues that the situation for MBAs is actually worse

I-Banking Job Seekers: Receive free e-mailed job postings matching your interests & qualifications! Register at www.vaultreports.com

VAULT REPORTS™

www.vaultreports.com

233

in the firm's London offices, partly because "the MBA is a very new concept" among European firms. Says that contact, a former associate in London: "In the past, Warburg has hired college graduates and they would grow them in-house. As an MBA, you're labeled 'a graduate,' but these guys do nothing but analyst work. There would be 24- or 25-year-olds, calling you up and using you like analysts." Shudders that contact: "Any MBA who's thinking about going to Warburg in London is out of his freakin' mind."

As for the actual hiring process, WDR posts recruiting schedules on its web site at www.wdr.com. The firm has recently instituted a snazzy online application procedure that is required for all candidates outside of the U.S. and Switzerland. Don't expect the hiring process to include all of those expensive dinners other banks may throw at you. Says one recent MBA hire: "That whole initiation into the firm is radically different from other banks. They didn't wine and dine me like the other banks."

What may not be different is the stress level of interviewing with WDR. Says one insider, who was hired for one of the firm's Asian offices: "The questions were mostly finance-related. Questions included: Can you explain to me how discounted cash flow works? When do you think debt would be better than equity?" "I had one intimidating experience where a high executive said nothing, but asked 'Do you have any questions for me?' I asked one and he said, 'Give me another one.' And so on."

OUR SURVEY SAYS

BITTERNESS ABOUNDS

Just as was reported in publications that follow the finance industry, insiders tell us that SBC Warburg Dillon Read came out ahead in the merger with UBS. Reports one associate: "UBS was just about decimated – I know a lot of very bitter UBS people." Another, while agreeing that SBC came out ahead, does not see the conquest as absolute: "Things are consolidating –

the merger is complete. There are remainders from both organization. Swiss Bank generally came out ahead in the management structure, but it depends on the group. "There's a big culture difference, and they're still sorting it out."

So what does it mean to current insiders that Swiss Bank came out ahead? It's difficult to say, culturally. "Up until the merger with UBS, the SBC part was like a lot of minifirms, strong together with a huge balance sheet," explains one insider. That contact explains with a history lesson of the former Swiss Bank's foray into investment banking: "Swiss Bank first entered into I-banking through the acquisition of a Chicago-based proprietary fund run by a bunch of whiz kids." This partnership, with a firm called O'Connor, took place in the early 1990s. "It was a classic case of a reverse takeover. O'Connor immediately took over and ran everything. They instituted a casual policy, so everybody was wearing jeans." That sort of loose, flexible culture, insiders say, continued in America throughout Swiss Bank's acquisitions of Warburg and Dillon Read. In London, it's something of a different story: "It's basically a lot of old Warburg people running the show," says one contact in London. "It's very much of a UK British culture, it's a bit stodgy." And in Asia: "I would describe the culture at Warburg Dillon Read as a relatively loose compared to the U.S. banks.

CULTURE CLASH

Despite this somewhat uneven culture within Swiss Bank, insiders remark on differences between the former Swiss Bank and UBS. "UBS culture, as far as I can tell, is much more militaristic," says one insider from the Swiss Bank side. "They had a lot of Swiss Army people – it's a lot more conservative, it's a lot more rigid, whereas Swiss Bank was a lot more American. How they're going to work that out remains to be seen," reports one insider, noting that "a lot of people" have left the firm. Despite Swiss Bank's overall edge in management structure, the UBS culture has influenced the new Warburg Dillon Read. For example, at WDR's trading floor in the U.S., sneakers and jeans no longer rule. "They said no more jeans, and it was such a huge thing on the floor," says one insider. "It was 'No more sneakers, no more jeans, no more this and no more that.' There's been a lot more meetings, a lot more managers, a lot more in-your-face management."

I-Banking Job Seekers: Receive free e-mailed job postings matching
your interests & qualifications! Register at www.vaultreports.com

VAULT REPORTS™

235

www.vaultreports.com

AT LEAST THE NAME IS SET

The constant barrage of mergers and acquisitions has certainly unsettled employees with the firm. "I mean, the name changes all the time. They finally settled on the name, but clients don't know that," says one sales and trading insider. "I have so far worked for Swiss Bank Corporation, SBC Warburg, SBC Warburg Dillon Read, and now Warburg Dillon Read. It's crazy." As for the most recent merger, "I think it's going to take a long time to really define now, and come up with a corporate culture and communicate that around the world who we are."

Warburg Dillon Read's U.S. headquarters are in Stamford, Connecticut, a New York suburb in wealthy Lower Fairfield County. Reports one insider: "The younger people tend to all live in New York. People with families tend to live in Connecticut – for them, it's an ideal situation. Anyone who doesn't live in Connecticut better think twice [about joining WDR]. It just adds on almost three hours to an already long day."

A couple of insiders report that WDR's pay scale lags behind its U.S. competitors. "The rumor is that we pay less" says one contact. Says another source: "The bankers at WDR feel they are definitely underpaid relative to the U.S. banks. It goes U.S. banks, then European banks." Those just starting after graduating from business school or undergrad looking for a quick hit in the wallet should note that "we also pay our bonuses in March, rather than in December"

Wasserstein Perella

31 West 52nd Street
New York, NY 10019
(212) 969-7836
Fax: (212) 969-2674
www.wassersteinperella.com

LOCATIONS

New York, NY (HQ)
Chicago, IL • Dallas, TX • Los Angeles, CA
• Frankfurt, Germany • London, England, UK
• Paris, France

THE STATS

No. of Professionals: 250 (worldwide)
No. of Offices: 7 (worldwide)
A privately-held company
CEO: Bruce Wasserstein

KEY COMPETITORS

Goldman Sachs & Co.
Lazard Freres & Co.
Merrill Lynch
Morgan Stanley Dean Witter

UPPERS

- Generous pay
- Job training
- Company subsidized plan to join outside gym
- Free meals (after 8:30 p.m. weekdays and lunch on weekends)

DOWNERS

- Long hours
- Poor diversity for women

EMPLOYMENT CONTACT

Frances Lyman
Recruiting Coordinator
Wasserstein Perella & Co., Inc.
31 West 52nd Street
New York, NY 10019

(212) 969-2649
Fax: (212) 969-2674
fran_lyman@wasserella.com

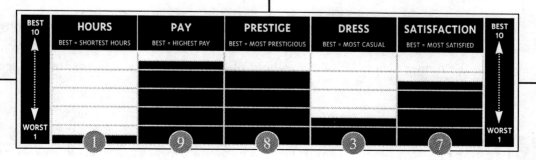

BEST 10 ↕ WORST 1	HOURS BEST = SHORTEST HOURS	PAY BEST = HIGHEST PAY	PRESTIGE BEST = MOST PRESTIGIOUS	DRESS BEST = MOST CASUAL	SATISFACTION BEST = MOST SATISFIED	BEST 10 ↕ WORST 1
	1	9	8	3	7	

THE SCOOP

M&A CENTRAL

Although it offers other traditional I-banking services such as debt and equity underwriting and investment management, Wasserstein Perella is known primarily as an M&A firm. In recent years, the firm has advised on major deals like the $25 billion UBS and Swiss Bank Corporation merger, which created the world's second-largest bank; the joint acquisition of Conrail by CSX and Norfolk Southern for $11 billion, and the acquisition of Capstar Broadcasting by Chancellor Media, which will create the largest radio broadcasting company in the U.S.

The firm was co-founded in 1988 by I-banking whiz Bruce Wasserstein (whose sister is Pulitzer Prize-winning playwright Wendy Wasserstein). Wasserstein, who enrolled in Harvard Law School at age 19 (eventually receiving both JD and MBA degrees from Harvard), left First Boston in 1988 with Joseph Perella. The two had clashed with other executives at First Boston, where Wasserstein had been co-head of investment banking. The bankers' reputations in the I-banking world served them well. Within six months of its founding, Wasserstein Perella had inked an alliance with Japanese powerhouse Nomura Securities that called for Nomura to pay $100 million for a 20 percent stake in the firm – thus valuing it at $500 million. Now employing 250 bankers, the firm maintains its strategic alliance with Nomura, which immediately established it as an M&A force. The firm was ranked in the top five for M&A activity in the late 80s. However, it dropped a bit in the rankings in the early 90s, as it concentrated on hostile takeovers (and developed a reputation for arrogance), before rebounding in the past few years to the top of the business.

THE RAIDER

As one might have predicted from the way it was founded, the firm has thrived on splashy hirings of top bankers from competitors. Most recently, the firm hired away Kenneth Tuchman, the former Lehman Brothers co-head of M&A in 1997, and Bruce Hackett, the former co-head of equities at Salomon Brothers in 1998. Tuchman joined the firm as vice chairman. One big name that has left the firm is Joseph Perella – after working with Bruce Wasserstein for 16 years, including on legendary deals like Philip Morris' $13 billion acquisition of Kraft and the $25 billion takeover of RJR Nabisco by Kohlberg Kravis Roberts, the name founder left in the early 1990s. Wasserstein and Perella ended up working on a deal together in 1997, albeit on different sides of the table. Perella, as head of investment banking at Morgan Stanley, advised the firm in its acquisition of Dean Witter, Discover, which was advised by Wasserstein.

The firm has also established strong equity and fixed income underwriting and research practices, and has an especially notable high-yield (junk bond) market making business through its Grantchester Securities division. But the firm's business that most often lands the firm in the papers (other than the M&A business) is its merchant banking arm. For example, the firm acquired cosmetics company Maybelline, which it sold to L'Oreal. And in 1998, the firm bought Steve Brill's *American Lawyer* magazine, a move that, observers note, is the first link in Bruce Wasserstein's plan to create a media conglomerate.

GETTING HIRED

Wasserstein Perella firm posts a schedule of its on-campus recruiting visits (which at some schools includes a talk by Bruce Wasserstein) and interviewing schedule on its web site, located at www.wassersteinperella.com. At on-campus school visits, the firm reportedly prefers to conduct two-on-one interviews. The candidate then makes a visit to the New York office. For analysts, the interviews last "all morning, with a lunch afterward." Candidates should know that "we get back to them very shortly."

More than other banks, Wasserstein Perella reportedly recruits candidates with legal backgrounds, as legal training comes in very handy for M&A work. "There's a fair push to get either laterals or people at the top law schools," reports one insider. Bruce Wasserstein is reportedly "actually closer to [Harvard] Law School" than he is to Harvard Business School.

I-Banking Job Seekers: Receive free e-mailed job postings matching your interests & qualifications! Register at www.vaultreports.com

VAULT REPORTS™
www.vaultreports.com

239

In part because Wasserstein also has ties to ultra-prestigious law firm Cravath, Swaine & Moore, "Wasserstein Perella actually has a lot of Cravath people."

Wasserstein Perella offers a "limited" number of 12-week summer analyst and summer associate positions. "They'll only hire a few summer associates, maybe four" reports one insider. These summer hires are far from guaranteed a full-time spot, insiders say: "It really depends on the quality of the summer associates – some may get offers, some may not."

Our contacts give advice on what Wasserstein is looking for in its applicants. "It obviously helps to know about the recent deals and that sort of stuff," reports one insider, but more importantly, "you definitely want to have someone who knows what they're getting into. I don't think its advisable to say I'm looking at all the bulge-bracket firms – plus Wasserstein. You want to see people who are very focused."

OUR SURVEY SAYS

SWEATSHOP REPUTATION

Wasserstein Perella, like other M&A shops, is known for working its bankers hard, but insiders report that the workload is better characterized by periods of intense work with some lulls. "The nature of M&A is more cyclical than anything. Sometimes, you could be working from 4 to 5 in the morning fairly constantly," reports one Wasserstein insider. "But other times, there may not be anything to do." Another insider agrees: "For all the long hours, much of the day is spent waiting for work to trickle down.

Still, candidates for the firm should be prepared for all-nighters. Says one insider: "They're definitely looking for people who can work the late hours, people who understand the differences between the small firm and a large firm. It's not a firm where you can sort of hide in the corner and do one small part of the deals."

POOR NUMBERS FOR WOMEN

There are few women at Wasserstein: in a recent analyst class, there were reportedly three women as compared to 30 men. "It's almost entirely male – very, very, very undiversified," reports one insider.

However, because of the firm's affiliation with Nomura Securities, the firm at least has a strong Asian presence. Reports one insider: "At all times, Nomura will have about five people in New York, going through training, with the firm. In Japan, we have a joint venture, where there might be one or two Wasserstein people, an associate or VP-level in one of the Nomura offices."

GOOD TRAINING

Unlike other mid-sized firms, Wasserstein Perella has a well-developed training program for new hires which lasts "about a month." The first two weeks include classes taught by an accounting professor and a finance professor. The other two weeks feature modules, M&A training, and valuation techniques. The firm will also bring in outside speakers. For example, the bank brings in a partner from famed law firm Cravath, Swaine & Moore to talk about legal issues involved in M&A.

All analysts take part in the training. "Associates have the option. If they've been an analyst before at another firm before business school, sometimes they'll just sit in on speeches by Bruce Wasserstein or other senior members."

GET TO KNOW THE SUPERSTARS

As with other smaller firms, insiders at Wasserstein report that "the best thing about the firm is you do work with very senior members." "What Wasserstein has done is picked up very senior members of these bulge-bracket firms," explains another contact. "They're giving them a lot more flexibility – and of course, they're getting more compensation."

I-Banking Job Seekers: Receive free e-mailed job postings matching your interests & qualifications! Register at www.vaultreports.com

VAULT REPORTS™
www.vaultreports.com

241

As for Bruce himself? "He's obviously a very, very bright guy," reports one banker who has worked with him. "He can be in a room, and he doesn't have to say a whole lot. But when he does speak, the whole room will listen to him. He's very, very good on the sell-side, no one else in that room is on the same level. He's very, very good at getting to the point quickly."

SPEND THIS MUCH TIME WITH EACH OTHER? YEAH, WE'RE CLOSE

Wasserstein insiders report that the firm is a pretty chummy place, though not a party. "People will typically eat together or watch TV in a conference room," says one former analyst. "People dress down, go to the gym for half an hour or an hour together. At night, it's a different firm, everyone knows everyone. You're very close with the analyst class." Says another insider: "It's almost always quiet. People work really hard. But the guys are just generally nice. They're friendly and jovial, but it's not a party type atmosphere."

Wasserstein Perella's New York headquarters are located in the same building as the Museum of Modern Art museum shop, in Midtown Manhattan. "[Wasserstein] rents offices from Deutsche Bank, and Deutsche Bank really wants to kick them out," says one insider "But Wasserstein, he's got this thing about where he wants the office to be. There's only about six blocks that he wants it, and therefore we have to stay."

Dining choices in Midtown tend to be somewhat limited. "There's a cafeteria in the building, its Deutsche Bank's. Nobody's really encouraged to go there," says one insider. "Most people go out – there's a soup place across the street where lots of people go."

Dress is surprisingly varied. Although during the week, insiders say, bankers at Wasserstein wear "conservative suits – there's nothing adventurous going on," on Fridays, "people wear jeans. Basically they look like college students again."

A RIVER OF FREE LIQUID

"All in all, the benefits outweigh the detriments," says one insider "And we get free sodas." Although that contact isn't necessarily talking about "benefits" in the sense of perks and HR policy, others are happy to oblige. One insider also enjoys the free liquids: "On every floor they've got a pantry, and it's stocked with drinks, soda, cranberry juice, lemonade, apple juice, and it's billed to clients." Reports one contact: "If you work past 8:30 at night you get a car service home, which is standard." Late nights also get bankers a free dinner, and "you get free meals for weekend work." Wasserstein also offers a "401(k) with match. The firm will even pay for your GMAT course at Kaplan."

I-Banking Job Seekers: Receive free e-mailed job postings matching your interests & qualifications! Register at www.vaultreports.com

VAULT REPORTS™

243

www.vaultreports.com

"The guys are just generally nice. They're friendly and jovial, but it's not a party-type atmosphere."

– *Wasserstein insider*

VAULT REPORTS™
www.vaultreports.com

Wheat First Union

901 East Byrd Street
Riverfront Plaza
Richmond, VA 23219
(804) 782-3516
Fax: (804) 782-3440
www.wheatfirst.com

LOCATIONS

Richmond, VA (HQ)
126 other operating offices in CA • CT • DC
• DE • FL • GA • KT • MD • MI • MO • NC •
NJ • NY • OH • PA • SC • TN • TX • VA • WV

THE STATS

No. of Offices: 128 (U.S.)
Subsidiary of First Union
CEO: Marshall B. Wishnack

KEY COMPETITORS

A.G. Edwards
Morgan Keegan
Raymond James Financial
Robinson-Humphrey
U.S. Bancorp Piper Jaffray

UPPERS

- Good opportunities for advancement
- Employee-owned firm
- Expected growth because merger with First Union
- Better name

DOWNERS

- Pokiness of Richmond

EMPLOYMENT CONTACT

Human Resources
Wheat First Union
901 East Byrd Street
Riverfront Plaza
Richmond, VA 23219

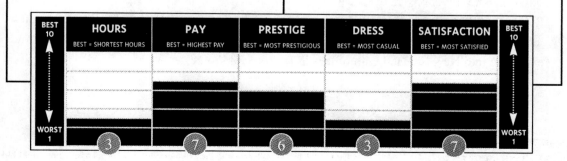

	HOURS	PAY	PRESTIGE	DRESS	SATISFACTION	
BEST 10 / WORST 1	BEST = SHORTEST HOURS	BEST = HIGHEST PAY	BEST = MOST PRESTIGIOUS	BEST = MOST CASUAL	BEST = MOST SATISFIED	BEST 10 / WORST 1
	3	7	6	3	7	

THE SCOOP

THE BLIND LEADING THE SUCCESSFUL

Since its humble beginnings as the one-man investment firm J.C. Wheat & Co. in 1934, Wheat First Union has grown to a national full-service firm offering a range of financial services. The founder's son, James C. Wheat, Jr., blind from the age of 24, is credited with much of the firm's success. From the time he joined his father's firm in 1945, Wheat pushed for expansion into brokerage, investment banking, and asset management services. Wheat also fostered growth through mergers, including the 1971 merger with First Securities that created Wheat First Securities, Inc. Wheat's successors, John L. McElroy Jr. and Marshall B. Wishnack further expanded the firm through a 1988 merger with Butcher & Singer, a successful Philadelphia-based securities firm established in 1910; the firm was then called Wheat First Butcher Singer In August 1997, the formerly privately-held Wheat First Butcher Singer agreed to be acquired for just under $500 million by the Charlotte, North Carolina-based First Union bank, one of the nation's largest commercial banks. The bank changed its name to Wheat First Union, creating an unprecedented event in the history of finance – a merger that actually improved a firm's name.

MERGIN' TIME

Headquartered in Richmond, Virginia, Wheat First Union offers investment banking products with a concentration on equities and M&A. Unlike other recent combinations of investment banks and commercial banks (such as Bankers Trust and Alex. Brown), First Union and Wheat First decided to initially keep their respective I-banking businesses largely separate. First Union's homegrown securities arm, called First Union Capital Markets, integrated Wheat's fixed-income division, but Wheat's equities and M&A practices remained housed in Richmond. The firm has experienced major growth in recent years, with annual revenues increasing more than 50 percent from 1990 to 1997. In 1998, the firm's brokerage army expanded into New England with offices in Boston and Worcester, Mass.

GETTING HIRED

Wheat First looks for team players who can work effectively with clients, and have prior investment banking experience. Recruiting at several top business schools, Wheat First conducts second- and third-round interviews in Richmond. The firm has two associate "Super Saturdays" – one in December and one in late January – during which prospective associates interview one-on-one with associates and senior bankers in half-hour sessions. Wheat First typically hires two to four associates and one to two summer associates each year. Send or fax resumes to human resources at Richmond headquarters. The ambitious should take note – the merger with First Union is expected to set off a hiring surge at Wheat First.

OUR SURVEY SAYS

LET'S GET DOWN TO BUSINESS

Employees describe a "terrific" working environment at Wheat First Union, praising the "slower pace" of living and working at headquarters in Richmond. With "intelligent, ambitious, and enjoyable" co-workers, one banker notes, "the intellectual challenge is rewarding." Insiders say the firm is "very progressive" in its hiring practices, "looking for the best people it can find without regard to race or gender." The diverse crew at Wheat First works at offices that differ from each other culturally. The offices "that work on the revenue side of the business" are "formal dress and have a let's-get-down-to-business attitude," while branches with "operations, support and data services have more fun and dress business casual; they tend to be younger too." Regardless, the firm offers "frequent company get-togethers."

I-Banking Job Seekers: Receive free e-mailed job postings matching your interests & qualifications! Register at www.vaultreports.com

VAULT REPORTS™
www.vaultreports.com
247

HAPPY ABOUT MERGING

One contact recounts an impressive history of advancement within the firm: "I started in the company in an entry-level clerical position in the benefits department, and I am now at the vice president level. Wheat First is very open to people with drive making their own way within the company." The recent merger with First Union "should be a good thing for Wheat First," say employees. "We do expect the creation of many jobs and many new opportunities available as a result of the merger."

Ed Shen: Ed is managing editor of Vault Reports. He graduated from Harvard University with a BA in English. Previously, he was a reporter with *The Advocate* of Stamford, CT.

H.S. (Sam) Hamadeh: H.S. Hamadeh is co-founder and managing director of Vault Reports. He holds a BA in economics from UCLA and a JD/MBA from the Wharton School of Business and the University of Pennsylvania Law School, where was an editor on Law Review. He has worked at the law firms Cravath Swaine & Moore and Skadden Arps and at the investment banks Goldman Sachs and Morgan Stanley. He has authored three books on career-related subjects.

I-BANKING JOB SEEKERS:

Have job openings that match your criteria e-mailed to you !

VAULTMATCH™

FROM VAULT REPORTS

A free service for I-Banking job seekers!

Vault Reports will e-mail you job and internship postings that match your interests and qualifications. This is a free service from Vault Reports. Here's how it works:

1. You visit www.VaultReports.com and fill out an online questionnaire, indicating your qualifications and the types of positions you want.

2. Companies contact Vault Reports with job openings.

3. Vault Reports sends you an e-mail about each position which matches your qualifications and interests.

4. For each position that interests you, simply reply to the e-mail and attach your resume.

5. Vault Reports laser prints your resume on top-quality resume paper and sends it to the company's hiring manager within 5 days.

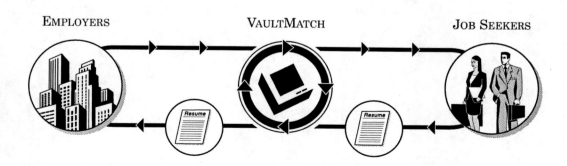

www.VaultReports.com

JOB INTERVIEWS ARE COMING!

Your competition is prepared...are you?

Vault Reports Employer Profiles are 50- to 70-page reports on leading employers designed to help you ace your job interviews. **Vault Reports Industry Guides** are 100- to 400-page guides providing in-depth information on leading industries, including industry trends, sample interview questions, and snapshots of the top firms. Filled with "insider" details, the Profiles and Industry Guides provide the hard-to-get company info that no recruiting brochure would dare reveal. Profiles are available on hundreds of leading companies.

> **Price: $25 per Employer Profile***
> **$35 per Industry Guide***

EMPLOYER PROFILES

American Express
American Management Systems
Andersen Consulting
Arthur Andersen
Arthur D. Little
AT Kearney
Bain & Co.
Bankers Trust
Bear Stearns
Booz Allen & Hamilton
Boston Consulting Group
Cargill
Chase
Citicorp/Citibank
Coca-Cola
Credit Suisse First Boston
Deloitte & Touche
Deutsche Bank
Donaldson Lufkin & Jenrette
Enron
Ernst & Young
Fidelity Investments
Ford Motor
Gemini
General Mills
Goldman Sachs
Hewlett Packard
Intel
JP Morgan

KPMG
Lehman Brothers
McKinsey & Co.
Mercer
Merrill Lynch
Microsoft
Mitchell Madison
Monitor
Morgan Stanley Dean Witter
Oracle
PricewaterhouseCoopers
Procter & Gamble
Salomon Smith Barney
Sprint
Walt Disney

.......*100s more!*

INDUSTRY GUIDES

Advertising
Brand Management
Fashion
Healthcare
High Tech
Internet and New Media
Investment Banking
Management Consulting
MBA Employers
Media and Entertainment

To order call 1-888-JOB-VAULT or order online at www.VaultReports.com

Founded by Wharton, Harvard, Yale and Stanford alums, Vault Reports is dedicated to helping job seekers ace their interviews.
Copyright © 1998 Vault Reports, Inc., 80 Fifth Avenue, 11th Floor, New York NY 10011.

VAULT REPORTS INDUSTRY GUIDES

The first career guides of their kind, Vault Reports' Industry Guides offer detailed evaluations of America's leading employers. Enriched with responses from thousands of insider surveys and interviews, these guides tell it like it is – the good and the bad – about the companies everyone is talking about. Each guide includes a complete industry overview as well as information on the industry's job opportunities, career paths, hiring procedures, culture, pay, and commonly asked interview questions..

Each employer entry includes:

 The Scoop: the juicy details on each company's past, present, and future.

 Getting Hired: insider advice on what it takes to get that job offer.

 Our Survey Says: thousands of employees speak their mind on company culture, satisfaction, pay, prestige, and more.

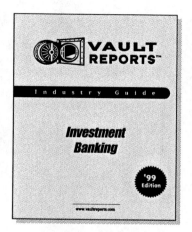

PRICE: $35 PER GUIDE

GUIDE TO ADVERTISING™

Reviews America's top employers in the advertising industry, including Bozell Worldwide, Grey Advertising, Leo Burnett, Ogilvy & Mather, TBWAChiat/Day, and many more!

100pp.

GUIDE TO FASHION™

Reviews America's top employers in the fashion industry, including Calvin Klein, Donna Karan, Estee Lauder, The Gap, J. Crew, IMG Models, and many more!

100pp.

GUIDE TO HEALTHCARE™

Reviews America's top employers in the healthcare industry, including Amgen, Eli Lilly, Johnson & Johnson, Oxford, Pfizer, Schering-Plough, and many more!

120pp.

GUIDE TO HIGH TECH™

Reviews America's top employers in the high tech industry, including Broderbund, Cisco Systems, Hewlett-Packard, Intel, Microsoft, Sun Microsystems, and many more!

400pp.

GUIDE TO INTERNET AND NEW MEDIA™

Reviews America's top employers in the Internet and new media industry, including Amazon.com, CDNow, DoubleClick, Excite, Netscape, Yahoo!, and many more!

130pp.

GUIDE TO INVESTMENT BANKING™

Reviews America's top employers in the investment banking industry, including Bankers Trust, Goldman Sachs, JP Morgan, Morgan Stanley, and many more!

400pp.

GUIDE TO MANAGEMENT CONSULTING™

Reviews America's top employers in the management consulting industry, including Andersen Consulting, Boston Consulting Group, McKinsey, PricewaterhouseCoopers, and many more!

400pp.

GUIDE TO MARKETING AND BRAND MANAGEMENT™

Reviews America's top employers in the marketing and brand management industry, including General Mills, Procter & Gamble, Nike, Coca-Cola, and many more!

150pp.

GUIDE TO MBA EMPLOYERS™

Reviews America's top employers for MBAs, including Fortune 500 corporations, management consulting firms, investment banks, venture capital and LBO firms, commercial banks, and hedge funds.

500pp.

GUIDE TO MEDIA AND ENTERTAINMENT™

Reviews America's top employers in the media and entertainment industry, including AOL, Blockbuster, CNN, Dreamworks, Gannett, National Public Radio, Time Warner, and many more!

400pp.